Sandy's Gift

Sandy's Gift

Walking with The Light

One man's journey of love, tragedy,
spiritual redemption, and freedom

Bill Dunn

Cedar Forge Press
7300 West Joy Road
Dexter, Michigan 48130

Published 2015 by Cedar Forge Press
Printed in the United States of America

19 18 17 16 15   1 2 3 4

ISBN 978-1-943290-12-3
Library of Congress Control Number: 2015956163

In loving memory of Sandra Ann Dunn, loving wife, mother and daughter

and to the approximate 15 million adults and their immediate families and households in America today coping with a patient suffering from a severe form of Mental Illness.

Those families are not alone and there is no outlet today for those families seeking help. My hope is that sharing this story may bring about change.

Contents

Prologue: Dragon Slayers 1

Part 1: Building a Life Together

You Shall Meet a Stranger
Across a Crowded Room 5

The Dating Game 9

A Time for Mourning. 15

The Jersey Shore 19

The New Year 23

Our First Home 29

Bo of the Beverkill 39

Working, Playing and Moving Along 45

Moments in Time. 53

A Change of Plans and Stroke of Luck 57

Down on the Farm 2002-2003. 65

A Year of Rest 2004 75

Missing Clues 2005 85

The Calm before the Storm 2006 95

Part 2: One Hundred and Sixty Days

Signs 107

August 2006 113

Seventeen Days of Hospital Care 125

September 2006 145

No Means No Mommy, October 2006 157

The Whisper 161

The Gales of November 169

The Last Day in November 187

Part 3: Hocus Pocus

Merry Christmas 195

Happy New Year 2007, Right? 203

Happy Birthday 213

2008, The Second Message 221

The Blue Dress 225

Time Passages, 2008 231

More Messages 237

A Final Message from Beyond 245

Epilogue: My Final Words 251

Appendices

The Sins of ZIP Code 07976 265

Public Servants? 271

A Court Hearing 279

DYFUS, a State Agency 285

Mental Health in America 297

Acknowledgments 305

Prologue:
Dragon Slayers

A long time ago in a far off kingdom once known as the Garden State, a young boy was born. He was the oldest of three children, raised by good parents in this long ago lost land within the Hamlet known as Florham Park. This lad's father served his country, America, in the Pacific Ocean during a great conflict and told his young son about the beautiful islands of faraway lands he'd seen during that horrible conflict.

The young lad would play in the nearby fields, woods, streams, and farms, pretending to slay dragons during his youth. While on these journeys, he discovered the wonders that nature offered in his nearby kingdom, a then-seemingly magical place today known as New Jersey.

Mentored by his father, the young boy was told that he needed to work hard if he were to make a name for himself. The young lad listened and worked hard. His first occupation was that of a news carrier while in the fifth grade. He later took on the lawns and snow during wintertime. By the seventh and eighth grades he was employed at his father's stable, West Orange Riding Club, which catered to the local nobles and their children.

By ninth grade this young lad tried a new endeavor: human mule, known by some today as golf caddie. In eleventh grade he became self-employed, parking cars for Ed Ponek, the Harding

Township chief of police, and tying trout flies for the local nobles and merchants.

When the young man was in the twelfth grade, he was determined to leave the area, as he wanted to become a Forest Ranger and see the canyons west of the Mississippi.

The father had a talk with his son. The young lad listened and attended a local community college. He continued to park cars and tie trout flies, and also found work in a local mill making preserves during his summer breaks.

Four years after he received his high school diploma, he emerged from college with a degree economics in hand. The year was 1979. The lad then embarked on a journey that lead him to the canyons of lower Manhattan instead of the faraway canyons of his dreams west of the Mississippi. Wall Street was different from the mountain stream that had been his first choice.

In 1981 Lee Wulff asked him to join him at the Wulff Catskill Fly-Fishing School to become a teacher. God (i.e., fly-fishing) had spoken to the young man, but he declined the offer. His late father had won the Maclay Cup in 1942 at age 16 and never rode a horse again upon the sale of his business. The young man learned a lesson from his father.

In 1985 he met his Cinderella at a party. She was the guest of a nobleman's son from Short Hills. He picked up her glass slipper and never looked back. This memoir is their fairy tale, and sometimes fairy tales get different endings.

Part 1:
Building a Life Together

You Shall Meet a Stranger Across a Crowded Room

My story begins on a Saturday evening in March 1985. My friend Tom was having a party at his parents' home in Morris Township. His parents were away in Florida for the winter. They were, as many retirees are called in the northeast, snow birds. Tom had an apartment nearby, but his parents asked him to stay in their home during the winter because they felt more comfortable with their son at their home rather than it being empty all winter.

I, William Dunn, told Tom I would arrive with Chris, Big Ed, and a few of my other friends. I had never been to Tom's parents' home as we had met socially and had not attended school together. Tom and I had met about a year earlier, and would get together socially and chase skirts together as all normal young men in their mid-to-late twenties do.

I was twenty-eight, in the best shape in my life and working in lower Manhattan on Wall Street as an institutional government bond broker. Life was good when I was a young bachelor. The last thing I was looking for was love. As fate would have it, that was exactly what happened that Saturday evening.

Chris, Big Ed, and I arrived at the party. The house was a Colonial, larger than most in the neighborhood, and the party was full of young single working professionals. I followed my friends through the door and there she was: a redhead with striking blue eyes. We immediately locked eyes. It was one of those moments we all experience every once in a while, but there happened to be one problem: she was with someone else.

As I closed the door, I knew her date or boyfriend had seen our connection since he was standing right next to her, and I figured that was the end of it. Throughout the evening, this redhead and I kept getting into that eye thing when we were in the same room or passing by each other. I had never been attracted to redheads, but there seemed to be something different about her, or maybe that attraction just occurs every once in a while. Call it chance, fate, or whatever.

I now had one problem: how to meet this pretty gal who was with a date who had seen our looks at each other and was tailing her every time she and I shared that glance.

After about two hours, I figured it was not going to happen, but then I finally got my chance about 11:30 P.M. It was just plain luck. The party was very crowded. I would estimate more than 150 people and perhaps as many as 200 were there. I was in the kitchen. The next room was the dining room, which had been emptied and turned into a dance floor. Music was playing, and there she was again, dancing with her boyfriend or date. She was facing the kitchen, and his back was toward me. I figured it was now or never, so I entered the dance room, grabbed another gal by the hand and asked her to dance with me. She declined, but I told her to not be a wallflower, didn't let go of her hand and started to dance with her.

I danced toward the redhead, and by the time I and the other gal were next to her, she and I were back-to-back. I kept bumping my butt against hers, but the next thing I knew, the next bump was with her boyfriend's or date's ass. I grabbed my dance partner's hand and swung around so that I was facing the pretty redhead again.

I didn't have much time and wasn't sure what to do. As we looked at each other, I looked into her eyes and mouthed, "Meet me downstairs in five minutes." I held up my left hand with my five fingers splayed and my right hand with one finger pointing to the nearby stairway.

She blushed.

I mouthed the same words with the same gestures, then I left the dance floor with my partner in hand, thanked her for the dance, and went to the kitchen. I then casually headed towards a downstairs den that also had a bathroom as if I needed to use it. I was nervous as I had never in my life been so bold or was having butterflies in my tummy. I didn't think she would show.

Minutes passed, and then there she was. She came down the stairs.

Before she had a chance to say anything I said, "My name is Bill Dunn, and I'm sorry to have bumped into you like I did, but I couldn't think of anything else and decided to take a chance."

She said, "My name is Sandy Fushi."

We both paused and looked into each other's eyes and then I put my arms around her and gave her a really deep long kiss.

She responded, then after a few moments started to freeze up.

I immediately let my arms drop.

Sandy looked down, and I placed my hand on her chin to bring her eyes to mine again.

Sandy was blushing.

I said, "I am going to give you my business card and a second business card. If you wish, please write your number on one and give it back to me."

Sandy started to hesitate, so I added, "I cannot tell you what to do, but if you do not give me your number and you go back upstairs to the other guy, you might miss the best thing that could happen for the both of us." She smiled at me and gave me one card back with a number on it.

Later, my friend Chris said, "That redhead is still looking at you, Billy. What are you going to do about it?" I didn't say a thing, but figured that when we left I would show my friend the card.

Throughout the remainder of the evening, Sandy and I

continued to make eye contact across that crowded room. Then she left with her date, as I would later find out, and I remained a few hours longer with my friends.

Fate is sometimes what we make of it, and sometimes the choices we make can determine that fate.

During that evening one other gal, a very attractive blonde with a great figure, seemed to take an interest in me, and we had spoken a few times throughout the night. When it was getting late and soon time to head out, the next thing I knew here was this blonde again, and she wanted to leave. Basically she said to me, "Please take me home with you," and it was clear to me what she also implied. My friends stood in disbelief as I declined her invitation.

On the ride home, my good friend Chris said to me, "Billy, that beautiful blonde asked you to take her home tonight."

I said, "Chris, I know that blonde was very hot, but I think that I met someone very special." Then I showed him my business card with Sandy's phone number on it.

Chris said, "Whose number is that?"

"The redhead."

"How did you get that?"

"Just sheer luck."

Fate is a very funny thing. Sometimes it can pass us by and other times we can grab it. If for some reason, my fate had gone to a seductive blonde that night, my life with Sandy would never have happened. That, however, was not the fate I choose. I am eternally grateful of the choice and blessed because that chance meeting on that special evening changed my life forever. Many never get that chance or miss it or let it pass them by. I was a fortunate young man who that night did not.

The Dating Game

My first date with Sandy was the following Friday evening. I drove to where she was living, which was her parent's home in New Vernon. It was dark that night as there were no streetlights on the road. I found the long driveway, knocked on the door at the appointed time and heard dogs barking. The door was opened by her father, an older man about 6' 3" and in really good shape for a man his age.

Mr. Fushi looked down at me and asked where I lived and what I did for work.

I answered both questions.

He asked where we were going, and I replied, "Freddies in Bernardsville for dinner."

Then Sandy appeared. She was dressed very nice, and with her long beautiful flowing red hair and beautiful blue eyes, she was just striking.

I was feeling a little awkward.

She jumped into the conservation with both her dad and me. Then she looked at her father and said, "We are leaving now, Dad."

It was apparent that she was the apple in his eye and could probably get her way with her father and do no wrong.

We said goodbye and left for the evening.

We arrived at Freddies. Dinner arrived around 8:30 P.M., and by 11 P.M., a band was to play.

Sandy informed me that she had just moved back home after

leaving an apartment in South Orange. She had attended Seton Hall University, majoring in art history, and was 25. She worked in Morristown at Compton Press in the production area. Compton Press was one of the larger high-end sheet-feed printer's in New Jersey, employing perhaps a hundred employees.

We had a very nice evening. Conversation flowed easily and everything seemed to go right. My premonition from the night when we met seemed right.

Sandy was very outgoing, pretty, and just a naturally really likable gal, and we just seemed to click right from the start. It continued to move that way all night and get better as the night progressed.

When the evening came to an end and it was time to leave, I dropped her at her home, and we made arrangements to spend Sunday afternoon together. I gave her a goodnight kiss and left in a really happy frame of mind, wondering how in the world did I get so lucky.

Sunday was one of those rare almost spring-like days we occasionally get in New Jersey in March. Temperature was in the low 70s. The ground was soft and the first smell of new spring hung in the air. We had an early spring that year, as it turned out.

I picked up Sandy at her parents' home and met her mother as her father was out with a friend playing golf or the driving range.

Sandy asked where we were going, and I replied that it was a surprise and asked her to change her shoes, which had heels, to some that were more comfortable.

She looked at me a little strangely, but agreed.

As we drove off, I told her I'd packed a picnic. I drove west to a very pretty place known as Ken Lockwood Gorge, a State Park located in Califon, N.J., about 40 minutes away and one of two gorges in the state. The South Branch of the Raritan River runs thru this park, which runs approximately two miles along the entire length of the gorge.

Sandy and I had a picnic lunch on a very large boulder overlooking the river. We sat on an opened sleeping bag for comfort.

She asked me how I knew about the place, and I told her I was a trout fisherman and fly fisherman and spent my free time fly-fishing for trout. For me, trout fishing was a break from the trading screens and pressure of Wall Street. On the river I could forget the workweek.

The trout in the river start feeding. I pointed out a few to Sandy and gave her my polarized sunglasses so she could view them.

We had a nice day, kissed a bit and on that rock she looked me in the eyes and said, "You're going to marry me one day, Bill Dunn."

I looked at her and laughed it off. I wasn't looking to settle down and was having too much fun for such serious thoughts.

Sandy and I continued to date, seeing each other on weekends for the next few weeks and one evening during the week. Things were going pretty good. I met her friends and she met mine.

By that time May was arriving. It was springtime, and time for me to begin the rites of passage that all self-respecting trout guys do: they go fishing. That means packing gear, going to bed early Friday night, getting up at 4:30 A.M., donning waders, going fishing, arriving home late Saturday, and then going out with friends or in my case Sandy.

This went on for a few weeks, then one Friday evening Sandy stopped by my place. I guessed that she was checking to see whether I was really out chasing other gals with my friends, as much to her seeming surprise, she found me at my desk tying trout flies for the next day's outing. Sandy had a puzzled look on her face when she saw what I was doing and I guessed that she figured out I really was staying in and getting up as I said I did. She said, "You really do this, Bill, don't you?"

I looked at her and said, "Yes, I do."

The following Thursday while we were in Summit having dinner together, she asked me whether I intended to go fishing Saturday morning.

I responded yes, and she asked who was going with me.

I said I was going alone as most of my friends wanted to go out and didn't make it the next day as they'd stayed out late the night before.

Sandy said, "I want to go with you."

I looked at her and said, "No, you don't. You don't know how to fish. What will you do all day?"

She said, "I will bring my camera and take pictures." She asked whether I would take her back to the beautiful place where we'd had that picnic on that Sunday in March.

I told her I would be happy to and said I would be by at 6:30 A.M. sharp to pick her up.

Friday night, Sandy called me and reminded me to be there by 6:30 A.M.

I said, "See you in the A.M."

When I arrived the following morning, she was dressed in jeans and looked great, and in her hands were a picnic basket she'd packed the night before and her camera.

If I'd been her mom or dad, I don't know what I would have thought of a guy arriving at my home at such an early time, but Sandy just popped out through the front door upon my arrival as the dogs were barking in the background.

I headed back to the Ken Lockwood Gorge with a beautiful red-head, picnic basket, and smile on my face. I caught some trout that morning. We had a nice lunch on that boulder and then I asked Sandy whether her father liked fresh trout. She said, "Yes, he does," and told me he'd said so when she'd told him of her plans.

Ken Lockwood Gorge was a fly-fishing-only stretch with a slot limit, and I always released the fish I caught there, so we headed up river and stopped by another area where I fished and creeled two trout for her dad.

When I dropped her off that night, she showed her father our gift and later she told me he had the trout for breakfast the next morning.

Sandy and I started to really get to know one another. I found out that she'd grown up around competition horseback riding through 4-H as a child, the house where she lived had once been a working six-acre horse farm, and they'd showed and raised horses when she was young. She'd spent one summer during her college years living in Manasquan by the beach and had worked that summer at Monmouth Race track. She was a really pretty outdoor girl who'd met a young man who also preferred to spend his free time outdoors. We seemed to be a good match.

On Memorial Day weekend in 1985, Sandy and I decided to go up to Northern New Jersey and go camping and fishing. She said, "Bill, I know you want to get away with your buddies, but I want to go with you."

I said, "What will your parents do when I show up?"

She said, "Everything will be fine."

When I showed up that Saturday, her dad gave me the look.

I mumbled a few things.

Sandy was her usual outgoing happy self.

We were gone for two nights.

When we got back to her house, her father was there.

Before he could say anything, Sandy pulled out a stringer of about six-to-eight trout and said, "Daddy, look what we brought home for you." She beamed her smile at him, and all was okay.

I was relieved.

Mr. Fushi asked me to join him for a drink outside on the deck. I stayed about an hour and we talked about golf. He'd found out that I played, was surprised to learn I'd played on my college team and suggested that we play a round together. We set a date for Saturday, the day before Father's Day as my father, brother John, and I always played on Father's Day and my game with Mr. Fushi would be a good warm up the day before. Up to this point, I really had not been in Sandy's daddy's good graces. Now he seemed to like me and think more highly of me. Perhaps I was passing the test.

It was now June 1985, and Sandy and I were spending more

time together. Her father seemed to like me. Her mom was okay, but seemed a little squirrely. Sandy's mom Harriet was a big animal lover, involved in rescues and such and tended to her cat rescue program.

On the Wednesday before Father's Day, Sandy called me at my office. She was upset and in tears. Her dad had had a heart attack and been taken to Morristown Memorial Hospital.

I met Sandy at the hospital and spent time with her.

Mr. Fushi said we would have to postpone our golf game. He wanted me to know that when I got back from my trip to Hilton Head Island—I was scheduled to leave Monday and return Sunday—that he would be back to normal and ready for our match.

I visited Sandy's dad with her every day as she brought him a good dinner every evening, and I saw him with her on Father's Day after my golf outing with my dad. Mr. Fushi asked me how I played that day, and we had a nice chat. Then I left Sandy with her dad, as I had to pack for my flight to Hilton Head, a trip I'd planned with friends the previous fall.

I flew out the next morning, arrived in Hilton Head, and played a round of golf that afternoon. I called Sandy each day when she was on her lunch break or before dinner to see how her dad was doing.

Thursday afternoon I got a message that was very hard to understand, but I thought Sandy had said her father had passed while I was out golfing that day. I called her and my fear was true: her dad had had another heart attack while he was in the hospital waiting to be transported to another facility. I told Sandy I would make arrangements. I called the airline and was on the first flight back to Newark Friday morning.

A Time for Mourning

I arrived home from Hilton Head late Friday afternoon. I went to see my mom and dad, gave them hugs, and told them I loved them.

They looked a little surprised.

I said that I really never tell them I love them and I felt that I needed to do so.

Driving over to Sandy's home, I hadn't been sure what to say, but I knew that I wanted to be there for her and her mom.

When I entered the house, I meet some other of the Fushis' neighbors and friends who I hadn't met before. I looked around and saw Sandy. I went to her, gave her a hug and said, "Let me know what I can do."

Sandy looked at me and said nothing, but the look in her eyes said it all.

The next few days I tried to be as helpful as possible. The viewing and mass were in nearby Madison, N.J., and Mr. Fushi was to be interned in upstate New York, outside of Rochester in the small town of Livonia.

The drive to Livonia was a long one. I made the journey with Sandy and her mom a week later, when we took Mr. Fushi's ashes with us. Mrs. Fushi wanted to drive the old route she and her late-husband had always taken. I looked at maps and thought the journey would take a long time, but that was fine because it would make Mrs. Fushi happy. The drive up took more than ten hours since we took Route 80 west into Pennsylvania to Route 15 north, eventually arriving at major highways, and finally to Geneseo, N.Y, where we stayed at a Holiday Inn. Genesco is a college town and home to a SUNY teachers' college. Mrs. Fushi had graduated in the early 1930s with a degree and moved down to Baldwin, New York, on Long Island, where she'd met Mr. Fushi. This trip was the first time I spent a lot of time with Sandy's mom, and I got to know her better.

The burial service was held Saturday the following weekend, and I took Friday off from work to make the trip with Mrs. Fushi and Sandy. This part of New York state is a very beautiful area, lush and green with many rolling hills and pastoral farmlands. A service was held, and I was introduced to Sandy's mother's side of the family. Everyone was very nice. They were down-to-earth, salt-of-the-earth-type people who reminded me of people I've met from the Midwest. There were luncheons and dinners, and all the folks told stories about the past as one does at such times.

I was next to Sandy at the burial. She was upset at the gravesite, and I said a prayer while Mr. Fushi was being interned. In that prayer, I told Mr. Fushi I would stay by his daughter and be there to take care of her. I knew she was the girl for me, and I felt that someday we would become man and wife. Something in my gut told me she would be woman for me, and if that was so, I would be there for her and he should not worry.

It was a beautiful late spring day. The sun was shining, and a few clouds dotted the view of the blue sky to the east. In the distance were farms and hilltops. I understood why Mr. and Mrs. Fushi had choose this place to be their final resting spot.

Monday morning we left to drive back to New Jersey. I told Sandy we would be taking a different route, staying on the Interstate system. We got back in about six hours' driving time, arriving by mid-afternoon Monday.

During this drive I became aware that Harriet really did seem a little bit odd at times. I knew she was 70 years old and just figured her oddities were due to age. Some of the things she said ran on and did not make a lot of sense. She seemed to lose her place at times when she told her stories. She'd start to tell one story, forget where she was and start another story. When asked about the first story, she was unable to remember the answer. If Sandy knew the rest of the story, she would finish it for her mom.

A few days later I spoke with Sandy about her mother's confusion. Sandy said that was just the way her mother was, and that was the end of that discussion for the time being.

The Jersey Shore

The summer of 1985 arrived in New Jersey. It was late June and beach weather. I was fortunate that my Nana Dunn had a home in the beach community of Sea Girt, N.J. Nana's home was a modest four-bedroom Cape Cod that my grandfather had bought in the early 1950s about six blocks from the beach. I worked in the city, commuting from Summit, N.J. Sandy was living with her mom, and we started to head to the shore about every other weekend, staying at my grandmother's.

The routine was simple. Friday Nana was at her home, and when we arrived, dinner was ready. Saturday was my turn to take her out for dinner early, and then Sandy and I would head out for an evening with friends. Sandy and I went to the beach, too. Sometimes I got up early and tried surf fishing, but I never did too well at that. Sandy and I spent time doing the summertime Jersey Shuffle on the weekends like so many other people still do. The Jersey Shuffle is a phenomenon--or shall I call it a migration?-- that occurs every year from Memorial Day until Labor Day. The Garden State Parkway becomes clogged as hundreds of thousands of people travel south every weekend to the Jersey coast for weekends away and summertime vacations when the school year ends in June. Once the Labor Day holiday is over, most of the cottages and summer rentals turn quiet as the "Bennie's," as the locals refer to the visitors, disappear.

Sandy and I were becoming a couple and were spending a lot

of our free time together. Summer was coming to a close. The days were getting shorter. Nana was fine and liked my new girlfriend.

September arrived. The shore visits came to a close, and it was trout fishing time again.

Sandy informed me that she wanted to go trout fishing with me.

I looked at her and said, "Are you sure?"

She replied, "Yes!"

The next thing I knew we were at Ray's Sports Shop looking for ladies' waders and some equipment. I explained to Sandy that she would use one of my spinning rods, and I'd teach her the basics on our next outing, I would bait the hook for her, and she would have to learn how to cast the spinning rod.

She informed me that she wanted to fly-fish like I did.

"Now, Sandy," I said, "first you need to learn the basics, and if you enjoy the sport, next year in the springtime, we will give the fly rod a try."

I am sure most ladies probably think this is a crazy arrangement, and quite frankly, I thought Sandy would give it a go once and then not want to go again. Well, a funny thing happened: on our first outing, Sandy caught a few trout. She called me over, and I took them off the hook and let them go. On the ride home that Sunday, I thought for sure that she would tell me she did not want to go trout fishing again, but much to my surprise, she informed me that the next Saturday we had a date at the South Branch of the Raritan River in Califon again.

It seemed my fate was now cast, hook, line and sinker, one might say.

The fishing thing certainly wasn't all we did. My job in the city required me to entertain clients with many social occasions. I went out probably two nights a week with clients, and Sandy sometimes joined me on such outings. My clients liked her. She was attractive and very outgoing on social occasions.

Sandy also had a circle of girlfriends, and we would spend time with them and their boyfriends as well.

In the fall of 1985, I also spent a lot of time working at Sandy's mom's home. Her late father had taken pride in their property, but it was quite a bit of work, six acres, for one man to do. Mrs. Fushi hired a service to keep the grass cut, but there was always a chore to do.

There was Sammy, a pony, in the barn, and Skippy, a horse, still at home from the days when Harriet and Sandy rode both. The animals were semi-retired, although Joanne still rode Skippy on the property on the ring. There were a few pastures for the horses. The fencing was getting old, as it had been installed more than thirty years earlier. There was a lot of maintenance to do, and large mature trees that needed pruning as well. I really didn't mind. The exercise was good for both mind and soul. Despite being a guy who worked on Wall Street, I really enjoyed getting my hands dirty and "playing farmer," as I called it, part-time on some weekends.

Fall was coming to a close, and the holidays would arrive soon. Sandy and I spent Thanksgiving Day at her mother's home with a traditional early afternoon dinner. It was just the three of us. Later that evening, we arrived at my Aunt Eileen's home in Scarsdale, New York, for another dinner. I told Sandy there would be a rather large gathering of my immediate family--mom and dad, brother and sister, aunt, uncles, and cousins—more than twenty people.

When we got there, Sandy was her usual outgoing self. Everyone seemed to like her. On the way back to New Jersey that evening, she commented that she'd had a nice time and my family was different from what had been the norm for her family of just her grandmother, mom and dad. Sandy had been accustomed to small gatherings during the holidays, and she seemed to thrive with all the activity of the large group setting.

Christmas was the next holiday, and we had the same type of arrangement, spending the morning with her mom, then going to my parents' home and following that with a trip to my cousin John's home in Pelham, New York.

That Christmas Day was special, as we had been dating for

about nine months. Sandy told my parents to get me some camping equipment because she knew I wanted to start to travel away next spring into Pennsylvania and the Catskills, a few hours away, to expand my trout fishing.

By this time I had gotten involved in a conservation group called Trout Unlimited and was the current vice president of the local chapter called Hacklebarney. We met once a month in nearby Morristown, N.J., so I was meeting some of my fellow trout fishermen in the area.

I was really surprised when I opened up some boxes of camping supplies—a tent, stove, lantern and so on—and learned that Sandy had gone out with my mom and helped her locate the items. I bought Sandy some type of jewelry and a few other girly things as young men do for their girlfriend for their first Christmas together, and she got me the boy things that young men want.

The year was coming to a close. Things were going fine at work and play with Sandy, who was turning out to be not just my girlfriend, but starting to become my best friend as well. We attended a New Year's Eve party that year, toasted one another, as all couples do, at midnight, followed by a kiss and awaited the next year to be.

The New Year

It was now 1986, and things at work were going fine. The desk I was working on was doing a good business. We all anticipated a good bonus, and I also expected a large raise as well. At the end of February, we had our reviews. I received the large bonus, almost as much as my salary had been the previous year, and I believed it was merited; however, my raise was not what I had expected. This was really the first year that the desk I worked on had made a good profit. I had expected more and was concerned that if I was to ever want a future with Sandy, I needed to see what I was really worth. I found out it was quite a bit more and I left the company to go to a competitor's desk a few blocks away. That was how things were back in those days in downtown Manhattan. It was the 1980s, and the U.S. government bond market was the place to work prior to the takeoff of the equities markets in the 1990s.

Spring arrived. Work was going fine. Commuting into the city from Summit was easy, and I could be at work in less than one hour from door to desk. Some might call the forty-five minute train ride the commute, but to me, time spent from doorstop to desktop was the full commute time.

Sandy and I started to get ready for some springtime fishing again and she pestered me about the fly rod thing again. I told her if she really wanted to try it, we would wait until mid-May when the weather was a bit better. Once again I thought her interest would pass and she would forget about it, but she didn't, and finally in mid-May, after her birthday, I said okay. Again we were off to outfit her for the next sport she eventually mastered, much to my surprise.

On our first outing I gave Sandy casting lessons in the backyard of her mom's house. She picked up the motion fairly easily. One thing I have learned over the years is that it's easier to teach the casting motion to women than to men. The reason is quite simple: women do not try to overpower the equipment and they learn to use finesse over strength, while their male counterparts seem all too constantly to use strength when they are first learning the sport.

Casting a fly requires a motion, balance, and rhythm. Once one has mastered it, it can become an enjoyable and relaxing pastime. I believe another reason some women take to the sport is that most trout fishing takes place in truly beautiful outdoor settings that are wonderful to behold.

Sandy was an art history major in college and worked in a printing plant that produced some very high-end prints and catalogs. Her eye for color was useful while she was at work and she truly enjoyed the settings where we fished together.

This season Sandy and I started traveling into central Pennsylvania and up into the western Catskills near the towns of Roscoe and Hancock, New York. These locations were approximately a three-hour drive from Summit, New Jersey, where I'd been living for the last few years while I was commuting into the city for work. I commuted rather than live in the city, because once it became green and warm, I need to get away to the woods, one might say, and back then a box, by which I mean an 18 x 30-foot apartment would have been all I could have afforded if I'd chosen to live in Manhattan.

I have always enjoyed being outside, fishing, hiking, or on the golf course during the good weather months. Sandy, having been a horse lover, was happy outdoors as well. We made many trips together that year. It is always fun to discover new places and quaint little inns along the way. Some were great, and some were duds.

Fishing wasn't the only thing we did on these trips. Antiquing and hiking were common as well. Many of the items we placed in our first home eventually came from many of these trips. Notable trips that year included Bar Harbor on the coast of Maine and Lake Placid in New York.

Summer arrived and we returned to Sea Girt on the Jersey shore. Nana was happy to have company, and Sandy and I had friends who either rented or stayed at family homes in the area.

Our outcome was becoming pretty apparent. I just need to continue to work, save money and enjoy life as all young adults who want to move forward do. By the end of the year I had been elected president of the Hacklebarney Trout Unlimited chapter. I was also a State Council delegate and actively involved with the organization on the local level and state level.

The following year, 1987, Sandy and I continued the routine, doing all the same things we'd done the previous year. However, we did also take a trip that year in July to Yellowstone Park in Wyoming. We both had a grand time. My nana had told us she and pop had traveled out west when pop retired and spent time there. She told me to stay at the Old Faithful Inn, and we did. Another placed we stayed on that trip was Chico's Hot Springs near the banks of the Yellowstone just north of the park in Prey, Montana. We fished the Madison River by drift boat for a few days, fished the Yellowstone in the park, and concluded our trip with a day at Depew's Spring Creek while we were staying at Chico's. We purchased some prints and knick knacks and took many wonderful pictures as well. The year 1987, the year before the fires hit the park the following season, was also the first time Sandy and I went horseback riding together. It was Western, which was fine by me. My late father had once owned a stable in West Orange and as a boy I'd had the pleasure of spending a few summers working for dad. Needless to say, it was the back end of a horse that I had gotten to know during those summers when I was in the seventh and eighth grades. That was before I discovered I could make a little more money as a human mule called a caddie.

When we returned from the trip, Sandy put together a photo album, including our boarding passes and tickets on the first page. She did a great job, and I still go back to that album from time to time to remember those happy days.

Once again summer ended, fall turned to the holidays, and the routine of our work and life together was apparent. Sandy and I spent all our free time together with both family and friends, and I am sure she started to wonder whether we would become man and wife. I was a little cagey with her. She knew I worked in the city and probably did well, but those were things I did not discuss with her. We went out to dinner on Fridays and she joined me when I entertained clients in the city for work, probably twice a month. Who wouldn't want to head into Manhattan for a show and good meal, particularly when a limo came to pick you up for a special event? I received a good bonus again that year, saved it and started to think that sometime in the spring things would become serious between Sandy and me.

By April of 1988, I had purchased a marquee-shaped engagement ring, 1.9 carats, and was ready to propose marriage.

The ring was the price of the Jeep I wanted instead, but you are supposed to do this only once and do it right, so I headed to the diamond district. My brother's brokerage firm had just done a private equity placement for a diamond house, and that was where I bought Sandy's engagement ring. I rode the subway uptown, went through three locked doors and found an elder Jewish diamond merchant who showed me quite a selection, explained the different grades, and even showed me investment-grade diamonds that at the time cost a small fortune. It was all quite a learning experience.

I made my choice for Sandy and picked up the ring the following week after it had been placed in a platinum and gold band. I was quite nervous on the subway ride back to my office with this very small Jeep in my pocket. The day I picked up the ring, De Beers announced a 12 percent increase. The merchant explained that I'd been lucky with my timing and would have paid much more if I'd waited. Later I had the ring appraised and it came in about 50 percent more at a few different merchants. One of the gals who worked on my desk asked to see it. She said it was beautiful and asked if she could put it on. I said no, the first person to wear it would be Sandy when I placed it on her hand.

If Mr. Fushi had been alive I would have asked his permission to propose to his daughter. Since he was gone I decided it would be appropriate to ask Mrs. Fushi for her daughter's hand. I told Mrs. Fushi I loved her daughter and wanted to spend the rest of my life together with her. Mrs. Fushi was very happy and seemed very pleased, so I showed her the engagement ring.

The following Friday night I had planned to take Sandy to dinner and pop the question. We had a nice meal, but I couldn't find an appropriate time in a crowded restaurant. We left, and while we were in the parking lot I, finally got the courage to ask Sandy to marry me. It had rained earlier that evening while we'd been at dinner.

Sandy said, "You need to get on a knee and ask me properly."

So I did.

Sandy said yes.

I had a wet knee. My fate was set and life would make a change for the better.

Our First Home

Summit was an easy commute to the city, and once Sandy and I were engaged, I figured we would just look for a larger place to rent nearby since I had been living with a roommate all along. By May 1988, though, Sandy started to get the itch to start looking for a home to buy. I hoped we would not find anything since the interest rate for a conventional thirty-year mortgage was over 10 percent. I really didn't think we could afford a decent home or that we really needed one.

Sandy, however, had a different idea and started to drag me out to look at homes, most of which were too far from my standpoint for me to commute every day, too big, or just too expensive. After about six weeks of these outings, I was tired and said, "No more!" I was sick of seeing houses and wanted to spend some time at the beach.

I got my wish, and everything went back to normal.

Sandy picked a wedding date, the following May just before her thirtieth birthday. I figured we would find an apartment prior to our wedding and then settle in.

Much to my surprise, it was Mrs. Fushi who located a small home which just happened to be around the corner from her home where she and Sandy were living. Apparently she'd run into an old neighbor at the Post Office, got into talking with her, and this neighbor had told her that she and her family were selling her parent's home, as both of them had passed and the family had decided to sell it. Mrs. Fushi and her neighbor went to see the home and then Mrs. Fushi told Sandy about the home.

A few days later Sandy got to see it and decided it was for her. She called me and described the home and explained that it would be easy for me to get into the city because the home was in the Green Village section of Harding.

All I could think was that the home would be expensive due to the location.

She took me to see the house the following weekend. It was the end of June or early July and I really was not in the mood for a house since we weren't even married yet. For the last year and a half we'd spent weekends together, living at my place or so it had seemed to me, but I figured, what the heck, it can't hurt to look. I was sure I really wouldn't like the home.

We arrived Saturday, and the woman who lived next door greeted us and then showed us into the house. The home was a small 1920s colonial. Later, while doing repairs to the home, I would find out that it was a Sears home that the woman's father had built himself as it had arrived by train to Madison and then been trucked to the location in Green Village. That was quite an accomplishment, though many homes were built that way back in those days.

The house had about an acre of property with a small working kitchen, pantry, and adjacent mudroom, dining room, den, and foyer downstairs. The second floor had one decent-size old bathroom and three bedrooms, the smallest of which had no closet. There was also a small non-winterized front porch and a basement, where the washer and dryer were with an old oil-fired furnace.

The location was lovely, but boy, did this house need work. There was no heat on the second floor and all the duct work was on the first floor. The woman explained that the furnace worked fine and the heat rose to the second floor.

I thought the house need to be gutted and updated first, and it would be too much work and expense for us to do. All the walls were plaster and lath, which was standard building code at the time.

There was one saving grace: the place was on a dead-end road, which was very quiet, and to me one other great thing was the four-bay detached garage in the back behind the home, which had a lot of room for items. An attic above the garage also had plenty of room for storage. Another important feature was that the home was surrounded by about six other homes that encompassed approximately 60 acres, and those lots could not be subdivided so the location would keep its rural setting as it has to this day.

The house had potential, but required a lot of work and I was concerned that it might be out of our reach due to these additional costs. I kept quiet while I looked at the home with Sandy on that first viewing. That afternoon, we went back to Harriet's home, sat outside on the deck and discussed the house.

Sandy said she liked it.

I told her I needed to think it over and explained that I thought the additional work necessary to upgrade the home would probably put us over the top as far as affordability. All the repairs that would be necessary were my major concern.

My situation was similar to my late grandfather's choice in Sea Girt. Sandy saw the home like my Nana saw hers, liked it, saw all the potential and probably knew I would agree just as Pop had for Nana. The difference was that we had not been together for more than thirty years of marriage. We were not even married yet.

I said to my bride-to-be, "Are you really sure this is what you want? It needs to be gutted, new furnace, just a lot of work."

Sandy looked me in the eyes and said, "I really do, Bill, and know we will be happy together there. I promise to help you with as much of the work as necessary to make this happen." I responded, "Sandy, we can purchase a home in the next town over in Madison, larger with four bedrooms, three baths and no work for the same price. All you will have to do is change the paint and maybe the carpeting colors to match and if you want to start a family, it will be turnkey."

Sandy said, "My mom is getting older, Bill, and will need help before we know it. She is 73 and will be 74 when we are married. Mom has this large six-acre place that I want for myself and my family someday, and when we have children, we will probably need to be with her eventually as this will become too much for her someday due to her age." I said, "Let me think this over for a few days, we will talk it over later and one more thing, please do not call me until I have enough time to digest all of this."

Sandy honored my request.

I did a lot of thinking over the next few days and then had a talk with my dad and kind of went over the details as I saw it. Sandy's mom had been diagnosed earlier in the year with early stages of Alzheimer's disease, and now her oddities were a reality and something that Sandy and I would need to address in any future plans as I saw it. Harding Township is very pretty, and I thought it would become a very desirable place as New Jersey was experiencing a fairly fast growth rate as the highway system that had ended in the middle of nowhere was to be completed in the next few years. Route 78 had just been finished from Summit to Route 287 in Bridgewater, and Route 24 was soon to start construction from Short Hills to eventually connect to Route 287 in Morristown. The finish date, about four years out, was slated for 1992. Harding was located right in the middle of the two.

My problem was that I needed about six months more in savings to have my down payment. My dad asked me to take him over to see the home. I called the neighbor and arranged to show my parents the home without Sandy's knowledge. My dad thought it was very expensive, and on the way home, we saw a home nearby that was just about the same size in nearby Madison and it was one-third less in cost. I repeated to my dad the words Sandy had said to me about her mom's condition and I told my dad that I thought Sandy and I should buy the home. I was very aware that this purchase would tap me out and we would be doing not much else but work on the home for the next few years for the necessary upgrades, but I thought it was important for Sandy to be nearby to help her mom. I then asked my dad what he would have done if he had been in the same situation as myself when he'd met my mom.

Dad thought of all the things I'd said as well and then said, "I agree with you, Billy, and I think your mom and I would like to help you out."

I told him not to worry and that would sell some stocks in my retirement account that had done well.

Dad said he and my mom wanted to give us a gift to help with the down payment.

That gift was a very nice gesture. I still would not have enough to avoid mortgage insurance, but it would make the numbers work a little easier. I knew this was going to be tough and hoped my year-end bonus that year would help. I figured it would be spent the following year on upgrades to the house.

About two weeks had passed since I'd first seen the home with Sandy. I called her and asked her if we could go back together and see the house again.

She made the arrangements.

We went back, and I believe Mrs. Fushi was with us. After we looked at the home again, we went back to her mom's home and I then said to Sandy, "Let's go out for dinner tonight and we can discuss all the pros and cons together." I was not really sure what she thought I would say over dinner. We went out someplace local and I said to Sandy that I thought that if the home were available in another year it could work, but I was afraid that the cost would be just out of our reach as I estimated how much the mortgage payment would be.

Mostly I was concerned about the costs of the upgrades, and that even though I was very handy and could do a lot of the work myself, we would have no life other than work, house, and work on the house for the next few years. I also showed her the numbers and told her that if she could find a similar house after our wedding date, we would be ready next year.

Sandy was disappointed, but she got the message and I thought that would be the end of it.

The next day, I called my dad and told him that I had thought it out and believed we would be better off if we waited until we were married. I said that I appreciated the help that he and my mom had offered, but I thought I should save a bit longer, I was sure another home would surface the following year and I would not need his help with a down payment by then.

A couple of days later, Sandy called me at work and said she wanted me to come over to her mom's home to discuss the house around the corner again.

I said, "I did the numbers with you and it just doesn't work right now and you agreed with me. We decide we would rent a home together away from Summit and close to your mom for this next year so you can help out with any of her needs."

Sandy replied that she had a way that would work and that I should just come by and she would go over it that evening.

I replied, "Okay, see you tomorrow," as I had a client to take out that evening and I really thought the matter was over.

The next evening, Sandy and I had dinner with Harriet, and then Sandy and Mrs. Fushi hit me with the bomb: Mrs. Fushi wanted to give Sandy the money so we could purchase the home around the corner.

I said we couldn't take it as she was a widow and living on a fixed income, and we should not need her help and that Sandy and I would wait until after our wedding and save our money until next year.

Mrs. Fushi and Sandy persisted, saying the house was probably the only nearby place that was available and that, one, I knew they were right, and second, if we bought the home Sandy would be near her mom if any help was necessary and I would also be nearby to assist with any odd jobs at her place.

I said to the two of them once again to let me think this one out and I would get back to them.

I spoke again to my dad and he said, "It's going be tough for a few years if you take this home, but I can see their point."

A few days later, I called Sandy and said, "If this is what you really want, I am willing do this for you as long as you are committed to this and realize that we will have an awful lot of work ahead of us."

Sandy said she understood.

I said, "What do we have to do next?"

She replied that she had made arrangements for us to meet an attorney, that we would need to sign a buyer agreement as we were not married to protect both of us if something happened and she would get me the details later.

A few days later, we met the attorney who drew up the necessary documents and then we moved forward with our purchase. Our closing date was set for September 15, and we started to prepare for the move.

We had been dealing directly with the one of the home's owners. When we decided to place our price, the neighbor called the family and said she had a young couple who were local and wanted the home. The family said the house had been listed with a local realtor and we would have to place our bid through him.

He asked questions about my salary and told me we could afford the home at the current asking price.

I informed him that we would pay a certain amount and no more, and that we had negotiated the price with one of the owners as it was an estate sale.

The realtor called me at work a few times about the price, and I finally told him if he bothered me at work one more time I would pull my bid. I called Sandy and told her I didn't want to speak to him again. I told Sandy that he kept telling us we should be paying more than our current bid price, and that he didn't want to discuss all the costs associated with the upgrades that would be necessary to bring the home to current standards.

On September 15, I received a call from Sandy who said there was one problem with our closing, but she was taking care of it.

I asked her what the problem was and she replied that we needed flood insurance.

I was at work, sitting on the 105th floor of the World Trade Center. It was about ten in the morning, and I was scheduled to leave at noon for our closing. At the time, I was employed at Cantor Fitzgerald, working on the long bond desk in very high-pressure position. I blew a gasket as I found out the flood insurance would cost an additional two thousand dollars per year, I told Sandy that over the course of the loan it would just continue to go up, that I would not be there for the closing, and that she should call the realtor and cancel the closing.

A few minutes later, the realtor called me. I said to him that he had not disclosed to us, the buyer, who he was also representing, a material fact and that I would not purchase the home under these conditions, and I hung up.

He called again, and I hung up on him again. I called Sandy and told her to let him know I would go to our attorney tomorrow and demand our deposit be returned. I was really pissed off.

That day I also called our mortgage rep, who was a personal friend, and told him the sale was off and that I wasn't willing to add flood insurance towards the home.

A few days later, he called me and said he was able to have the insurance waived. It turned out that the flood plain was more than 150 feet behind the dwelling and the insurance would not be necessary.

One reason why I had blown up that closing day was that I had moved out of my place in Summit on the last day of August. The current owners of the home had allowed us to place most of my furnishings in the garage until the sale closed. I was staying at my parent's home, awaiting what was to be a happy move-in day in two weeks, and now I had no place to live, all my furniture in the garage of a home we were not to buy, as it looked, and wondering what else could go wrong.

All's well that ends well, as they say, and we wound up closing two weeks later on September 30th. The rest is now history.

I had to endure two more weeks living with my mom and dad. I decided to make the best of it and, after having lived apart from them for some time, let's just say it was interesting. I had forgotten my mom's and dad's little quirks. We all have them, myself included.

Sandy and I spent the next few weeks getting all the usual things in order to move to our new home, moving furniture, filling dressers, and all the rest.

I realized we needed a lawn mower and purchased a small push one for the fall season. Next came the rakes. It was backbreaking work with a large amount of mature trees, so a leaf blower came next, and then the fall season cleanup was complete and November was soon to arrive.

Sandy and I took a few fishing trips upstate to the Salmon River just north of Syracuse for steelhead trout as we had done the past few years together, and soon the holidays were to arrive. For Thanksgiving and Christmas, we were back to the normal travel arrangements we had been doing the last few years, although we did not exchange much that year as the house had been our big purchase.

I received a good bonus, which enabled us to purchase a new bedroom set. Sandy and I agreed on it, and she cut a deal on the price, as she was always a good shopper. We also set aside a good amount for work to be done in the future and I kept an amount for our future honeymoon. Sandy also received some money that spring as her father's mom, her grandmother, passed, and we set that money aside as well for the house.

One item Sandy wanted was a fur. She showed me one locally, and I suggested that we take a drive to Flemington Furs down in Flemington, N.J., about an hour's ride. She got herself a beautiful blush fox jacket that she would wear on special occasions. I said to her, "If that's what you want, go ahead and get it for yourself. Your grandma would want to see you happy."

By now springtime was soon to arrive, and our wedding date

was set for May 6, 1989. I tried to be involved, but found, like all men probably do, that a wedding is the ladies' day and if you want to make your bride happy, just agree with what she wants and all will go fine. That's exactly what I did. A few times I was asked what I thought only to learn that what she wanted would always win out. The only decision we men have is to show up and say, "I do."

I did a little local trout fishing that season before our wedding, but it was just to some close-by local streams early on Saturday mornings so I could be back before noon, as there were household chores to do and Sandy was busy planning the wedding. Spring seemed to fly by as we had a lot on our plate with both a new home and wedding. Things were going well for the two of us.

Bo of the Beverkill

Sandy and I were married May 6, 1989, at Christ the King Church in New Vernon. Christ the King Church is set at a beautiful location, elevated on a hillside overlooking a pond that has geese and ducks as residents. The grass was green. Tulips were in blossom, and cherry trees were in bloom with their pink blossoms for all to see at the church. A sign across Blue Mill Road read: Duck Crossing.

We were married by Father Mannon, who'd taught Sandy some classes while she attended Seton Hall University. She liked him quite well. It also happened that Father Mannon had graduated from Seton Hall Preparatory School in 1944 with my father. Dad knew him as well and played golf with him occasionally. Sandy had called him and asked him if he would marry us, and he'd agreed. He was not a priest at Christ the King, but the church allowed us this wish.

Father Mannon was quite a character. One notable fact about him was that at one point in his career, he was the priest for none other than the New Orleans Saints during the late 60s and early 70s. While there, he was present when the longest field goal was ever kicked in the NFL—sixty-three yards by Tom Dempsey. During our wedding ceremony, Father Mannon gave a sermon about Dempsey, his physical stature and, for those who'd been unaware, his special shoe as he'd been born with a deformed foot, but was able to overcome that and one day set a record that lasted till broken December 2013 by 1 yard. When Father Mannon declared us man and wife, I kissed my bride and then she said, rather loud to everyone's surprise, including mine, "Let's party!"

We had about one hundred fifty guests for the wedding, and our reception was held at the Madison Hotel.

Sandy had no idea where she was going for her honeymoon and had been asking me where we were going. I wanted to go to Hawaii, but she had been there with her best friend Cathy, her bridesmaid, the year before we met, and I did not want to go somewhere where she already had vacationed.

I informed her that, as her husband, tradition said that all I had to tell her was what type of climate to pack and dress for, that the honeymoon is the groom's last gift to his bride and that I would follow that old outdated tradition. I assured her she was going to a very nice place and said to pack for warm weather and bring a bathing suit.

We spent our first night as husband and wife in the honeymoon suite of the hotel. It was a very beautiful room, finished off in early American New England-style furnishings and decor. I told Sandy we had to leave by 6 a.m. to be at Newark Airport the next morning for an early flight.

The next morning we awoke as man and wife for the first time.

I said, "We are heading to Sandy Lane."

She gave me a puzzled look and said, "Get real, Bill."

As we boarded our plane to Puerto Rico, I'm sure Sandy thought I was taking her there since she seemed a little confused when we landed and then I said we had another plane to board. This time we were on to Barbados, our final destination. If anyone ever visits Barbados or sees a TV commercial for the island, there is a very famous old hotel with a pink-colored limestone building with an archway that has a view of the Caribbean through the entranceway. It is a magnificent tropical paradise and it turned out that the travel agent from our town did a super job locating this place for us. The resort Sandy Lane had a golf course, tennis courts, beautiful beaches, and snorkeling just off the beach. There was a coral reef one hundred yards from the beach and beautiful floral gardens.

I decided prior to our arrival that we would not take the meal plan and just stay at the hotel, and if we wanted to eat all our meals there we could do so, but thought Sandy would prefer to try different restaurants. This was a good choice. We arrived at the resort by early afternoon Sunday and went to the beach to get some sun. On Sundays the resort had a traditional Caribbean dinner with rumba dancing and metal drums playing, so we decided to have our meal there. We were not all that thrilled with it, but a few nights later, we had a fine meal. We just were not big on flying fish or curried goat, the local fare for that evening.

While we were at the resort, I played golf a few times. Sandy drove the cart and putted on the greens. She was always good at miniature golf. We played tennis, did some sightseeing and snorkeling, which was very neat, and we went horseback riding on the beach. We stayed at Sandy Lane twelve days and eleven nights, then headed back to New Jersey the following Thursday.

We arrived home Thursday afternoon. The weather was fine. We did a walk around the house and everything was fine at home as well. Sandy asked me what I wanted to do since we were still off until the following Monday.

I said to her, "Would you care to do some fishing upstate in the Catskills?"

She thought about it and said yes.

She had not fished with me at all that spring and did truly enjoy the sport.

I thought she would say no and we would stay home for the weekend, but that was not her choice. I believe she did this for me as I had been itching to get upstate to fish the bigger rivers. It was the third week in May and probably the best time of year to be on the Beverkill and Delaware river systems.

Friday morning we packed the car, headed to the village of

Roscoe, and located a motel for the next two nights. We spent the next few days on the rivers with fly rods in hand next to our wedding bands.

Saturday evening we had dinner in the Antrim Lodge, a famous local watering hole for all the fly-fishing trout bums and hobnobs. I sat facing the entrance, as we were seated near the bar, a good distance away from the entrance, and Sandy faced me with her back towards the entrance. We were just about finished with dinner, when I noticed an old fishing buddy of mine Dick Hepper arrive with some friends. Dick saw me and had a big smile on his face. Dick is now in his late 80s, currently widowed. At the time, he was in his 50s. He winked at me and said nothing, but had this funny grin on his face and I couldn't understand why.

Dick was with two other gentlemen that night. It turned out that on Friday one of them had returned to their camp and told the other guys that he'd seen Bo Derek fishing on the Beverkill River that day. The other guys had told him, "You're nuts." He'd sworn to them that he was certain he'd seen her and the following Saturday he repeated his tale, saying he'd seen her again fishing with the same fishing guide. They'd said, "No way," and told him he was crazy, though Dick also said to Richie, "You're right. A few years ago, I also saw her," just to humor him.

This town is the birthplace of American fly-fishing for trout. When you get off the highway, Route 17, there's a sign that says, "Welcome to Trout Town USA." This area has been frequented by some very notable figures, including past U.S. presidents, and it is quite common to see people walking around town in their waders and full equipment.

Dick saw Sandy and me in the restaurant that evening and noticed that Sandy, who had her back to him, had her red hair done with braids and beads at the end. He said to Richie, "Remember you told us you saw Bo Derek?"

Richie said, "Yes, I did."

Dick then said to Richie, "I told you I met her a few years back and it was while I was fishing, but I never told you I gave her a fly and helped her land a trout and she told me if I ever saw her again that she would give me a kiss as she'd landed her first trout while on the river and her guide did not have the right fly."

Richie said, "You're full of it."

Dick then replied, "She's sitting over there with her back to us."

Richie said, "You're right, Dick, there she is again with her guide from this afternoon. I told you guys I saw her. You didn't believe me and quite frankly I don't believe your fish tale of knowing her."Dick said, "I bet you dinner and drinks that if I go up to her, she will give me a big hug and a kiss as she promised she would if I ever ran into her again."

Richie said, "You're on!"

With that, Dick started to walk toward our table with his finger to his mouth to let me know not to say a word and be quiet.

I thought he wanted to surprise Sandy.

He tapped her on the shoulder with his back toward Richie, and she turned to look up to our longtime Hacklebarney Trout Unlimited member and friend Dick. She stood up, gave Dick a big hug and kiss on the cheek and sat back down.

The look on Richie's face was shock. Dick knew Bo Derek! And he'd just gotten a hug and kiss from her as he'd said he would.

Dick turned with a grin on his face, walked calmly back to his friend and said, "Pay up. Let's eat, pal!"

A little while later Dick said to Richie, "Would you like to meet her?"

They walked over to our table and Dick introduced Richie to Sandy and me.

Richie then realized he'd been had and started to laugh.

They all then sat down at our table and had a drink with us.

Dick said, "I want to introduce you to Sandy Dunn. That's really her name and she is not named after a dry fly called a Sandy Dun." This fly pattern is fished in the area during the fishing season and is know as a Sandy Blue Dun as well.

A nice evening was had by all, and when I saw Richie a few years later or bumped into him from time to time when I was fishing or in town, we would have a laugh over the evening he met Bo of the Beverkill. That was how I wound up a very lucky man married to Bo of the Beverkill. Sandy was a very unusual lady, ahead of her time.

Sandy's picture graced a few publications of the time as well. While heading to work one day, I picked a copy of the February 1989 issue of *Sports Afield* at a newsstand in the World Trade Center before I headed up to the 105th floor at Cantor Fitzgerald, and there she was again in print on page 83 with the following caption: "Changing flies and retying knots and leaders are all part of the game." The picture was just a headshot taken the previous season, but I could tell it was her because I was by her side at the time and I recognized the hat she was wearing.

A few years later I found her again in the April 1991 issue of a magazine called *Fly-fishing*. She was the centerfold, and she had her waders on. She was on page 39. The picture is a full page and shows her standing alone, fly rod in hand, on a quiet pool of a great eastern river not so far from our backyard. This photo was taken the previous year, as I found out after I called the magazine to locate the author of the article titled, "The Beverkill." The gentleman sent me a copy of the picture, which I had laminated to a nice wood frame I still have to this day. The picture had been taken the previous spring around Memorial Day as the flowers blooming in the bottom of the picture arrive at that time of year.

Sandy was a rare gem who I was blessed to fall in love with. Not only was she beautiful, happy, and just a wonderful gal to be around, but she also, because of her love for me, gave up her time to make me happy doing the things that I really enjoyed. There are very few ladies who give to that degree, but Sandy was a giving and caring woman, who did so for her love for me and to see me happy.

Working, Playing and Moving Along

The first thing done to improve our new home in the spring of 1990 was the exterior: a new roof, replacement windows, new gutters, and vinyl siding to the entire house. Sandy wanted to put new wood on the exterior, but the cost and the fact that painting would be needed about every six years were major considerations for the siding. She picked the colors, and by the end of May the place from the exterior looked new. The contractor was a local man from town. Sandy grew up with him and they went through both grammar and high school together.

Holidays were soon to arrive, and we took a few trips upstate in November to go steelhead fishing near Pulaski, New York. After that we settled down for the holidays and winter.

After the New Year, 1990, Sandy informed me that we needed to put in new carpeting.

I said, "We need to leave the old as we will soon need to start the interior." We were seeing some cracking of the plaster walls. The house was built in the 1920s and the walls were 70 years old and in need of repair.

By fall we got started. We got a few quotes, which seemed high, and I said to her, "Look, I have always been handy. Let me give this one a try."

She said to me, "You don't know how to do this."

I responded, "You don't need a college degree to ripe out walls and such."

I said, "Look, Sandy, let me give the dining room a try and if I cannot do it, we will then just have to hire someone to finish the job."

She reluctantly agreed, and by the end of September work was soon to begin.

One of my good friends arrived on a Saturday morning, and we got started with the task at hand. My friend and I had a fan going. We put plastic over the doorways and started ripping the walls apart. It is a very messy job, but we were finished by the end of the day. All plaster was off the walls and most of the lath was removed as well.

Sunday I finished the rest of the job, removing the remainder of the lath and taking out all the small nails. The house was somewhat dusty, but I then headed off to the Home Depot and purchased the electrical wire, boxes, and insulation. I also ran ductwork to the bedroom to be hooked up sometime in the future.

Monday I was off to work, and by the following Friday evening during the week I had finished rewiring the room and putting in the insulation. A friend of mine hooked up the wiring to the new 200-amp box that was installed prior to this phase of work.

I hired a man to sheetrock the room, worked with him the following Saturday, and kind of learned how to do this work from him.

He said, " Measure twice, draw your lines to be cut and measure a third time. If everything measures correct, the sheetrock will fit in place."

It was good advice. He also did the spackling, as that was one job that requires experience, and once the walls are up, the only thing one can see is a bad spackling job. I realized this job was beyond my experience and it was best to hire out for now and probably in the future.

Sandy found out I was able to get this work done and I did know my limitations, mostly spackling. She was quite happy with the finished job. From start to finish it took about a week and a half, with both weekends, all day, and me working late into the evening during that week. She wanted wallpaper and picked it out, and a few weeks later we had a very nice dining room.

One room down and a few more to go.

We repeated this process after the New Year in 1991 as Sandy informed me that she was pregnant with our first child, due sometime by the end of July. I redid the bedroom above the dining room, this time by myself, and there was much less mess as the room had a door that could be closed off. I still hired the same man to do the spackling and had the duct work attached so we now had heat for our newborn.

Sometime in March Sandy picked out new carpeting for the room.

Work was fine, and life was about to change with the arrival of our first child. An ultrasound indicated that we would be expecting a girl, and Sandy seemed quite content with her new role as mother to be.

Sandy and I took one trip that springtime to the Catskills around Roscoe over Memorial Day weekend and that would be our last for a while as I could see it. We purchased larger lightweight waders, and she was a trooper as we fished a little with me holding her hand while she got into the stream and only where there was easy wading for her.

By June she had gotten all the baby furniture and a crib and had her baby shower. We were now in the waiting game for a few more weeks.

Our first child arrived July 20, 1991, and I was present for the delivery. For a first-time dad, watching the whole process was incredible, something I will never forget, and once that child is born, it brings husband and wife closer together.

Our daughter Jenny was healthy, and we were very grateful for our special present. Our lives together had just changed for the better. I took a week off from work to help Sandy the first week after Jenny was born and enjoyed the company of my wife and child.

We settled down to a new way of life as all new parents do. Sandy had been moved from the production department into sales, which allowed her flexibility to be a mom and work out of the house, and she did a great job at both. I continued to work in the city, commuting, and was quite involved with Trout Unlimited at both the local and state level, even more so now that fishing time was no longer a priority. Sandy and Jenny were my priority, and I settled into that role comfortably.

Holidays were to arrive by the fall, and we traveled as we had always done on Thanksgiving Day, having dinner first with Harriet in the early afternoon and then to see my side of the family later by dinnertime up in Westchester County, N.Y.

After traveling so much that day, I did some thinking, and said to Sandy that now that we had a family we should stay home for Christmas Day this year. It was our first Christmas as parents. I spoke to my mom and dad and asked them if they would mind, and so that first Christmas, 1991, we started a new tradition in which we invited family and friends to our home Christmas Day to exchange gifts. I purchased a honey-baked ham that Christmas Eve and put it out for the family and friends Christmas Day.

The next year was uneventful except for the passing of my grandmother Dunn, who I'd called Nana. She was just shy of 100, passing at the age of 99 where we had spent many memorable days at the shore with her.

Winter turned to summer. I had just finished gutting the living room next to the completed dining room and duct work was placed for the bedroom above, that being Sandy's and mine.

Summer turned to fall. In September 1992 we went back to Roscoe, New York, staying at Twin Island campground. We stayed in a friend of mine's camper. We took the dogs and Jenny and just had a relaxing time. I fished a little, and Sandy fished also as we traded off baby-holding time.

One of our first evenings there I put Jenny to bed, and Sandy and I had a campfire out front in the fire pit, seeing Jenny looking out at the two of us from a window. After about half an hour of going in and out to tend to our fourteen-month-old child, Sandy brought her out to sit with us, and we did that during each evening's campfire while we were there for the remainder of the week. We found a thank-you gift in town for my friend and left it for him to find on his arrival when he visited his camper after his trip to Canada.

The New Year, 1993, brought a bit of funny news and it came from Sandy. She said to me, "Bill, I know you are working very hard to provide for us and you really do not do much anymore for yourself."

I said, "That is what I am supposed to do now."

Sandy replied, "I have been thinking and we really had a nice time while up the camper. I think we should get one."

I was in shock and thought she would just drop the issue, but much to my surprise by February she had started looking without my knowledge.

One Saturday she said to me, "I want to take you out for a drive and show you something I have found for us to buy."

I thought it was a new couch or something like that.

She took me to a R.V. dealer as she had located a nice used unit. It was about twenty-four feet long, the maximum we would be able to tow with our vehicle at the time.

I was concerned that it would probably kill our Bronco II and would require upgrades to the transmission and hitch. I also was not interested in pulling a camper around all the time, and I figured that would be the end of it.

That was not the end of it. By July 4, 1993, we had a new camper located in Roscoe, New York, in Twin Island Campground. A new chapter was soon to unfold for the two of us.

We spent the remainder of that summer and fall spending our weekends in the area. Sandy was happy as there were other young moms with families there, and I was able to get some fishing in with my friend and made some friends at the campground.

We closed that season on Columbus Day weekend, driving up Saturday morning. The weather was looking bad, so we came home that Saturday evening. We made a good choice as eight inches of snow fell that evening, and we were home warmer and dry and did not have to close up with a snowy mess.

That fall I gutted our bedroom, going through the same process as I had for the other rooms and now we had heat in our bedroom for the winter season.

In the spring of 1993 Sandy was pregnant with our second child, due in early December. We spent time this season from May until Columbus Day weekend again in Roscoe, known as Trout Town, USA. Leslie was born December 9, 1993, and we had another healthy beautiful little girl. Her room was finished, painted as the others had been and with heat as well.

By early November Christmas was soon to arrive. We had a nice, happy, and healthy family. Life was good, and I decided it was time to break away from my responsibilities with Trout Unlimited. I had been local president of our chapter for seven years, highly involved in the state council, fundraising and doing other activities, my family was growing and the organization needed some new blood and fresh ideas.

As 1993 came to a close plans for the next year moved ahead. We would finish the remainder of our home—bathroom, foyer, and stairwell, hiring out the job as it was just too much work for me to do myself. We attended my cousin Paul's wedding in June 1994 in Vermont, and the gutting and dirty work was done while we were away. When we got back, we had about a week while at home until the work was completed.

Sandy picked the wallpaper and finally got that new carpeting for her home. It was carpeted to match her decor, which most visitors said was very well done. She had a good eye for colors. We had only the kitchen to work on next as we were anticipating adding an extension in the next few years.

By summer 1995 our cute house was becoming rather small, and by the end of the year I started discussing the addition. However, work was becoming slow. The U.S. government bond market was not the business it once was. Surpluses were on the way under a Republican-controlled Congress. Bill Clinton was president. The equity markets were becoming the real moneymaker on Wall Street. Our market was contracting, and I was not sure how much longer there would be work for me.

Sandy and I decided to hold off on the addition and instead decided we should finish the basement, which would become a playroom for the girls with built-in storage closets and desks and an office area for Sandy.

This was a large project and although it did not require any demolition of plaster and lath, it did require me to frame out and build a vapor barrier between the concrete walls and studs. The project was started in the fall of 1995 and completed shortly before New Year's. Furniture and carpeting were in place shortly afterwards, giving the girls a place to play inside during the bad winter weather. They were now two and four years old.

Sandy also got an office downstairs complete with a new computer, fax machine, and business telephone line into the house, so she could work from home and just go to the office for press checks with clients when her jobs were being printed.

Sandy's work was going fine. Mine was starting to slide. Firms were closing their operations in the government bond markets. In 1988 there were fifty-five primary dealers in the government bond market. By now there were quite a few less and the industry was shrinking. Salaries stagnated and for some, went down.

It was 1997, I was working a night desk and it was very difficult. The market opens Sunday evening (Monday morning in Japan), is open until Friday afternoon in New York and trades twenty-four hours a day. We had a mortgage and bills to pay. I figured there would be a turnaround in a few years, but that was not the case, and by 1998 it was time for me to start a new career. It was not by my choice, but due to necessity.

I did a lot of research, and after much thought, I felt a new career as an advisor would be suitable choice. I wound up as a financial advisor, working at Summit Bank in Ridgewood, N.J. about forty minutes driving time from my home.

I worked very hard and everything went fine. I was making a good income, and Sandy and I were now getting ready for the addition to our home. We also had our well replaced in the summer of 1999 as there was no city water. The old well was about twenty feet away from the house and we had it moved to the back of the property, as we had our plans in place for the addition and figured that construction would begin sometime in the summer of 2000.

In the spring of 2000, something happened to change these plans and give us even more work ahead.

Moments in Time

In the fall of 1997, by looking at a map, I located a special lake, secluded up a dirt road in the peaks of the Catskills about forty minutes from our camp in Roscoe. This little gem is called Alder Lake. It was once the private estate and summer home of a wealthy New York City railroad man, Samuel Coykendall, who developed it, placing a grand mansion and damming a small steam to create the lake. In his day, the owner had lavish parties, and notable guests would frequent his summer retreat, which was built in the late 1800s. Today the location is just a few hours by car from New York City. In that time, it was quite an undertaking to get there, as travel was done by train and then a carriage ride. The road trip apparently took an entire day over unpaved wagon trails, a two-day trip in total for visitors of that era.

I took Sandy and the girls to Alder Lake for the first time Columbus Day weekend, the closing weekend of our camp season, for a picnic lunch. It was one of those truly beautiful rare fall days. The sky was blue with not a cloud in the air and the full peak colors of fall foliage that the northeast has were in full splendor. The oranges and reds were present in all different shades, with the greens of the conifers as their backdrop, as were the beautiful blue shimmering lake and magnificent blue sky.

When we arrived as a family, the winds were gone and the lake was a mirror reflecting all the fall colors. It was as if we viewed two sets of the peaks only in reverse that special day. We decided to take a walk around the lake. The trail was well marked, and as we followed it our family received many special gifts from the forest that day. The first was what appeared to be an old apple orchard in a low area as we went around a bend in the trail, complete with delicious apples for the picking. They were McIntosh apples, smaller than the store-bought variety and a bit tarter in taste. We then located some rough campsites. A little later down the trail we crossed a small bridge built over the only intake stream into the lake. We peered into the pool below the bridge and saw Brook trout in their spawning colors preparing for their annual ritual.

Other wonders also appeared to us on that special day. My youngest daughter Leslie started to get tired from the walk, so she rode on my shoulders for about the last two miles or so as we made our hike. She was not quite four years old yet. It was one of those special lasting days that families sometimes get to have. Sandy and the girls loved the place and we promised that, next season, we would return.

The following season we did return to our special little gem a number of times. We brought our dogs as well, and I brought my fishing rods to give it a go while we had our picnics and sometimes evening meals there, bringing along a portable grill. There were afternoons at Alder Lake when I caught over thirty Brook trout and Sandy fly-fished as well. The girls played nearby, catching newts and crayfish with nets and placing them in buckets to see who could land the most in an afternoon or evening. That was how we spent our days and afternoons here while the girls were small. There were trips again in the fall to pick apples in the cool fresh mountain air and other trips over the years while we had our camper.

Alder Lake sits at 2200 feet above sea level and nearby Balsam peak rises to 3,723 feet. The lake is approximately forty-five acres and has its own genetically distinct Brook trout, according to the park ranger who frequented the lake.

Below the spillway of the dam were the remains of an old caretaker's house and the remains of a small hatchery that Mr.

Coykendall built. The ranger explained that Brook trout eggs had been brought from Maine and raised in Mr. Coykendall's private hatchery to be stocked in the lake for his guests while they visited, and that Alder Lake was the only location where this strain of trout were located in New York state. The trout have a distinct blue hue in color and tend to be small, and no trout are stocked in this lake as all the fish are a now native since the original transfer from Maine. A fifteen-inch fish is a monster, and while I was there with my family I landed a few monsters, releasing all of them back to their native home.

The mansion was boarded up when we first visited. The lake is a somewhat remote spot still as the area has no facilities, keeping it forever wild, part of the Balsam Lake Mountain Wild Forest within the boundaries of the Catskills Forest Preserve. We were fortunate to find it as a family. Alder Lake for me holds my fondest memories of happy family outings while my children were young and Sandy and I were building our life together.

The other treat the area of the Catskills holds is a wonderful county fair, the Delaware County Fair held every August in Walton, New York. This fair is one of the oldest continuing fairs held in the country, now more than one hundred sixty years and going strong. It takes place about the third week of August, and we generally went to the fair from Thursday until Saturday evening, the last night, weather permitting.

Sandy and the girls enjoyed all the critters in the 4-H area, rides, games, and all that is to be seen at such an event. It was an event we went to every year after we purchased the camper in 1992 and something the girls awaited every summer. This event is truly one of a kind for this part of the country, and can bring one to a time and place that seems to have vanished in so much of America today.

We as a family were truly blessed to have such wonderful times and make some very lasting friendships with people from different walks of life while we were in this beautiful part of the country.

A Change of Plans and Stroke of Luck

Sandy's mom Harriet, who had been living around the corner from us, had been diagnosed with early stages of Alzheimer's a few years prior and had been doing fine, was now getting worse and one day a neighbor found her in the local supermarket. She apparently was lost and did not know where she was. This woman took her home, called Sandy, and that was the end of our house expansion plans. We had Harriet checked out and it was apparent that she was now in need of help.

Sandy said to me, "Bill, it's time now for us to help mom. I think that we should not continue with our plans now."

I asked what she wanted to do, and she said, "Let's start getting her home back in order and we should prepare to move in and I will take care of her. Your work is going fine, and we can either rent our home or sell it."

I asked Sandy, "Is this really what you want?"

She said, "What choice do we have?"

I said, "We could rent your mother's place or have someone stay with her and help her."

Sandy would have none of that and said, "It's now time."

I agreed with her wish and now we were back at it again, doing another home repair.

This time we did not have to do any demolition, just a good old-fashioned clean up while our plans for our first home and addition were on hold. Harriet's home needed to be painted. Sandy selected the colors, and we started from the bottom and worked our way up.

I was over there probably two or three evenings during the week, working after dinner, and Sandy helped when she was available during the daytime. We started that fall of 2000 and decided to enjoy our summer with trips to the Catskills and Jersey shore as well.

Work started inside the home that fall and by March the downstairs was done. Painting continued until about the end of May 2001. Then the second floor was finished, and the house was cleaning up and looking nice.

We took a few trips after Memorial Day to Roscoe with the girls and were ready to enjoy the summer after school was out in late June. New carpeting was installed and appliances put in the kitchen as well as having the exterior of the house painted. All in all we spent a fair amount of money on Sandy's mom's home. Financially we had no worries. Mrs. Fushi had helped as when we'd purchased our first home and now it was our time to help her, it just arrived a few years earlier than we'd expected.

Sandy was now maintaining our house, helping her mom with her needs daily, shopping for her and just keeping an eye on her. I told Sandy not to worry about work, but she still saw her clients when necessary, though she was concentrating her time more at home.

My dad's health was deteriorating during this period. Dad had been diagnosed a few years back with prostate cancer. He'd had it treated, then a few years later, he'd had bladder cancer and then trouble in his kidneys, and it was spreading again. Dad was not doing very well in the summer of 2000.

My work had been going very well, and in that same year I left Summit Bank and went to work much closer to home at First Union Bank, about twenty minutes away in Livingston, N.J. and one town away from my parents' home in Florham Park. I was spending my early mornings with Dad from about 8 a.m. until about 9 a.m. weekdays, just talking with him, and then heading to work. I would stop and get him *The Wall Street Journal* and he enjoyed reading the paper each day as he was not able to get around very well. He was confined to his bed and a wheelchair and was using oxygen. He had been a heavy smoker as a man, starting during his time in the Navy during World War II. He had stopped too late and been diagnosed with emphysema about fifteen years earlier.

Sandy and I had Thanksgiving at my parents' home that year, Harriet joined us and our children when we went to my parents for dinner later. All of us thought that Dad would not be there for Christmas. He did not look good. He was to start radiation and chemo the following Monday after Thanksgiving.

Christmas arrived, and we were again celebrated after Santa's arrival at our home. Later that morning we went to Harriet's home and then went back that afternoon to my parents' home. Dad was doing a little better, but was off the chemo for about a week and was to go back after the new year to check on the progress. We all were saying prayers that the cancer would stop that Christmas Day in 2000. I continued to see Dad every morning in the new year, 2001, and hoped the chemo would work. We were looking for a miracle.

Dad went back in mid-January to have his progress checked, and the news was not good. The doctors scheduled another round to start soon, and I was coming to the conclusion that Dad's outcome was looking bleak.

I said to my boss at the time that I would arrive at work by 10 a.m. and stay late, explaining that I needed to be there and make Dad as comfortable as possible. I am now very glad that I took this time to spend with him.

He worried that I was not spending enough time at work and probably not making enough money.

I told him not to worry, all was fine and it was. We had a mortgage still at the old house and it was not a problem.

Dad started the chemo in late-January and after a week or two decided that he wanted no more.

I guess that he had now come to terms with his illness.

On June 20, 2001, my father passed in his sleep. We had started, as a family, with a round-the-clock vigil with him about four days prior to his passing. Having worked a night shift in the city a few years back, I volunteered to do the evening shift from 11 p.m. to 6 a.m. My brother, sister, mom, and I were staying at the house as we awaited the final days.

Dad did get his final wish as his lifelong friend Marty Horn arrived from Florida a few days before Dad's passing. It cheered him up and brought a smile to his face to see his lifelong friend. I had called Marty and explained to him Dad's condition, asking him to come ASAP. Marty and his wife had arrived shortly to say goodbye and were in my parents' home when Dad passed.

Three days before Dad's passing I brought my daughters over to see their grandfather and said, "It is time to say goodbye to Popup," and at seven and nine years old, they said goodbye for the last time. We had our time for mourning, and I thought of Peter, Sandy's dad, and of the hurt that she had experienced, and I now knew that same feeling truly for the first time in my life. Dad was gone, and I would never be able to say, "I love you" again, and I had an empty place in my heart. The passing of a loved one creates memories that do not go away, and with the passing of time your heart can heal, but the memories do not fade.

Dad's funeral was held a few days later, and I met some of his childhood friends from his Seton Hall prep school days. Dad was laid to rest nearby at Gate of Heaven in East Hanover, N.J., where his father's family's cemetery plot was located. The service was nice, and Mom was now by herself for the first time in her life. She seemed bored as she had been Dad's nurse for some years as his health deteriorated. Mom started to stop by more often, spending some time with her grandchildren, and I visited a few days each week either on my way to work or my way home.

That summer of 2001 Sandy finished getting her mom's house ready for our planned arrival prior to the start of school in September. She picked out new carpeting for the house, new appliances were installed in the kitchen, and some furniture was added as well. We planned to move in before Labor Day weekend, as school would begin the first week of September 2001. A good deal of time and money had been spent getting Harriet's home ready for our now extended family.

The movers had all of our furniture moved the Wednesday before Labor Day, and we moved the small stuff ourselves. The children shared a bedroom, Sandy and I had the master bedroom, and Harriet was in another. We converted a bedroom downstairs into an office for Sandy and tried to settle in.

We soon discovered, after living with Harriet, that her disease had progressed much further than we had thought and we were having difficulties with her. Many patients with this disease have odd sleeping patterns. They fall asleep during the daytime and can wander around in the middle of the night. Harriet was one of them.

Things continued to deteriorate while she was with us. We were all being woken up in the middle of the night. One night I located Harriet in the kitchen and found that she had turned on all the burners on the stove, so finally I went to the hardware store and bought a deadbolt and placed it on the outside of Harriet's door. We all slept well that evening, and from that point on I made sure Harriet's door was deadbolted every night.

On the morning of September 11, 2001, I was at home on a conference call. Sandy called me from upstairs and said, "Bill, come up here and look at the news."

I said I couldn't as this call was on.

She said, "You have to see this. They are saying a plane hit the World Trade Center."

I went upstairs, thinking a small single engine plane had crashed, and as I saw the TV set the first thing out of my mouth was "This is a terrorist attack!"

Sandy said, "No, they were saying a plane just crashed."

I remembered my past, sitting up there on the 105th floor when I'd worked at Cantor. I looked at Sandy and said, "There is not a cloud in the sky. Two hundred yards away is the Hudson River and New York harbor. The only way a plane could hit the building would be a deliberate crash and it was not a small plane either. The next highest building downtown is half the size, and a small plane could not cause all that smoke."

The next thing I knew the model with a mouth on TV said, "It looks like there is going to be another accident." And with that plane number two collided into the South Tower.

I have said before that life is about the choices we make and sometimes we make the right choice or it just passes us by. I had just turned down an offer to go back to work at Cantor for a second time. A gentleman from town ran the energy desk, knew that I had worked for them on the bond desk and wanted me to go back. I had thought about it. The money was very good, but I had changed careers and said to him, "I am forty-four now. If I take this position, I will get about a five-year run on it and then this market will be replaced by computers just like the bond market was."

Sandy thought I should take the position, but I really did not want to be out of the house at 6 a.m. and home by 7 p.m. on a good night when I was not out with clients. I was happy with my new-found vocation, and if I wanted to see a play at school that the girls were in, I could do so. Financially we really had no problems. For myself this decision was about the lifestyle we had and I was very happy with that decision that I made. Had I made another choice that summer of 2001 I would not be here today. It could have been me that fateful September day. By choice or fate I was spared.

My last conversation with John was Saturday before 9/11. I saw him that morning while I attended the soccer clinic for Leslie. Both he and I had second-graders, and in our town the recreation department starts soccer in kindergarten. I had met John there as his son was in Leslie's grade and the clinics were co-ed at that time until the third grade when they split. This year John had decided to be a volunteer as I had the prior two years.

He and I discussed the normal things, made small talk, and he again asked if I was interested in going back into the city. He said a local young man from town had just joined his group, was looking for brokers and felt I would be a good fit.

I said one last time to John, "That part of my life is over and I really do not want to go back into the city. It's a young man's game now, and I am happy with my career path."

That was Saturday morning.

The following Tuesday life changed forever in America. Many people saw the events that followed and viewed them in disbelief. I thought of my past coworkers who were probably gone forever and started to cry on our front steps as I was sure that no one had survived and I considered myself very fortunate to be out here somewhere in New Jersey.

My family and I went to only one memorial service after 9/11, and it was for John. It was held at Christ the King, where Sandy and I had been married back in 1989. We attended that service as a family that day. It was a very somber experience. Many people from town were there.

John's wife walked down the aisle of the church just prior to the beginning of her late husband's service. She was alone now with four young boys, the youngest just under one year old. I could not even comprehend what she and her family could be going through and said a prayer for her and all the others who had lost someone that day.

The normal words were spoken at the service, and there were many in attendance. I really knew John only from the soccer clinic in the fall, where we'd met a few years earlier, and when we'd bumped into one another at school events for the kids. He was a very likable man and a good provider for his family. They were his first priority.

There were very few dry eyes during the mass that day. I held up until the priest spoke and wanted to talk to John's boys about their dad. They were nine, seven, four, and just an infant. The words were beautiful and then the tears welled up for me as I thought of the many other families going through this same ordeal by the thousands from the area.

I had two clients who lost their children as well. America would never be the same, and I started to think about what was really important to me. It was my family: Sandy, the girls, and their happiness. We had lost my Uncle Bud that March, Dad in June, and now in September 2001, something worse. As a country we had lost our innocence, if that is the right word. Something changed forever that tragic day.

Down on the Farm
2002-2003

A few weeks later, I talked with Sandy and I said, "What is it that you would like to do?"

I was not asking her about the next few weeks, as the holidays were a few months away. It was the end of September 2001, and the events that had occurred during the first nine months of that year had me thinking about what was really important to me: Sandy and our children's happiness. I had an idea that she wanted to get back to horse riding, which she had done as a child, with our girls and I asked her if she wanted to that.

Sandy said she did. The girls loved the horse and pony that Sandy's mom had had when the children were younger. But she had to have them put down due to the animals' ages a number of years ago. Skippy had been retired by the time Sandy and I first met and were dating, and she and her mother and children had visited him while the girls were very young. We had pictures of the girls riding while being led around the ring in Mendham where Skippy was retired many years earlier.

I then said to Sandy, "Okay, it's time for you to do so."

I remember that she had followed me on all those fishing trips and been a trooper and became quite the angler. She became very good at the sport and could out-fish most men I knew while we had traveled upstate over the past years. She and the girls occasionally went riding somewhere at a public barn and had done so a few times in the last few years in the Catskills.

We then had a discussion regarding our now empty home around the corner. Originally we'd thought of renting it out, but I said to Sandy that due to tax law changes, we could put it up for sale and have a very large profit with no taxes to be paid on the sale. If we did so and her mom needed help, we could use that money if necessary to assist her. I asked Sandy to think it over and said that if we decided to sell, I would gut the kitchen and do a simple remodel as the kitchen was small and the house would probably be ready by spring 2002.

That was what we decided to do, so I was back at it again in the evenings after work during the week and took the weekends off. By the holidays work on the house was close to being done, and we had a nice Thanksgiving and Christmas with a few missing family members that year. My father was no longer with us nor was Uncle Bud. I got Sandy a gift certificate to a nearby stable as one of her gifts. She took Jenny along with her to ride and eventually let her daughter use all the sessions. It seemed the horse thing was on the horizon.

That fall of 2001 and winter of 2002 I spent my weekends working on Harriet's property as well. I removed all the brambles or pricker bushes along the western edge of the property line. This area was about 700 feet in length, and with just a chainsaw and gloves on, it was a lot of work and good exercise. I could not even see the old fencing underneath the brambles.

Sandy questioned me as to why I was doing all this work, and I said to her, "If we are to bring this place back, I can do most of the work."

We had rebuilt the old place around the corner, and this project would be something that if I couldn't do it then we would hire someone. I had shown I was handy and did not mind getting my hands dirty.

By March 2002 we had the house around the corner ready for

sale. We decided that we would try to sell it on our own until the end of June, and if it did not sell by then, we would list the home with a realtor.

Sandy had started to look around for a horse for herself, and by April 2002, Jack, the first horse to be back on the property in more than fourteen years, arrived.

For Sandy and the girls, this was a happy day and for Harriet as well. For myself I just figured that a new chapter in our lives was to start to unfold.

The barn on the property was usable, but really in need of repair. I told Sandy, "If all goes according to plan I will get to it in the fall."

I enjoyed the work and the fact that I could always envision how a property would look before it was actually finished. Sometimes the finished version might change a little bit, but for me the pleasure was the self-accomplishment of the finished project and that I did it myself.

I continued to work on the old fencing throughout the summer. Harriet's mental health was deteriorating, and we were having our hands full, one might say. I had already placed a deadbolt on Harriet's bedroom door so we could sleep at night, and now the children were being affected. Leslie was slapped by her grandmother, and we had to keep a constant watch on Harriet as kitchen appliances were turned on and left on. Basically we had a new four-year-old in the house, but this one could reach everything. We took a few trips upstate to Roscoe that summer and had Harriet cared for while we were away over those few weekends.

That summer another critter arrived, Twister, a pony for Jenny. He arrived in early July and was a birthday present for her eleventh birthday, he just arrived a little early. It now seemed our dice were cast, but this time in a different direction. I was to become farmer Bill, Sandy was happy, the girls were happy, and we almost sold the house on our own, but then listed it in July as we had discussed.

Mostly everything was good except Harriet's health, and we discussed what needed to be done for her. All day long Harriet would say, "Where's Sandra?" even while Sandy was sitting in the room with her. God above only knows why, but it was the one thing she said all day long. Sandy was having a very difficult time with her and I was of the opinion that she needed to be placed into a facility. When we'd first arrived the previous fall Harriet had been manageable, but now was almost impossible to deal with her as she needed constant care and really was no longer making too much sense of things. Otherwise why would she have looked at her daughter and asked her "Where's Sandra?"

Anyone who has dealt with Alzheimer's knows that one day, it becomes time when you can no longer take care of your loved one. It was my opinion that it was decision time.

Sandy was very distraught and said, "Let's try to get through the summer and then we will see where we are."

We had planned to take the kids on a trip to Bar Harbor, Maine, in August. That was arranged that winter, but by the time it was time to leave, I took the kids and Sandy stayed home, watching her mom. She did not want to leave her mom alone somewhere even though we had located a facility to care for Harriet during our week of traveling.

I wasn't happy with Sandy's decision, but she said that with the horses and her mom it would be best if she stayed at home and that the girls and I should go. That was how our family trip of the summer 2002 became the girls and me in Maine and Sandy at home that week with her mom, her horses, and friends around the corner at the public barn. I was disappointed that she would not be traveling with us. The girls and I left. We had a very nice time while we were away. We took many pictures, ate lobsters, and went whale-watching. We had a *National Geographic* experience that day as the whale breached more than twenty times around the boat. That day was spectacular, and I still have the video of the trip.

We also traveled to North Conway in New Hampshire, and I drove the minivan up Mt. Washington and placed the sticker on the bumper of the van. It would have been better if Sandy had come. She put together a nice photo album for us after we got back in late August, and we gave her some nice gifts that we'd picked out for her on that trip while she stayed home for her mom that summer.

School was about to begin, and by late September we seemed to have a buyer for the house. I started to work on the exterior of the barn that month, residing the entire barn myself and by the middle of October the painting had been completed.

Harriet was becoming more of an issue and very difficult to handle.

I said to Sandy, "It's now time."

Sandy was very emotional over this statement, and I said to her, "The children are being affected by Harriet's behavior and you have to locate a facility for her now."

Sandy did not want to move her mom, and I finally said, "You either move her or I will cancel the closing that is moving forward with a closing date of December 1 and take the girls back to our now empty home. You and I can no longer handle Harriet any longer."

Sandy finally agreed that I was right. I had said to my wife that no person could have done any more for a parent then she had. Sandy had helped her mom since the day I had met her, raised a family, worked, and done a superb job with all and now needed to take a break as she was really now unable to care for Harriet.

I told Sandy we now had a plan to look for a facility nearby and to pay for her mom's needs if she exhausted her funds. I said, "Look, we are set to close on our old home by December 1 in a few months, and all will be fine."

We could have canceled the closing and paid the realtor the commission if we'd wanted to since the house was almost paid off and had doubled in value, but I knew that Sandy wanted to give her daughters the lifestyle she'd had growing up. The girls, especially Jenny, loved horses and so we, as a husband and wife, decided to let the old place go. I really loved my first home and had wanted to do an addition, but the decision was now about how to best cope with Sandy's mom. I knew Sandy and the girls really loved horse riding and I remembered that conversation Sandy and I had had many years ago when she'd said, "One day it will be time to take care of mom and I do want to live in my old home again and give my children what I had as a child."

By the Tuesday two days before Thanksgiving in 2002, Mrs. Fushi was in a nearby facility in the Alzheimer's wing located nearby in Florham Park, my hometown.

One other thing arrived that October 2002. About 250 sections of split-rail fence came by tractor trailer. One neighbor said to me that it was the biggest pile of wood he had ever seen and he asked where we'd located the fence and who we'd found to install it all.

My response was that Sandy had found a supplier from Pennsylvania and gotten us a good price and the installer was a very reasonable man we'd located locally. The neighbor asked who this man was, and I said, "You're looking at him." For most people installing a fence might seem a large task to do, but it was almost November and I had another project to keep me busy that fall and early winter.

A doctor who'd lived across the street from us at our old house had done this himself, and he'd been in his 50s when he'd done so. I was in my 40s, a younger man, and I knew if the doc could do it, so could I.

The job was actually quite simple. All I had to do was cut all the old posts at the base, as most were more than forty years old and rotting at the base. The slow part was moving everything. All I had was a twenty-five-horsepower lawn tractor and a cart to pull from behind to move all the old posts out and place them into a large pile on another location on the property.

I started to bore all the post holes, measured out the distance, and estimated the amount necessary to complete this portion of fence. I'd added an extra ten percent for insurance when our order was placed. I next ran a line and placed a stake every ten feet, four inches. I rented a post hole digging machine one weekend and had all the holes bored. This work was done by late March 2003 and then all I had to do was move the pile of fence. That was easier said than done using just the tractor and attached cart. Just before Memorial Day weekend the side pasture, riding ring and smaller pasture were complete.

I said to Sandy, "I need a rest. Let's get up to Roscoe for the weekend."

We did. A local gal named Peggy, who ran the public barn around the corner, took care of our animals and we got a break or I guess I did. Sandy wanted me be happy, she knew that fly-fishing in the Catskills was what I needed and I guess she figured I deserved it.

Life was good. Sandy visited her mom a few times a week at the facility, although her mom was not ever really aware of where she was nor what was going on by this time. Sandy was frustrated when she came home from these visits.

I tried to speak to her, saying just stop by and be agreeable with your mom and do not try to be logical as there really was no point. I stopped by myself, unannounced, typed in the five-digit pass-code and saw how Mrs. Fushi was being cared for. She was bathed, cleaned, and treated well by the facility, and that's all one can do under such circumstances. The facility was run mostly by women. I remember only one man worked there the entire time Harriet was cared for. One resident named Millie stole all the other ladies' underwear and hid it in her closet, and others did funny things as well. One of the ladies would whistle at any man who came in while in the lounge when she was watching TV.

One day when I arrived one of the patients said to me, "Doctor, are you here for my appointment?"

I responded that I was there to see my patient down the hall,

Harriet Fushi, and I would be down to see her the next week and that she had the wrong day.

She agreed and seemed happy with my answer.

The holidays came and went that winter, as did school plays and the rest of the usual activities. By spring 2003 Sandy and the girls were really enjoying the place, and the farm was coming back to life as it had been many years ago when Sandy was a child growing up on the land.

The barn had six stalls, tack area, and an attached hay shed that could hold about three hundred bales of hay. I purchased a new horse trailer for the place and a thirty-horsepower New Holland Farm tractor. Bill had his Tonka truck now.

I regretted that I had not purchased the tractor the prior year. It would have come in handy for the first portion of split-rail fence that I had installed. In all approximately 350 sections eventually would be needed to complete this endeavor on the entire property.

Two more critters arrived that year. Fred was a gelding quarterhorse that Sandy had located as Jenny was riding almost every day. Leslie was also riding so she had the pony and Jenny had her own horse. The horse's registered name was Fancy By Fred.

The next arrival was not my choice. The girls had always wanted a sheep, goat, or something like that and somehow we'd arrived back from the Delaware County Fair owners of Bud. I had tried to get out of this one, but unfortunately since we had a horse trailer it was humanly possible to transport a sheep home.

Jenny and I took the trailer up to Sidney, New York, to bring Bud home the following weekend after the fair that summer and that was the end of that. However, Bud did make a hit at a Halloween party in the fall of 2003. It was funny as Sandy and the girls took walks down the road with two dogs on leashes and one sheep on a leash. Some passersby got funny looks on their faces as they drove by since sheep were not often seen in those days so close to Manhattan, though they'd been much more common in the days of my youth. Sandy used to say that the New Jersey of her youth was called the Garden State and now should be called the Guard Rail State.

Everything seemed fine. My work was good and Sandy and the girls were happy, but we did have one new pressing need, however. The septic system was really in need of replacement and pumping was not the answer we had hoped for, so a new system was in the works. Permits and plans were started in the fall of 2003 and took some time.

Harriet passed away that fall in late October in her sleep, and Sandy was distraught over her mom's passing. Her service was simple and was held at the house as Sandy believed that would have been her wish, and I believed her decision was correct.

Once again the holidays were upon us for 2003 and another member of the family was gone. Harriet's passing was a blessing, at least from my point of view, as Sandy had been caring for her since the day we'd met. It was my belief that Mrs. Fushi had had this disease from the day we met and that "just a little squirrely" issue I'd noticed back in June 1985 was the early stages of her disease as she was later medicated for quite some time. It was my hope that after the Christmas holidays all would be fine and such was the case.

A Year of Rest
2004

It was the New Year, 2004, and we were about to have what I believed would be a year of rest from some of the work, constant home repairs, and family illnesses we had experienced over the past few years.

I spoke with Sandy about the next year's game plan. A new septic system was to be installed, as the old system had not been working very well. It had been pumped a few times last year, and our plans and permits were now in place. We had located our contractor and by May work was to begin.

One other change for our home, which would begin in late March, was the installation of a new furnace. The current one was old and the boiler had developed a small crack. To repair an old system made no sense. We decided to install a system that would incorporate three zones available, though only two were needed because we felt that a few years out we would expand the home and if it were done, the third zone would take care of our future plans or allow a new owner someday that option.

Sandy now called New Jersey the Guard Rail State, and we had decided that once the girls finished high school it would be time to move to a new location outside the state. If we did not stay and expand the house, the new furnace would make the home more marketable.

Sandy and I also had a discussion regarding a family vacation for the summer. We knew the girls would want to attend the Delaware County Fair as it had become a family tradition, always around the third week of August. Since Sandy had not traveled that summer to Bar Harbor, I wanted to know where she would like to go. A couple of weeks later Sandy told me her idea for a family trip: Breyerfest in Lexington, Kentucky. I had no idea of what Breyerfest was, so she got online and showed me.

The girls had been receiving Breyer horses from Santa the last few years and apparently there was a festival in Kentucky every summer in late July around the time of Jenny's birthday. Sandy also said that she and her parents had taken a trip to see the horse farms in that area when she was a child and that she would like to share that same trip with her daughters.

I said, "Fine, why don't you plan the trip?"

And she said she would.

Things were going fine, and by the end of March or April, the new furnace and boiler were in place. Work was soon to begin on the septic system, but first I had to remove some of the split-rail fence that I had installed. When the job was completed, I would then make the necessary repairs and install a new line for what eventually would become a back pasture for grazing.

Work was fine, and life seemed good. In May my mother took a fall from the steps off the porch to the backyard patio. It was only three steps, but she was seventy-two. I figured that it was just a slip and all would be fine. Mom had a cast on her right leg from the knee down and did require some help as the doctors had said she was to be in a cast for about ten weeks. My sister, who lived about a half-hour drive away, and I would be available to help my mother. Sandy also stopped by a couple of days to assist her as well. I stopped by every morning and brought her the newspaper as she like to read the daily paper and the stop added just about fifteen minutes to my drive to work.

By Memorial Day, work had begun on the septic system. This was a rather large and messy project with heavy equipment on the property. Due to the fact that we were having a rather wet spring, the work proceeded slowly. The property lies on ground that is basically level and flat, perfect for a horse facility. It drained fine, but due to the type of soil, it could get soggy after a large rainfall and we'd had our share that spring.

One day I came home early from work to see a bulldozer stuck in the backyard. It had sunk under its own weight. The contractor had to attach a cable to his crane to pull it out and had to wait a week to move forward while the area dried out.

I spoke with him, and we decided to have the old ring on the property repaired, utilizing some of the old materials from the ring toward the mound for the leach field to cover the raised mound. When the work was done, we would have new sand brought for the riding ring. Once this phase was completed, Sandy and the girls would have a true riding facility to enjoy. That was what she had always wanted. The place was really starting to look like a true horse farm again.

Sandy ordered the four sets of tickets and secured lodging for the first part of the trip to Breyerfest in Lexington. We also discussed taking the girls to Mammoth Cave National Park, a few hours' drive from Lexington. From there we planned to drive to Gatlinburg, Tennessee, go to the Dollywood theme park in nearby Pigeon Forge, Tennessee, and from Gatlinburg take the Blue Ridge Parkway to Asheville, North Carolina, and visit the Biltmore Estate, the largest private home ever built in America. The trip would involve some driving, but would let us explore the heartland of the country as Sandy and I were thinking that in eight years, both girls would be in college, and we would be free to leave the Garden State of our youths that was becoming what Sandy was calling the Guard Rail State.

Fortunately for our family, our home was a true reflection of the state in which we grew up, and both of our daughters were very fortunate to have that experience as children. Sandy knew I was sick of the congestion and issues associated with the direction in which the state was moving, and we were starting to think about a departure date once the girls completed high school. Both of us knew that the area was changing rapidly, she wanted a horse farm and all I wanted was a nearby trout river, golf course, and her happiness, which of course meant being able to ride again on her own place.

I had always wanted to move to Wyoming, but felt we would end up in the southeast somewhere and western North Carolina seemed to have it all. This was to be our first trip together to look for what would someday become our next phase together in this journey called life.

My mom was having more difficulties. Her left arm was starting to give her some trouble. When I asked her about it, she replied that she was using a walker to get around instead of the crutches and putting all her weight on her left arm was making it a little sore. This discomfort seemed to continue after the cast was gone as well. I thought little of it and said that since the cast was gone and she no longer needed the walker that this soreness should also pass.

By the end of June school was out and the girls were enjoying their summer vacation. I spoke with Sandy about our planned trip in three weeks and asked her if she had made plans for the animals, horses, and dogs. She responded that everything was set to go--or so I thought.

The work on the septic system was completed, and the riding ring had been updated and finished as well. I often cooked dinner out on the deck, where I watched my wife and daughters riding while I prepared a meal on the weekends.

Two days before our departure I got the suitcases for our trip out of the attic. I told Sandy I would come home from work that night and see if everything would fit in the minivan the next day, the day before we left for Kentucky. We were to leave Thursday as the events started Friday morning for Breyerfest. When I got home that evening I packed my bag, and the following morning I wanted to load the car and get snacks for the trip. I took the day off as I wanted to get a day's rest before our long drive with an early morning departure as we needed to cover about seven hundred miles in one day.

Wednesday I took the girls out to get drinks and snacks, and when I returned home I asked Sandy where her bag was to load into the car. Then she hit me with a bomb: she informed me that she was not going as she had been unable to find someone to care for the animals. I was very upset and asked why she had not told me. She rambled on, making excuses that really just made me more upset.

I said that I would not leave again this year on what was to be our family trip and take my daughters by myself again. If she would not go, I would rather sit home. I asked her why Peggy, who ran the public barn around the corner and had watched the house in the past when we were upstate the last few years, could not do so this time.

Sandy said, "It was the dogs."

That seemed pretty lame to me, as Peggy had done that in the past.

I asked Sandy why she failed to inform me.

She had no answer.

I then told her that I would tell the girls the trip was off.

She pleaded with me not to and begged me to take the girls as they were looking forward to the trip and the Festival in Kentucky.

I agreed to take them and again go off by myself with two girls in hand to a plastic horse festival. The remainder of the day was not a good one for me, but I did not want the girls to see me angry so I kept a straight face as I was about to go away for the second trip in a row without my wife.

I said to Sandy that I would not do another trip like this one and that if pets and horses were to control our lives and not enhance our lives that we should consider getting rid of a few of these animals as I did not wish to be tied to our home.

"It's a big world out there," I said and added that earlier this year we had discussed this trip and agreed that once the girls were off to college it would be time to leave the Guard Rail State, and that this trip was to be the first of a few trips to perhaps find that next last chapter to park for the rest of our lives together.

Sandy apologized and said she was sorry, this would not occur again, please take the girls, make them happy and enjoy the trip and take many pictures as well.

I agreed to do so.

The trip went well. I was probably the only single dad in a world of moms, young girls, plastic horses, and the real thing trotting around Kentucky Horse Park in Lexington. We did the Breyerfest Fair, saw the farms around Lexington and one day drove over to Paris, Kentucky, and took a tour of Claiborne Farm where Secretariat was stabled and later interned with a gravestone in his honor. We then went to Mammoth Cave, Dollywood, Gatlinburg and finally on to the Biltmore in Asheville, N.C. It was a very fun trip with one missing thing: my wife, who stayed home for the second trip in a row.

I'd understood the rationale last time, but was not happy about it for this trip and decided that for next year's trip, I would handle all the arrangements, including the animals issue.

Sandy and I later had a talk in which I said that I really liked the looks of the Asheville area and next summer we should head there for a trip as I thought she would also like the area. There were horse farms, trout streams, golf courses, a longer warm weather season, and best of all, it was beautiful with the backdrop of the Blue Ridge Mountains within sight.

In early August, I went over to my mom's to show her pictures of the trip and noticed that her left arm seemed worse and she was having trouble holding items with her hand. She explained to me that she was working with her therapist who'd said she had a torn muscle in her forearm from using the walker instead of the crutches.

A few weeks later we all went to the Delaware County Fair in Walton and this time, Peggy looked after the horses. The dogs traveled upstate with us as normal and all seemed fine.

It was now September and Mom did not seem to want much help. She was getting around better, but when I asked her why her left arm was not doing any better, she said the physical therapy was causing the pain but the nurse had said it would take some time.

Just before the Columbus Day weekend, a three-day holiday in New Jersey back then, my sister called me and said she had called my mom for two days and not gotten an answer and so she'd driven over the second day to see if all was fine. She'd found my mother on the floor as she'd been unable to get up and into her bed the prior evening and had spent the night on the floor. She could not move as her left arm was useless and her right leg, although the cast was off, was still pretty weak from no use.

I arrived at the house and saw Mom. She was in bed. Her left arm was held in a half closed position and she could not lay her arm straight down

I said to her and my sister that we needed to get her to a doctor. She said that she was fine.

I replied that she could not even get herself into bed.

My sister said that she was going stay with Mom that night.

I knew that Mom did not want to leave her home, but she was unable to take care of herself and needed some assistance.

I called a service that can provide live-in care as I thought that she simply needed someone to help with the day-to-day issues of a home and really could not help herself up if another fall were to occur. My belief was that this arrangement would be temporary and that no other option was available. I then spoke with both my brother and sister. I knew I could not stay there and they could not either, so when I arrived back that Wednesday, I made arrangements to take my mom to the group to select a caregiver for Thursday.

I spoke to my mom, saying that we needed to have someone come in, and she said, "No!"

I looked at her, then I left the room, went to the attic, returned to her room with a suitcase in hand, went to one of her drawers and asked her to tell me which clothes she wanted me to pack.

Mom looked again at me, and I said, "If you will not have someone in here to assist you, we have no other decision but to take you to Brighton Gardens Assisted Living as there is also a room available now." I showed her the brochure. "This is where Sandy's late mom stayed until her passing."

Mom looked at me and knew I was right so she agreed that tomorrow that we would drive to Clifton and interview someone. A nice woman named Kasha was selected and by Saturday she was staying at my mother's home to help care for her.

Mom did not want to see a doctor, and we insisted that she see one. My sister made the arrangements. The appointment was to be the following week after Columbus Day.

My mother insisted that she was fine and did not want to go. Mom had always been very healthy, never needed to see doctors and saw enough while Dad's health was failing over the last few years of his life.

A few days later I received a call from my sister, who was very upset. She told me that at the doctor's office the doctors had discovered a very large lump on mom's left breast and there also was a lump by her lymph gland.

This really did not sound very good to me, and I thought to myself that now I understood why Mom had taken that fall and that she was probably in much worse shape than anyone had thought.

Unfortunately, after a week at the hospital Mom was diagnosed with breast cancer and a tumor in her brain, and most probably cancer had also spread elsewhere as it appeared that her lymph glands were also affected, a rather dismal change of her health in just a six-month period.

I spoke with Sandy and told her I was not very encouraged by the news.

I went to see my mom one day in November while she was in the hospital. She was alone. The doctors had said that they wanted to give chemo and radiation a try. Mom said that she did not want it, and both my brother and sister were very upset on this one.

I said to mom, "Why is it that you knew that you had detected a lump on your breast a few years back and did nothing?"

Mom looked at me and said nothing.

I said, "Mom, you miss Dad, don't you?"

She said yes, she really did and that she just wanted to be with Dad.

I then said to her, "Listen, Mom, you have to at least give the radiation and chemo a try. Based on what I see and believe it probably will not work, but I have a family and both John and Cindy are single. You are their family and you need to at least give this one try for their sake."

Mom told me she would think about it, and I added one other opinion to her regarding treatments. "Mom," I said, "if you do not give this a try, I will never forgive you as you need to give my brother and sister some hope. For their sake, please give it a try. Not for me, but for them."

In the end Mom decided to have treatments. This went on for about a month, and Kasha was caring for Mom's needs while she was at home in-between treatments.

Needless to say Thanksgiving at Mom's was a little bleak that year and Christmas was soon to arrive. I spent as much time as possible at my mom's home, visiting daily and watching for the second time in five years the ravages of cancer, not a very nice sight.

Mom had agreed to give the radiation and chemo a go. She was losing her hair, was bedridden and had to be moved every four hours so no bedsores would appear. It was just horrible to watch my mother deteriorate like this.

One day while I was at the house my mom said, " I wish you could just take me to the vet like I had to for my dogs that have graced our lives. We treat our animals more humanely than ourselves in our last months of life with this disease." I remember thinking to myself that she was right, but we couldn't do that.

Sandy visited often as well and about ten days before Christmas I asked her if she had taken care of Santa's duties for the girls. She said no, she had been too busy, so off we went to take care of that together and make the best of it.

I thought nothing of it and assumed that she had been too busy.

Christmas arrived and we had time together at our home in the morning and were to have dinner at my mother's that evening. Treatments had stopped about a week before Christmas. In mid-January she would need to go back again to monitor the progress of her treatments. It really wasn't looking good for Mom right now and at dinner I know we all had that sinking feeling that history was being repeated in my parents' household.

Missing Clues
2005

Shortly after the New Year began, Mom went back to see how the radiation and chemo had attacked her illness. The news was not good.

Mom, who was really not in good shape, decided that she would not continue any treatments and would wait for the time when she could be with Dad.

Watching her illness progress was very difficult. I looked at my mom, who had never been anything but there to help us all as a family, and now the ravages of cancer were destroying her. I prayed that she would pass as soon as possible.

Throughout the illness, she never complained about her pain, which was horribly apparent to all of us family members.

Hospice was brought in to make Mom as comfortable as possible, and Kasha was there to care for Mom.

On May 12, 2005, Sandy's birthday, Mom my received her wish and joined my father. Needless to say, it was not a very good day nor birthday present for my wife either.

My brother John called me that morning as I was leaving for work and said, "Billy, get over here as soon as you can. Mom looks like she is leaving us."

I changed direction and got to Mom's house as fast as possible. When I arrived, John was in my parents' bedroom crying. He said, "Mom passed a few minutes ago." I gave him a hug and then went over to the bed. I looked down at Mom and watched as the last bit of light disappeared from her open eyes as she left this world to go to the next world. I had never seen this happen before. I bent over her and watched as the color and spark of what we call life had just left her. I closed her eyelids, gave her a kiss on her forehead and said, "I love you, Mom. Be happy with Dad now."

Again we had the necessary arrangements to take care of. For the first time, I was named as executor of the estate by a will; however, I had basically handled this responsibility twice in the past. When Dad passed, Mom was named. When Sandy's mom passed, Sandy was named. You know who got all the details done.

This time there would be much to do. With fifty-plus years of lives spent by my parents and a household full of belongings it would take time and work, but it would get done. My brother, sister, and I sat down and came up with our plan, set it in motion, and started to move forward toward the liquidation of the estate.

Sandy and I had talked earlier in the year and she had said, "Let's do the trip to Breyerfest this year."

So this time I said, "Fine, you get the tickets and I will make arrangements with regards to the animals." I would not do this trip again alone.

She agreed and that was to be the end of it or so I thought. I was busy with duties at work and planning the liquidation of the estate. We decided to make improvements to the home since although it was nice, Mom had not done a thing since my parents had bought it new in 1962. It was of good size with 3200 square feet and five bedrooms, and it still had the original linoleum floor in the kitchen. The home needed to be painted inside and out. Carpets needed to be removed and the baths and kitchen needed to be updated to bring it back to life.

We decided to place the house into a limited partnership and spend the money necessary to make the improvements. Once again it was home repair time, and I knew what needed to be done.

We as a family would do some of the tasks ourselves and hire help for the bulk of the work.

One of Sandy's good friends, Peggy, was leaving the area. She and her family, who had been running the old horse facility around the corner, had to leave the barn and home that they had been leasing. The owner had passed away the previous year and the family was selling the property. It was approximately ten acres with an old dairy barn converted for horses and the home was also very old. Both the home and barn were in disrepair and would require a very large amount of money and work to make the place livable. Peggy and her family could not afford the price and had located a riding facility about forty miles west in Blairstown. They had decided that it was time to leave as New Vernon was losing its identity and had become a very desirable and rather expensive area in which to acquire a home or property.

It was now late June and school was out. Sandy was very upset about Peggy leaving and spent a great deal of time at Peggy's helping the family pack and move things at their barn.

I was concentrating on Mom's place, getting it ready for sale sometime next spring. Since Peggy would not be available to tend to our horses, I located a man she recommended who did some of the local barns in the area and another woman who would come in and care for our dogs while we were on our trip.

As the end of July was approaching, about a week before our trip, Sandy said she would stay home again.

I blew a gasket.

Sandy said she felt it wouldn't be safe for our animals to be left unattended.

I said we had someone who Peggy had recommended to clean the barn and care for the horses and another woman to tend to the dogs and small critters in the house.

Here we go again, I thought. This time I would not listen. Arrangements were made for our trip, and I called my cousin Cheryl, who knew of a young gal who would live in our home and do all the chores while we were gone. I wanted no excuses and would not stand for it. At last Sandy and I would take the trip together with the girls, and Sandy would see Lexington and the hills of Tennessee. We would not get to make the trip to Asheville as I had wanted to. My cousin Allen's son was to be married, and we would arrive home and then head out to Southold on Long Island's North Shore for a long weekend for the wedding.

It was now late July and we made the trip Breyerfest. I brought my golf clubs, as there was a county golf course next to Lexington Horse Park that I had spotted during last year's trip. Sandy was with the girls during the day while I snuck in two rounds of golf during part of the festival as I did not get to play much anymore, and I stayed with them all day for the last day.

We went back to Paris, Kentucky, and Claiborne Farm for a tour as we had last year and drove around to visit some of the nearby farms at the end of each day. We next headed to Pigeon Forge, Dollywood Theme Park and nearby Gatlinburg, Tennessee, having a good time. We then headed back to New Jersey, skipping Asheville, but thinking that next year we would return to make that leg together. It was a long drive back, and we got home late that night. Tomorrow we would be off again for the North Shore of Long Island for the wedding.

The trip to the wedding was uneventful, but took about four hours as one must maneuver around New York City and take a few bridges or tunnels, depending on the route.

We stayed at place called Santorines with other family members and relatives. This part of Long Island, with its farms, wineries, and a few bed-and-breakfasts dotting the way, was not like the South Shore with its homes on the beaches by the Hamptons and Montauk. The North Fork of Long Island is a really quiet area with very few lodging hotels.

As we pulled into the motel when we arrived, Sandy got a rather peculiar look on her face and insisted we could not stay there and must find another place.

We had just driven four hours to get there and the day before we'd driven about eight hundred miles to get home, and I was in no mood. I said to her that there was no other place to stay as all the rooms available had been booked as she knew and that she had booked the place months ago. The wedding was to be quite large as my cousin's son was to be married to a family that was quite large and the reception was to be on the grounds of the bride's grandparents' estate, overlooking Great Peconic Bay. In all more than five hundred guests were to attend.

Sandy continued to act very oddly, insisting that the motel was a "Mafia" place and we would not be safe there.

I said to her that my brother and sister were there as were almost all of my cousin John's other children and to knock it off, as we had no other option. I wanted to hear nothing more of it. The room was paid for and that was that.

The place was a little old and outdated and there were some Italian Renaissance statues about the grounds. If another place had been available, I would have preferred something a little newer. The location, however, was very nice as we had views of Long Island Sound and the sunsets were very pretty. In all about thirty members of our family were staying there. We unloaded our belongings and Sandy continued to act oddly and complain that she did not feel safe.

I was a little tired and said, "Let's just unload our belongings to our room and then go out for some lunch."

We unpacked and then headed to Green Port, the next town east, and sat down in a restaurant by the water for lunch. The restaurant was a local place. It was hot outside so we decided to sit inside for the air-conditioning and view looking out at the water of Long Island Sound.

Menus were brought by the waitress. I looked up from my menu at my wife seated across from me and the next thing I knew Sandy was the color of her coral blouse, beet red. I asked her if she was feeling okay.

She said that she was just feeling a little flushed.

That little flush lasted for about ten minutes. She was sweating terribly, and I was getting very concerned, as I had never seen her like this in my life.

She said to me that she was okay.

I asked her if she wanted to get up, take a short walk outside and get some fresh air, and she agreed.

I said to her, "I think that we should get you to a doctor."

She said that she was fine, was starting to go through the change of life and had been having hot flashes.

I asked if she had been to her doctor.

She told me yes.

I asked if any medication had been prescribed.

She said no.

I looked at her and said, "When we get home I want you to go see your doctor and if it is necessary for you to be prescribed that drug Premarin that comes from the horse foals raised to create the drug, take it. It not necessary for you to go through this if medication is available. Your behavior back at the motel when we pulled in was really very odd and somewhat frightening."

Sandy looked me in the eye and said, "Okay, when we get back home I will take care of it."

We then went back inside of the restaurant had lunch.

Sandy was in the same state for about fifteen more minutes and then her complexion came back to normal and she seemed fine. When lunch was finished and we headed back to the room, she was fine. I thought nothing more of what had happened as she'd assured me she would see her doctor.

The wedding was held at a local church and the reception was at the bride's grandparents' home, overlooking Great Peconic Bay. The grounds of the home were beautiful, encompassing about four to five acres, and on the property, right by the water, was a small old lighthouse about thirty feet in height that had been an operating lighthouse in its day. All in all the grounds were magnificent.

The home had been built in the early 1900s and was very stately with about 5000 square feet, which I thought would have been a very large home in its day. Catering tents stood among the outdoor floral gardens and fountains. The weather was grand.

The wedding reminded me of my youth. As a seventeen-year-old teenager I had parked vehicles at parties for the former Chief of Police of Harding Township, Ed Ponek. He was a good man, whose daughter was my late Mom's good friend living across the street of our first home in Florham Park. As a young man I also had worked at some weddings on similar properties in the New Vernon/Bernardsville area while I was in high school and college. The largest was William Simon's estate. He was former Secretary of the Treasury under President Nixon. Many high-ranking officials and dignitaries were present.

The reception was fabulous and Sandy, the girls, and I all had a wonderful time. The next day, Sunday, we headed home and all was to be fine, I thought.

In early August, Sandy was back to her horses and riding with the girls. Peggy had moved, and Sandy missed being around all the other horse ladies at Peggy's stable.

I told Sandy, "Look, the area is no longer what is used to be. The land values are just too high for someone to make a go of it in the horse business. Accept it and sometime in the future we, too, will eventually have to leave. Let's just get the girls through high school and then it will be our time again while they are away at college. If Lexington is your wish, then someday so be it." I thought she would really love Asheville, if she got to see it the next summer. "The Delaware Fair is coming in a few weeks and the girls want to go, so let's just get upstate in a few weeks and enjoy the rest of the summer. School will be here before you know it, and I have to get back to Mom's place again."

Sandy said she would locate someone to care for the animals while we went to the fair, and back to work I went at my job and Mom's place.

The day before we were to head upstate to the fair in the third week of August, it happened again. There was no one to care for the animals and I was off again with the girls. I was annoyed and really wanted all of us to attend the fair as a family. One of my favorite country singers was playing the last night and I wanted us to hear her sing that night together. I got to hear her sing with my daughters, looking at all the happy families together and wondering why my wife was not there with us. I was getting really sick and tired of animals as a reason for Sandy to be tied to our home.

School began and the girls were back to school. I was very busy with work and Mom's estate and home to be settled and seemed to do nothing else except attending the girls' school events.

Sandy was not spending any time at her job and was complaining that there wasn't much left for her as most of her clients had either left their jobs or their companies had closed.

I told her go out and look for something else to do. I reminded her that I'd done U.S. Treasuries in the primary dealers market for almost twenty years, starting out in the back office and working my way up, and that that industry had changed and was still in a contraction mode. Cantor had twenty-five people doing what almost four hundred fifty had once done. Computers had changed the industry. I said that printing was experiencing the same and much of the work was moving overseas. Gerrardi Press employed about ten full-time employees, while Compton once had more than one hundred.

I said to Sandy, "Why not look for something else?"

Our arrangement of our financial affairs was quite simple. I took care of all the bills, and I said, "All you need to do is make enough to pay for your horses, which really is not too much. They live on our home, and although you spend little time at work, I understand it, so just find another field for the next few years. Our finances are fine, and we really have nothing to worry about in those matters."

It was my belief that Sandy was getting bored as printing was fading as an industry and she need something else to do.

A few weeks later I told Sandy I had stopped by Seaton Hackney Stable as there was a new sign out front. It turned out that the Morris County Park System had purchased the facility and had been repairing it. I went over to see what was going on. It turned out that they were looking for someone to run the barn. The County Park Commission wanted to outsource the facility as long as it was open to the general public.

Sandy had always said she would love to run a barn, and I thought this would be the perfect chance for her to do something that she really loved and now was the perfect time to do so. I felt a career change would be good for her. I sat her down, laid out a business plan and said, "It's now up to you. All we have to do is form an LLC to protect ourselves and see if it works, and I am willing to commit the capital for you. If this is what you want, just let me know. It's close by and just five minutes by car."

I never heard a word back from my wife about this proposal and figured, what else can I do?

Sandy was complaining about the area, and I said, "What can we do? We are not uprooting our kids from school as you want and I'm not willing to head to Blairstown to be near your horse friends and add another hour a day to my commute. Our home is starting to look good and all you're doing is complaining. We have spent a small fortune and it's better now than it was when I met you twenty years ago while your late father was alive. All I do is go to work, work here on your home, and then work to finish up my Mom's house to list it next spring. You need to look at all the wonderful things you have to be thankful for. If printing is dying, find something else to do as I did in the late-90s. Very few people in the business world remain in the field they start out in and must adapt. The world has changed so much in the past twenty-five years and sooner than you know it, we will leave here for good."

About a week before Christmas I spoke to Sandy about the gifts for the girls as I'd seen their list to Santa, but had not done any of the shopping, assuming she had taken care of it as I was very busy with work and the other issues.

It turned out she had not done anything.

I asked her, "What do you do all day? It does not take eight hours to clean three horse stalls and that barn is really a mess from what I can see."

Sandy did not have much of a response and rambled on with some excuses.

I said to her, "Let's go take care of the Christmas shopping. I'm really not sure what we can even find so late." I also asked her what her doctor had said about her menopause condition as I had forgotten to ask her about it earlier.

She informed me that she had not gone to see a doctor.

I said to her, "You really need to go. Your behavior is starting to get a little different and I am sure it just a hormonal imbalance that with proper medication can be resolved."

Sandy assured me that after the girls went back to school she world see the doctor.

The Calm Before the Storm
2006

After the 2005 holidays were over, we were busy with our normal activities. That meant school for the girls. And work at my office and evenings and weekends at my late parents' house for me. Work for Sandy had dried up as she'd claimed that the print business was no longer very busy. Having lived through the contraction of the government bond business of the late-90s, I continued to encourage her to find something else to do.

She agreed to look as I told her it was not about the money, but about being somewhat active as she wasn't leaving the house much, and for her own sake she needed something to do as she had too much free time. The girls were in sixth and ninth grades and starting to become independent of Mommy's needs. Soon they would blossom into young ladies. Again I asked her to look into the stable at Seaton Hackney as the sign was still out front and the county was still looking for a manager.

Sandy and I discuss a summer trip. My thought was that we would head back to Kentucky for Breyerfest and Dollywood, and on this go-around we would get to Asheville for a few days to look over the area, as I had wanted to do the prior year but had been unable due to my cousin's son's wedding.

Sandy came up with another suggestion, saying "Let's go to the Outer Banks of North Carolina to the beach."

We'd both vacationed there years ago before we'd had children and she thought that a beach vacation would be great for the girls.

I said, "Great, if that's what you want, start looking for a house to rent and find one that we can bring the dogs to as we will have Alfredo handle the horses."

Sandy went online and located a nice house that had a dog run on the premises. She called the agent and mailed out a check paying for the house and hurricane insurance for the last weekend of the summer. The house had a pool and was just a short walk to the beach. Sandy said that the girls were now a little older and did not want to go to Kentucky again. We informed them of the plans and told them they would still go to the Delaware County Fair in Walton, New York, as traditional, and they seemed excited by the idea.

In early February 2006 I came home from work one day to find that my oldest daughter Jennifer's bedroom door was broken. I inquired, and Sandy said it just got loose, but to me it did not look that way.

Later in the evening, Jennifer informed me that she and her mother had had an argument, as her mom had been acting weird. She'd closed her door and locked it only to have her mom start trying to push the door in. Apparently Jenny had even placed a dresser in front of the door to keep her mom out, but her mom somehow pushed hard enough to open the door and knocked over the dresser as well.

I didn't know what the argument was about, but everything seemed fine at that time with the exception of my having to repair the door.

I asked Sandy about the incident the follow day after the girls went to school and she tried to brush it off.

I said, "You need to see a doctor about your menopause issue, Sandy. Your behavior is getting different. Please go see a doctor and just have some blood work done to check out your hormone levels."

She agreed with me and said she would.

A few weeks later I asked how her blood work went, and she replied that the doctors had said everything was fine.

I did not give it another thought since she had finally seen someone, but still thought she might need to go back. She informed me that Dr. Berger's office had told her to come back in three months for a follow-up.

Mom's house was listed for sale in May 2006 and finally there was some breathing room, or so I thought.

Shortly after the house was listed, another argument occurred between Sandy and Jennifer and again the door was broken down. This time, I arrived home early from work as my daughter called me, saying, "She's doing it again, Dad. Please come home."

I arrived to find Sandy very quiet and normal.

The door now needed to be replaced, which I took care of, discarding the old one in the hay shed of the barn. Again I said to Sandy, "Go back and see your doctor."

She was very calm and agreed to do so. I suggested that we get away and head to our camp for the Memorial Day weekend as I thought perhaps she just needed to get a break from things.

Sandy agreed, and we were set to go away.

Two days before the holiday weekend she again let me know that she was unable to find someone to care for the animals.

I said, "Alfredo will do the horses," and she said she could not find someone to care for the dogs.

I replied that we always brought the dogs upstate with us.

Sandy then said, "Why don't you just take the girls and go?"

My response was, "No, I'll let the girls know and we can just stay home. This place is nice enough, and I can fish at the club nearby over the weekend."

I was planning to be away for the first week of June to fish the Catskills during "bug week," as we all call it, and had three friends who were coming up to stay with me at the camper and fish that week. "Bug week," when all the insect hatches occur all day long, is the peak time to fish the rivers up in the Catskill region.

We all had a nice uneventful weekend. I did some yard work on the property and some trout fishing at the club. Sandy and the girls were out on some trail rides, and in the evenings I cooked dinner out on the deck overlooking the barn and ring. I remember thinking how lucky I was to live on such a beautiful place and watch my beautiful wife and daughters riding on the rebuilt ring while I was preparing our evening meals.

I got away for that long-needed week off to trout fish the Catskills during the first week of June. My buddies and I fished all week and I called home every day to see how things were going.

One day when I got back from fishing, there was a message from Jennifer saying, "Mom is doing it again, Dad."

I called home and spoke with Jennifer, who said everything was then fine.

I asked, "What happened?"

Jennifer replied, "Mom was acting weird again, but is now okay."

I then spoke with my wife and asked her to go back for her follow-up visit as it had been three months since her last blood work. I said, "Your behavior is starting to affect your relationship with your daughters and something needs to be done about it now."

She agreed and said she would go the following day and have blood work done again.

When I came home the following weekend, Sandy said she had been to the doctor and needed to go back during the week for a follow-up to see the results of the lab work.

My thoughts were good!

Leslie, my youngest daughter, was finishing sixth grade and wanted her bedroom done over. When we'd moved into the house Harriet was living with us and Sandy had painted the girls' room, which they'd at first had to share. The room was quite lovely. The carpet was dark green. One of the walls had a large mural of a tree with jungle animals and the other had stick-ons to give it a jungle look. It was very nicely done.

The girls had been seven and ten when we'd moved in. Now, five years later, Leslie wanted a teenager room, one might say, as next December she would be thirteen. Both girls had their own rooms again after Harriet was placed into the facility in 2002. Leslie also wanted a new bed as she had been climbing up to a unit that we'd purchased so both girls could stay in the room together.

Leslie and I went out and located a new bed, which was ordered, and I was told to expect delivery sometime in mid-August. Leslie also picked out new paint as she wanted the kiddie-look off her walls.

I asked Sandy if she would take down the mural and paint.

She agreed and said she would do so.

After finally being done with Mom's house, I really did not want to paint Leslie's bedroom.

Within a short time a buyer had come through for Mom's house. The closing was set for the third week of July 2006, and my thoughts were: it's finally over, the last leg of the estate is just about completed, it's time for a break and summer is about begin, Mom's house is in contract, and Sandy's late mom's house is looking good. By next year all work will be finished on this place.

I spoke with Sandy about the interior of the barn and showed her some pictures of high-end barns, saying that next year she would have a barn like no one else's. I wanted to take the remainder of the year off from more work as I was tired and wanted to relax and finally enjoy some time off and a slower lifestyle. Farmer Bill was seeing the light at the end of the tunnel. We really only had to finish off the interior of the barn and add a little more split-rail fencing and all home repairs would be over with.

Whiteface Mountain hiking 1986

Yellowstone Cutthroat 1987

First ride as husband & wife 1989

Bride and father-in-law

Skippy semi-retired 1993

Portrait fall 1996

Easter bunny Greenvillage 1997

Lambertville, N.J. Shad Festival carriage ride May 2002

Part 2:
One Hundred Sixty Days

Signs

Saturday, June 24, 2006, was Jenny's first day of work. About two weeks before school had ended she'd asked if it would be alright for her to get a job for the first time, and Sandy and I had said yes. Jenny was 14 and would require work papers, which she'd received just before school had ended Friday, June 23, 2006.

Jenny's first job was at the local Dunkin Donuts in nearby Madison. I dropped her off and was happy to see that my oldest was growing up. Next fall she would start her sophomore year of high school. She was growing up fast. Her younger sister Leslie would begin seventh grade next fall as well.

Summer had begun and all should be fine. The Fourth of July was around the corner, as was closing the sale of Mom's home in a few weeks.

The following week on one of Jenny's days off from work, I received a call from her complaining that their mom was bothering her and her sister and asking if I could come home.

I told her I could not, but we, as a family, would have a sit down after dinner to discuss things with their mom.

We had the conversation with Mom, though by then it seemed that all had been worked out between Jenny and her mom before I arrived home. Nothing much more was said. We then discussed the upcoming July Fourth weekend.

The first full work week after the holiday I again received a call from Jenny again with the same message, "Please come home. She's doing it again."

I asked Jennifer, "What's going on?"

Jenny replied, "Mom's acting weird again."

This time I decided that I needed to leave work immediately and I left the office to head back home. When I got home the door to Jenny's room had been damaged again and was in need of repair. I was not very happy as a new door had been installed back in May.

I asked Sandy what the hell was going on.

She made some type of muted response.

I then asked Jenny what had happened, and she stated that her mom was acting weird.

I then asked, "What do you mean 'weird'?"

Jenny responded that Mom was just acting weird again.

I thought about the incident I had witnessed the previous August when we'd arrived at Santorini's out in Long Island for the wedding. I then asked Jenny what specifically was weird, and Jenny said, "Just weird. Things and words that were not making sense."

Jenny had walked away from her mom, wanted to be left alone in her room and had locked the door.

Her mom had pushed in the door, opening it by putting a pin in the lock from outside the room.

They'd had a pushing match that her mom won.

When I spoke with Sandy about this incident, she said that they'd had an argument.

I looked at my wife, who was now nervous, but calm and normal, and I said, "I want you to go back to the doctor's office." I told her that this was the second time in three weeks that the girls had called me regarding her behavior and I didn't know what to do. I then said, "This is the second time that I have to repair Jenny's bedroom door. It would have been the third, but I had to get a new door the second time this happened back in May and the old door is out in the hay shed of the barn."

Sandy remained quiet throughout the evening while I spoke with her about her behavior while I was away at work. I was convinced that she was definitely in need of medication for menopause, and I demanded that she go back to the doctor's office.

She agreed to do so.

I was quite busy with work and the closing date was set for Mom's home in about a week. I needed to make all the small corrections over the weekend before the final inspection set for Monday, July 17.

I was present for that, closing was set for Wednesday, July 19, and both my brother John and sister Cindy had planned to come to our home that morning for the closing. The next day was Jenny's birthday. Wednesday morning my brother and sister arrived at our home before 10 a.m. John had hired an attorney he knew to draw up the documents, and they were to arrive by courier no later than 11 a.m. as the closing was to take place in Morristown at the buyer's attorney's office. We received a call from the buyer's agent saying that the documents had not arrived and we needed to make a few calls to the courier to locate them. Apparently they were to arrive later and the closing was moved to 2 p.m.

The whole morning Sandy's behavior was odd to say the least. She kept insisting that we were selling her home rather than our Mom's home. I told her that was impossible as my name did not even appear on the deed of her late mother's home, which was now in her name only as the deed had been transferred after her mom's estate had been settled.

This behavior continued as she repeated her claim and questioned both my brother and sister, insisting that we were selling her house. I was really pretty tired of all of this behavior and I again asked Sandy what the doctor had to say about her menopause. I explained that my sister and brother were there to collect their checks from the closing of our late mother's home.

The documents finally arrived that afternoon and we left for Morristown, for the final leg of closing Mom's estate. After the closing, I arrived home with a check and Sandy again insisted that I had just sold her home.

I just looked at her and said, "You better see the doctor tomorrow."

She said she couldn't as it was Jenny's birthday and she would do so on Friday instead.

My response was "you'd better."

Sandy's behavior that day was very odd as she continued to insist that I had sold her house.

I said, "Look, in the Victorian Era women were locked up and put in sanatoriums due to behavior from menopause. You are truly in need of help."

This was the second time I had seen this behavior and I started to wonder if this was how Sandy had been acting with her daughters while I was at work. I now believed that something was truly wrong as I was trying to speak to her and getting responses that made absolutely no sense. I showed her the documents from the closing, which listed the address as my mother's home and said, "I've had enough of this."

Sandy looked at me and that was the end of it. Tomorrow I would deposit the funds into the bank, and we would be off to the horse store to get my oldest her birthday present.

In our home we had a tradition that whoever celebrated a birthday could choose the dinner meal for that day. One year, my youngest selected pancakes and bacon for dinner. This year, Jenny wanted to go to the local Charlie Brown's restaurant about five minutes from our home and had made this request over the weekend.

That morning Sandy and I headed out to a horseman's outlet for some riding equipment and she'd seemed fine. Yesterday's issues were gone. I'd taken the day off as work was slow in the summer and I generally took only one long trip of ten days off each year and worked a number of long weekends throughout the year. That afternoon I did yard work and later in the evening as we were getting ready to head out for dinner, Sandy started acting odd again and refused to go out for dinner with her family for her oldest daughter's birthday. I was pretty angry and ended up taking my two daughters out by myself. A repeat of yesterday's behavior had just again appeared out of nowhere.

When we arrived back from dinner Sandy was fine and I repeated the words from the prior day, saying, "Go see the doctor now. This is just too much for both your children and myself."

That night I started to think of the most recent events and decided Sandy was truly having a very difficult time from her menopause. I was determined to make sure that she would follow up with the doctor again. At this point I had witnessed Sandy's odd behavior for the second time, back-to-back two days in a row with the first time having been back in 2005 while we were away for the wedding, I was beginning to perhaps grasp what the girls were going through while I was away at work from 7:45 a.m. until about 6:30 p.m. not to mention all the time I'd spent preparing Mom's house for sale. One moment all was fine and then another Sandy was not making any sense of things.

It was now the last week of July 2006 and we had called the store inquiring when the new bed frame would be delivered. The store informed us it was due in two to three weeks. I asked Sandy to start painting Leslie's room as her daughter had picked out the paint a month earlier. One day that week when Sandy finally started to take down the mural I arrived home to find her in tears and asked what was going on.

Sandy's reply was that she was upset about having to take down the mural and all the work she had done from years past.

I said, "Your youngest is no longer in first grade and will be entering seventh grade next fall. She is no longer a little girl. By December she will turn thirteen and soon become a young lady. Your oldest will be starting tenth grade and is now becoming independent of both of us. It's time to move forward. Leslie no longer wants a kiddies' room, but a bedroom suitable for a young teenage girl."

That evening I helped Sandy finish removing the mural and get the room ready for her to complete the painting. A few days later the room was painted and all we were waiting for was the new bed to arrive.

August 2006

I asked Sandy if she would like to get away for a few days upstate to our camp in Roscoe, New York, as I felt that a change of scenery would be good for all of us. She had not been away all year and the girls wanted to go away as well. It was agreed that we would head upstate early Friday, August 4. I had work that morning and said that I would be home by 11 a.m. and all we would need to do would be load the van, get the dogs and kids and leave. The weather forecast was for sunshine and we planned to go tubing down the Beverkill River together as a family on Saturday. I made arrangements for Alfredo to care for the horses as I wanted no excuses and I left for work that day. All the bags had been packed the night before and placed into the porch ready to be loaded when I arrived home before lunch.

I arrived home around 11 a.m. as planned, changed from a suit and tie to dress-down and started to load up the van and check out the property, making sure everything was ready and in order. I then got the dogs into the back of the van. The girls got in.

I asked Sandy to get in and again it started.

Sandy said, "Where we are going? Where are you taking me?"

I looked at her and said, "We are going to the camper up in Roscoe," and she again asked me the same questions with an odd look of distrust on her face.

This dialogue went on for some time. I finally said, "I've had enough of this. If you want to stay home, then I'm taking the girls away as we promised them the tubing for tomorrow. In two more weeks, we will be headed up for the Delaware Fair, we will not have time to go tubing and the girls want to get away."

Sandy pleaded not to leave her home.

I said, "Get in the car."

After over an hour she finally decided to go with us. I had gotten very upset as an hour and a half had been spent on the whole ordeal. She finally got into the car, and off we were, finally heading away at about 12:30 p.m.

We were halfway up our road when I heard my youngest daughter scream, as the door behind my seat opened and I looked out the side mirror and saw Sandy rolling on the roadside. I immediately stopped the van, got out and in bewilderment just looked at her and did not say anything. I was now really upset and afraid she had hurt herself. I calmly walked over to her to see if she was alright. Her pant leg was slightly torn and a small amount of blood appeared on her pants by her left knee. I asked her if she okay.

She was quite calm and said she was fine.

I then said, "Get back in the van and we will now take you to the doctor."

She begged me not to take her there, so we went back to the house. Her behavior was now calm and appeared to be normal. I told the girls to forget the trip upstate as we need to be home and that both their mom and dad would need to head to the doctor's office.

Sandy insisted that she was fine and said that the medication she was on was causing her some issues.

I said, "Let's go see the doctor now and have it changed."

Sandy said, "Look, I just won't take it anymore. Let's just go upstate now." She had bandaged her knee.

I did not want to leave.

She said, "Look, the girls want to go tubing. I will be fine and I promise that next week I will go see the doctor and get a new prescription."

I looked her in the eye and said, "I think we should stay home."

She then loaded up the dogs, rounded up the kids and said, "Let's go now."

Her behavior was completely different.

I finally agreed, and we were now off sometime around 3 p.m. I knew we would hit traffic. We did, and I felt that if one more thing arose on the drive I would immediately turn around and go straight to the doctor's office.

The ride upstate was uneventful, just long, well over three hours instead of what would have been just under two hours as our routine was to leave no later than noon Fridays to avoid the weekend traffic. Sundays we generally left right after lunch to get back home to avoid the traffic as well. This had been our routine over many years while we had our camp as it allowed us to attend to the chores and other household duties Sunday afternoons before the start of the work week.

That weekend all was fine. Tubing took place down the Beverkill River as we'd planned Saturday afternoon. The weather was perfect in the mid 80s with a blue sky and no humidity. The river was about 70 degrees, perfect to go tubing. We all had a fine time that Saturday afternoon and campfires both Friday and Saturday nights. Our drive back home was fine. Sunday evening at home Sandy said she would call the doctor for an appointment on Monday and have her prescription changed.

I thought thank God. She seemed to be better over the weekend since she had not had her medications.

The following week all seemed fine, and there were no issues at home. Friday, August 11, we received a call that Leslie's new bed was in the warehouse and could be delivered Saturday. We decided that Monday would work, as we needed to take apart the built-in bed unit that was currently in the room.

Sunday I removed the old bed unit, which had a built-in desk on one end, cabinets on the other end, and the frame and mattress about five feet up with a ladder to climb attached to one side. I spent most of the day removing the bed system, moving it to a storage area, rearranging the rest of the room to suit my youngest daughter's wishes, and giving the room a good cleaning. The mattress was placed on the floor where the new bed would be located. That night, she would sleep on her mattress on the floor.

That evening I finally got a chance to read the Sunday paper. It was after dinner and I was tired. On the first page was a picture of a twelve-year-old boy named Jack Kimzey. His mother, who had been separated from his father and given custody of him a year earlier when he was eleven, had apparently killed her son by suffocating him and then tried to kill herself by slashing her wrists and ankles. The article stated that the father had tried to have custody of the boy, contending that the mother was having mental health issues and that a judge had ruled in the mother's favor over the father's objections. The mother was located nearby in Basking Ridge, a wealthy and affluent town.

All of a sudden I got a sick feeling in my stomach as I started thinking about the last few months and the issues that Sandy was having. This horrible thought kept coming back to me: I hope it's just menopause or could she be suffering from something far more serious? Now I knew that something must be done.

A few moments later Sandy walked into the room and asked me what I was reading.

I did not want to show her, but she was insistent and wanted to see the newspaper.

I then showed her the paper.

She saw the article and read the article and then looked at me right in the eye and said, in a rather odd tone, "I would never do something like that."

Now I was truly worried. Her behavior had been really getting very odd. I thought about her jumping from the car, refusing to attend her daughter's birthday dinner, and a number of other things. A light went on and then that sick feeling hit me again. I decided she was going back to the doctor and I would also attend.

I went to bed that evening very worried and finally drifted off to sleep.

Monday morning I awoke and Sandy was not in bed. I got up, made the coffee, and looked around the house, thinking she might be up early and in the barn doing her horse chores. She was not there and the barn was a mess. I walked around the house and finally saw her: she was in Leslie's room with her back towards me. One of the dogs was by her side and she was asleep on the floor next to her daughter.

Sandy was curled up by Leslie's mattress on the floor, and Leslie was sound asleep with her head on her pillows. All seemed well. I thought perhaps Sandy had been up late, talking with her daughter, and fallen asleep.

I left for work and had decided that I had to call the doctor's office and discuss with him the past few month's events, whatever medications Sandy was now taking, and that perhaps something more serious was wrong. A few messages went back and forth that day, phone tag.

Tuesday, finally at the end of the day, I briefly spoke with someone at the doctor's office. I was told to arrive early Wednesday and they would speak with me.

Wednesday morning I went to the doctor's office and discovered that Sandy had not been to see him as she had claimed over the past year.

I then asked him what to do, and he replied I needed to get her in to see someone ASAP.

That afternoon I decided that I would find an OB-GYN doctor myself, schedule an appointment for Thursday for a blood draw and pray that she would go. The doctor's office gave me a few names to call. I made the calls and set an appointment for Thursday at 4 p.m.

When I got home I spoke with my wife with whom I had spent the last twenty-one years of my life.

That evening I told the girls that although we had planned to leave tomorrow and head upstate for the Delaware Fair, we would not be going, that mom and dad were going to a doctor's office tomorrow afternoon and that if everything was fine, we would go to the fair a day later.

That evening Sandy spent five to six hours explaining to me that she was fine and did not need to see a doctor.

My answer was simple. I said, "You have told me for a year now that you would see a doctor, and you have not."

In bed that evening Sandy continued to ramble on, losing herself at times and really behaving oddly and distrustful of my motives, to say the least.

I replied, "If there is nothing wrong, then we will find out and a simple blood draw will determine it. A few weeks ago you jumped out of our car. Something is wrong and for whatever reason you refused to join your family for Jenny's birthday meal at Charlie Brown's restaurant.

Sandy had no reply.

I was praying that a blood draw would find a hormonal imbalance.

That evening I went to sleep with a very uneasy feeling.

By 5 a.m. Sandy had woke me up, again insisting that she did not need to see a doctor.

This refusal went on all morning long.

I decide to speak with the doctor's office again and was there early as I was heading into my office for appointments I had for the morning and early afternoon.

I spoke with Dr. Berger's wife, who ran the office, and explained to her that I did not believe Sandy would go with me to her appointment and I asked, "What can I do if she refuses?"

The doctor's wife said, "Get her to the emergency room and that if she will not go, do not force her to do so."

I asked why and was informed that Sandy she could have me arrested for kidnapping her.

I said, "Are you kidding me?"

The answer was no and if she continued her behavior the only thing that I could do was call the police.

I drove back to the house, hoping that I could convince my wife to accept the appointment that I had made for her the prior day. I was unable to convince her. She now insisted that she wanted to see Dr. Nina Reynolds, a different OB-GYN doctor who had delivered both of our daughters.

That evening I was very upset and extremely concerned because my wife would not see a doctor, was in complete denial of having any problems, and continued to try to put off any medical help.

Sandy said she would call Dr. Reynolds in the morning.

I said, "I no longer believe you." And I confronted her about the fact that Dr. Berger's office had told me she had not been to see them in years.

Sandy said to me, "What do you mean?"

I said, "I went to see Dr. Berger and his wife told me you had not been there for a long time, and now I know that you have been lying to me for the past year regarding your menopause issues."

That evening I again had to listen to her jabber all night long about why she did not need to seek any help, but would call Dr. Reynolds next week after we'd headed up to the fair tomorrow morning. This night was a repeat of the prior Wednesday and I really was now trying to figure out what to do. I laid awake all night and decided that in the morning I would try one more time to convince Sandy to seek the medical help that I now determined she truly needed.

Friday morning I again had to tell the girls that they would now miss the Fair and we would be staying home. They were disappointed, and I could not blame them.

I then headed off one more time to speak with the doctor's office and they informed me to call the police if Sandy refused to go to the emergency room. I drove home and tried to convince Sandy to go to the emergency room.

She asked me where I went, and I said, "The doctor's office

again. They believe that you must make your appointment this afternoon that I have rescheduled from yesterday because you would not attend."

She said no and that she would see Dr. Reynolds next week.

Again I asked her to go and again the answer was the same.

I went downstairs to make a call.

Sandy followed me and asked who I was calling.

I said nothing.

When the police answered my call, I asked them to come to our home.

Sandy started getting upset and tried forcible to take the phone away from me.

I screamed into the receiver, "Please send some right now. We need your help."

Sandy said, "Why have you called the police?"

I said, "I believe that you are in need of help and since you refuse to see a doctor, I have spoken with our doctor about your behavior the last few months, and they instructed me to do so if you continued to refuse to go to the emergency room. I have no other option left to get you medical help."

The police arrive that day at around 10 a.m. First to arrive was Patrolman Irons followed by two other police officers named Gaffney and Gromek. Gaffney was a man of medium build about 5'8" and Gromek was a man about 6'3" who looked like he played professional football.

The police observed my wife's condition. She was rambling on, not making sense with what she was trying to say.

I explained the sequence of events that led me to reach out for help, that she had jumped out of a moving car and that Dr. Berger's office had recommended that I call if she would not get help. I stood by our car, begging her to just get in the car and go with me to the emergency room, which the police witnessed.

Sandy tried to speak with me, and I said, "You need help. I love you. Please, we need you to see a doctor."

The police also said to my wife that they thought she needed to see a doctor.

Sandy started to agree to go. Then as the police led her to our car, a look of terror appeared on her face and she refused to go to the hospital with me.

After an hour and a half of this behavior with Sandy agreeing to go and then changing her mind, I was at wits end. She was following me around, saying things that were not making any sense. The police witnessed this behavior, but said they could not force her to go.

During this time the police removed a pen knife and other sharp objects in Sandy's possession, forcibly when she refused to surrender them.

I told Officer Gromek, "I'm taking the kids and we have to get out of here."

He looked me in the eye and said, "Mr. Dunn, don't leave her alone. She's not right."

Just before the police left the house, my sister arrived and stayed with us as the police left our home. We could not understand how, now after they had witnessed Sandy's erratic behavior, she was still allowed to remain with us. I had a major dilemma. I had done everything that was humanly possible and yet still my wife would not seek any medical help nor could I force her to do so. The police had recommended not leaving her and now "what am I to do?" remain the question.

My sister and I spent the next few hours trying to convince Sandy to go to the emergency room.

She would finally agree to do so and then as she was about to step into the car that strange look would come across her face and she would refuse to go.

I was convinced that Sandy would not go for her blood work, which had been rescheduled from the day before, and was trying to come to grips with what to do next. In about an hour Sandy would miss her 4 p.m. doctor's appointment again, if she refused.

Sometime after 3:30 p.m. my sister called me over and said that she needed to speak with me about something. That something, I would find out, was that Monday morning my youngest daughter Leslie had awoken to see her mom lying next to her bed on the floor as I'd seen. The one thing I hadn't seen when I'd opened Leslie's door that morning was that Sandy apparently had the dog next to her on a leash wrapped around her hand and in her other hand she'd had a large carving knife approximately fourteen inches in length.

Leslie had disclosed this fact to my sister late in the afternoon. We then asked Leslie to show me the knife, which she could not locate in the kitchen as it had been removed.

That was it.

My sister called the police again and they arrived for the second time.

This time Sandy's behavior was off the charts as one might say.

The police informed me that they had made a few calls after they'd left earlier and that someone else would arrive shortly. I asked who, and the response was a DYFUS officer. DYFUS is the Division of Youth and Family Services.

The representative Nick Mangold arrived a few minutes later. He spoke with the police about what they had observed earlier in the day and Sandy's behavior while they'd been present for the second time. He then spoke with me and I went over the series of events over the past few months, including Sandy jumping from a car, having the steak knife we'd just found out about, and breaking the doors. I showed him the original door, which was in the hay shed. He then spoke with the girls individually as to what they had witnessed over the past few months. The DYFUS officer then informed me that someone from St. Clair's Hospital would arrive soon to evaluate Sandy.

The moment that the DYFUS representative arrived, Sandy's behavior immediately changed to very quiet and passive, a complete reversal from what we'd witnessed throughout the day and what was indicated on the police reports.

It was late in the afternoon and the clinician or doctor from St. Clair's, Dorothy Gergely, had arrived and spoken with all of us about what we'd witnessed today and in the past few months.

She then spoke with Sandy, came back to me, looked me in the eye and said, "Your wife is hearing voices and you have done the right thing calling help for her."

This was the first time a professional had said anything to me about Sandy's mental condition. Sandy was now to be taken away against her own will to St Clair's Hospital. I thought, thank God, I live in a country where I can get my wife the help that she truly needs.

One of the police officers said, "When I was here earlier today, we saw how bizarre your wife appeared. You have done the right thing. She is going to a good facility, where she will get the help she needs. She not the first person to go there. All will be fine."

Finally, Sandy would receive the help she needed. The same help that for a year now she had been telling me she was supposedly getting.

Sandy did not want to leave the house, was not willing to cooperate with the police and was now to be involuntarily moved from her own home to the psych ward at St. Clair's Hospital in Denville.

The police asked me to have the girls taken inside our home away from the windows while Sandy was placed into the ambulance. I did not understand why until she was asked to put on a straitjacket, which she did not want to do.

The police again asked her to put on the jacket or they would be forced to do so.

Sandy finally reluctantly agreed.

My guess for the jacket was that while the police had been there they'd had to remove from her possession a pen knife and other sharp objects that she'd refused to hand over to the local police who'd been dispatched that day.

It was after 5 p.m., and no one had eaten all day. I took my sister and the girls to Charlie Brown's for dinner and felt as if the weight of the world had been lifted from my shoulders, at least for now. I told the girls that we would miss the Delaware Fair this year, but Mommy would get the help she needed.

I again said a few prayers that night, knowing that my wife and family would be helped. We, as a family, were in unchartered waters, one might say, figuring that the cyclone of the past few months was over as we had survived the eye of the storm. That night I finally drifted off to sleep for the first time in about two nights. I knew that tomorrow was a new day and the start towards recovery for my wife and our family. Thank God, I thought, that I live in a country that has support for families such as ours in a time of crisis.

Seventeen Days of Hospital Care

I awoke still tired as it had been a sleepless night with my mind racing, but optimistic that Sandy was in the right place. It was time to talk with my daughters about their mom. I let them sleep in that morning as I thought that they probably need the rest, and I was trying to comprehend the past few months since the end of school and why I hadn't seen the truth about Sandy's behavior earlier. I did not have an answer, I but knew that once I had read last Sunday's newspaper that I had acted properly and that it was time to speak with the doctors at the hospital. I would do so today.

When the girls awoke I had a talk with them about their mom. I knew that they were only twelve and fifteen; I realized that both of them had probably been through a horrible situation in the past year or so, and I did not want to upset them about their mom's condition. I told them that Mommy would be getting the help that she needed, that she would probably be spending some time away and that she would probably go to another hospital after her stay at St. Clair's in Boonton, or so I thought. I also told them that we were very fortunate to live in a country that has the care available for people like Mom who are sick and that under doctor's care I was sure their mom would get better.

I also tried to recall events from my early childhood. At my current age of forty-nine I remembered few, but I knew that for both girls, about to enter the seventh and tenth grades, that this would be one of those days that they would never forget just as they would never forget the day when Mommy would come home better and well.

I arrived at the hospital sometime in the late morning or just after lunch that day. I had told the girls I would be away for a few hours, visiting their mom, and they should call me if there were any problems as I could be home in about twenty minutes.

The facility was on the sixth floor of the hospital and one needed to pass through two locked doors at which a guard was posted. The walls were padded throughout this entire floor and most of the people present wore slippers and pajamas or some other loose-fitting clothing.

When I visited Sandy, she was calm, but very reclusive and asked me why I had done this to her.

I said, "I love you and you need medical help. For the past year you have lied to me about seeing our doctor. I believe that you have a hormonal imbalance due to menopause and that hopefully once it is determined, proper medication will be the answer."

I was praying that this was the problem, but really very concerned that this was not the case. I asked to speak with the doctors, and was informed that I was to meet with Sandy's clinician Kellyn Lopez.

The doctors said they had done a blood exam and physical and were awaiting the results of the blood tests, and there was not much more they could tell me. My thought was okay, hopefully by tomorrow, Sunday, they will have an answer about her blood test.

I filled out some paperwork regarding our insurance, and then I said, "I want to speak with my wife again."

I spoke again to Sandy and told her I would be back in the late afternoon, as I needed to bring her some belongings from home.

She asked how long she would be there, and I stated that I didn't know.

The hospital worker, Kellyn Lopez, informed me that Sandy would be under observation for some time, however, and that I could bring nothing back that has a tie string belt. I understood why. The people here were under observation, and a belt or anything with a drawstring or shoelace could be a weapon in the wrong hands. This precaution was for everyone's safety, both patient and staff.

Later that afternoon I returned with bathing supplies that were inspected, as were the articles of clothing that I brought. It was pretty apparent that this floor of the hospital was run quite well and the rules for clothing applied to all, from my observation.

I was now wondering where all of this would take us as a family. I was informed that tomorrow, Sunday, was family visitation day, and I told Sandy that I would bring the girls to visit at 2 p.m. as that was when visits were allowed for the children.

Sunday morning I decided to head out to the barn. Since Sandy had been taken to the hospital Friday, the chores for the horses were now on my shoulders. When I saw the appearance of the barn Saturday, I truly knew that Sandy was in need of help.

Sandy, who had always been an animal lover and always cared for the pets, had let the barn go into such a state of—"mayhem" is about the only way I can describe it. Garbage was everywhere, piled up all over. Empty bags of grains and supplements were stacked all over the place. It looked as if nothing, not even garbage, had been thrown out in a few months; however, the stalls had still been tended to.

I thought, this will take me days to clean up, but I'll get it done. The question was where to start. I spoke with Jenny, the other true horse lover, and we started the process that Sunday morning.

This cleanup ultimately would take about three full days of work for me. I found multiple bottles of ointments, vitamins and all other things that were old, judging by the expiration dates. The amount of garbage was incredible and would take weeks to get rid of. Looking at how the barn had fallen into such a mess indicated to me just how ill Sandy had fallen.

In our household I was responsible for the yard care and helping with the household duties, but as far as the barn was concerned

I'd wanted nothing to do with it. My late father had once owned a very large riding stable, the West Orange Riding Club. I had spent a few summers working for Dad in the sixth through eighth grades and my knowledge of a horse was from its back end, one might say. I really never took to horseback riding as a young boy, and I really had not been in Sandy's barn since school had ended, as I had been very busy with both work and getting Mom's house sold. Now I had more work to attend to.

In the afternoon we went to the hospital to visit as a family. When we got there, I was informed that my youngest Leslie would not be allowed into the hospital as she was only twelve and the hospital's policy was that only children fourteen and up were allowed in. My oldest Jenny was not happy to see her mom and my youngest really wanted to see her mom, but was only allowed to look through the two locked doors.

If I had known of this policy, I would not have taken either child. Looking back, I can say I understand why that policy existed, but at the time I did not understand it. That entire visit was a very sad event that I now regret. My oldest saw her mom in a padded facility and my youngest just got to wave to Mommy from a glass window.

Very little was said on the way home. I wanted to just get the girls back home and attend to all the household and animal duties that were to be my responsibility for the next few weeks or months as I now saw it.

Sunday evening I received a call from one of Sandy's closest friends, Terry Sandello. She lived in the next town over in Madison. She and Sandy had met while Sandy was in print sales. Terry had become her client first, but later one of her closest friends. Their friendship had now lasted ten years, if not longer. Terry had just returned from a vacation at her sister's home down in Virginia Beach. Terry asked to speak with Sandy and I gave her the news that Sandy was up in St. Clair's Hospital in the psych ward.

Terry said, "Thank God, you got her there, Bill."

She then told me that over the last few months she'd observed Sandy's behavior getting increasingly odd. She said that about two weeks ago Sandy had arrived for a visit just before Terry's vacation trip. Sandy had one of the dogs on the leash and would not enter her home for coffee and was acting totally strange. Finally, at one point, Sandy said to her closest friend in the world, "You and Bill are having an affair."

Terry responded, "You are my best friend, and I would never do so, and your husband Bill would never do so as well. Bill loves you Sandy."

Terry said that while she'd been away she'd kept thinking about Sandy, that she was very worried about what she had witnessed, that she and her family had just gotten back from their trip and that she'd wanted to call to see how Sandy was doing.

Terry said, "Bill, you did the right thing. I will make a few calls for you to her friends and we will go visit her."

My thoughts were that I wasn't the only one who seen Sandy's behavior, that I was glad she would have a few other visitors and that it should be helpful for her to know that her friends cared for her.

Monday morning I had to call into work and speak with my manager about what had transpired over the weekend. I said I needed to be out for a few days; I was in unchartered waters, one might say. I had to get a game plan together and would go again to the hospital to speak with the doctors and clinician who was caring for my wife.

I arrived at the hospital and asked if the blood results were in. They responded yes.

"What are the results?" I asked.

They informed me that they could not tell me.

I asked why.

The answer was that Sandy had not, after three days, signed a consent form, and they were not allowed to tell me anything.

I thought, my wife is in the hospital, not in her right mind, and again we are going through this. What the hell is going on? This makes absolutely no sense whatsoever.

The doctors said that Sandy must consent and sign a paper so they could speak to me regarding her condition. They also informed me that she was refusing to take any medication and that in order to do so she must sign paperwork as well.

I could not comprehend what was going on. My wife was in the insanity ward and nothing could be done. This was the most absurd thing I had ever heard of, and why was it so? The answer was an act of Congress: the HIPAA law or patient's privacy act.

I was in absolute shock.

Sandy was in a facility, non-compliant, and nothing could be done until she agreed to sign paperwork, similar to laws that would have arrested me if I had taken her against her will to the hospital.

Kellyn Lopez told me to come back tomorrow, as I was to join Sandy in a one-on-one open session with the doctor present.

I agreed to do so, and I spoke with Sandy later and asked her to sign the paperwork so the doctors could help her. Then I left to head home.

That night after dinner the girls asked me if we were going to go to the beach down in outer banks of North Carolina as planned.

I told them that I really did not think so as I needed to be home for their mom. I said, "Look, I know you missed the Delaware Fair this year and the house at the beach is paid for, but your mom needs help now and next summer we will get away."

They were disappointed, but what else was there to do? I felt bad for them, as there was to be no trip for the summer and I did not know if their mom would ever sign her consent forms.

The following day, August 22, I arrived for our joint session with the doctor at the hospital.

The joint meeting between Sandy and I occurred in a small office located on the same floor of the hospital. The doctor, Sandy, and I were present.

I spoke with Sandy prior to the meeting when I first entered the floor of the hospital and asked her if she had signed the consent forms.

Sandy told me she had.

I thought, good, now she's medicated and was starting towards some progress.

We had a few words, then it was time to speak together with her doctor and we were moved into the office. This was the first time I had actually spoken with a doctor at the hospital as all other conversations had been with her assigned clinician.

Doctor Patal introduced himself to me and began the meeting. He instructed Sandy and me that he would ask each of us questions and we were not to interrupt each other while we answered his questions. The doctor asked if we both understood what he had just said.

I responded yes, and Sandy said yes as well.

The doctor first asked Sandy if she knew why she was at the hospital.

Her response was muted.

He asked her about some of the incidents of the past month.

Again she was in denial of anything being a problem and insistent that we just needed marriage counseling and all things were fine otherwise.

Then the doctor asked me if I was okay with marriage counseling.

My response was that I would do whatever was necessary and I would agree with his recommendations.

Then the doctor asked me my opinions of the past months' events.

I expressed my concerns and said, "I believe that marriage counseling is not the issue here."

Sandy started to interrupt me and continued to do so until the doctor said, "If you do not stop, I will end this session right now."

Sandy stopped talking and I thought that would be the end of it and we would continue the session.

Doctor Patal again asked me to go on.

I spoke to Sandy about her jumping out of the car and sleeping next to her daughter's bed with a fourteen-inch carving knife.

As I was speaking, she continued to interrupt. The doctor asked her to stop, and she would not. The doctor again asked her to stop interrupting me, and she again would not.

Finally Doctor Patal rose from his seat and looked at Sandy and said the meeting was over.

I was quite shocked and did not know what to do. I looked at Sandy and said something and then asked to speak with her doctor privately about what had just occurred. The doctor said there really wasn't much he could tell me and again, I asked why and said, "Look, she signed the forms and is now medicated."

The doctor's said, "No, she has not signed a thing and so far has not cooperated with anyone while here."

I said, "She just told me she had signed the forms yesterday."

He said, "No she has not. Your wife is ill and in denial of the events that got her here."

I could not believe my ears. She was lying again, and I had just wasted another day and now I doubted if she would sign anything.

As I drove home, I wondered what the hell I would do now. Nothing had changed. Sandy was in a facility in need of help and refused to get help.

The one bright spot was that according to New Jersey law, there must be a public hearing before a judge within twenty days when-ever someone is involuntarily confined to a mental institution. At least when that occurred, based on her lack of progress, I thought Sandy's need for help would be clear.

The following day I spoke with Sandy by phone as that option was available for the patients. I confronted her about the fact that she'd lied to me, was not taking any medications, and had not signed any paperwork since she'd been at the hospital.

Once again she was in denial and said that she had signed the paperwork that day. Later I called her clinician, who informed me that Sandy had not signed anything. I told the clinician what

Sandy had told me, that she had been in the hospital for six days with no change in her behavior and no medications, and that she still insisted that she was fine and wanted to come home.

That evening I had a talk with the girls and again they asked about the beach. These kids needed a break away from all that had occurred, and really, I did also. Their mother was not willing to sign anything to help herself and I had made arrangements for the horses a few weeks earlier. I told the girls that Mommy was not well and if she didn't seem to get better by tomorrow we would decide by dinnertime whether to go. All we need to do was pack and load the van Friday morning for the drive down. I said that if their mom's doctors said she needed help, we would need to stay home. I had not discussed their mother's non-compliance with them, and I told them I would see their mom tomorrow and speak again to her doctors.

Thursday was visitation day, and I would go alone.

On Sandy's seventh day at the hospital, I arrived and asked to talk first with her clinician. I explained our current issues and asked if she thought Sandy would sign any paperwork.

The answer was no.

I then told the clinician I would tell my wife that if she still refused to sign any paperwork that I would take the girls away to the beach house that she'd selected earlier that spring and that her choice was either to sign her forms and I would stay home, or I would go.

I spoke to my wife again and discovered that one of her friends was also in the hospital in the same ward as Sandy. I could not believe it. I later found out that this woman had been in the hospital many times due to mental health issues that I was unaware of prior to that day.

I decided to speak with my wife again and I said, "You have not signed anything. You have lied to me repeatedly while here at the hospital and you continue to refuse any help. I cannot make you sign any forms, but the girls want to take the trip to the Outer

Banks to the house that you selected in Nags Head. I have decided that if you do not sign your papers for the doctors, I will take the girls on the trip, and if you sign the papers, I will keep them home. It is up to you to make a decision."

Now Sandy had a dilemma. She sat in her chair and said, "I will sign the papers."

I said, "Fine. Let's do it now."

She said, "I will sign them after you leave."

I said, "No, you will not. They need to be signed now!"

This discussion went on for quite some time as she would first agree and then say, "I'll do it later."

I remembered the hours we'd spent in a similar pattern the day she'd jumped from the van, so finally I said, "Okay, you can sign them when I leave and I will call to make sure that you have signed them. Otherwise I will take the girls away."

I arrived home that afternoon convinced that in the morning we would be leaving for our trip.

By Friday, August 25, nothing had been signed and off we left for our trip, once again without my wife, for another family vacation and this time with three dogs along.

Friday evening we got as far as a nice motel about a mile from the entrance to the Chesapeake Bay Bridge-Tunnel, staying at a motel on the bayside. We had a nice dinner at a place overlooking the sunset on the bayside.

I had not received any calls from the staff at the hospital or from my wife all day long on my cell phone and figured that nothing had changed.

Saturday, our rental was to be available by around noon. We would be there on time, according to our timetable.

We got up Saturday and there were still no calls, so we headed south to the beach house, picked up the key and groceries and unloaded the van.

That afternoon I checked my voicemail and there was a message from the clinician Kellyn Lopez at the hospital.

I called back and spoke to the Sandy's clinician, who I had last talked with late Thursday night, only to find that Sandy had still refused to sign her papers. Much to my surprise, Sandy finally had verbally agreed to allow the staff to speak with me regarding her condition and said she wanted me to see her tomorrow as Sunday was visiting day.

I told her clinician that was impossible as I was now at the beach with her daughters as I had told them I would be if she did not sign the papers. Apparently, Sandy finally had agreed verbally sometime Friday while we were en route to the Outer Banks. I thought perhaps she had finally started on some medication, and that when we got back Sandy would, after some time on meds, appear better.

I spoke with Sandy that day and so did her children. We told her that we would stay and be back in about five or six days.

She asked about the house she had picked out, and I said it was fine, but that there had been quite a lot of development since both we'd traveled here years ago before we had children.

The girls seemed to be fine. All of us needed a break from every-thing, the weather was nice and we called every day to speak with the girl's mom.

One day I received a call from Nick Mangold, the DYFUS agent who had arrived at our home the day Sandy was taken away to the hospital.

He asked me how the girls were.

I responded that we were at the beach in North Carolina and they were flying kites and asked whether he would care to speak with them.

He said no.

I then explained that Sandy had not cooperated with the doc-tors at the hospital and since the beach house had been paid for in advance, I thought a break from the home was needed.

He seemed to agree and indicated that he knew that Sandy had been refusing any treatment during her stay before we'd left.

We took a few drives to see the wild horses north near Corolla, visited the Wright Bros. Monument, went boating, and had a nice relaxing time away from home. During the week, I was able to speak with Kellyn Lopez as to Sandy's progress, and Ms. Lopez indicated that Sandy was now on meds. But the clinician really did not indicate that Sandy had been making any real progress. I also was told that Sandy's judicial hearing was set Friday, September 1, at the hospital, and I told the girls that we would be leaving early from our trip as I need to be at the hospital Friday morning.

I packed the van Wednesday evening, and we headed out just before sunup on Thursday, August 31. I figured we would be home by late afternoon.

We arrived home Thursday. The trip home was much shorter as I took 95 north instead of the Chesapeake Bay Bridge Tunnel route. The van was unloaded, and there was a letter in the U.S. Mail from the courts, also indicating that Sandy's hearing was to take place tomorrow and that I was invited to come.

Of course I intended to be present.

Sandy's clinician, Kellyn Lopez, had said that the doctors would recommend that she be sent away to a facility, that the hearing would be necessary to facilitate the doctor's recommendation, and that this was standard procedure.

Thursday evening I called Sandy and spoke with her and asked her if all was well.

She said everything was fine and asked me how the beach was today.

My reply was we were now home.

Upon hearing this news, Sandy became very quiet. She said nothing to me about her court hearing as if I did not know of it.

I then asked her if I could visit with her tomorrow.

Her response was that the next visitation day was Saturday.

I knew this information was correct, since when she'd entered the hospital Kellyn Lopez had told us that visits were allowed Tuesdays, Thursdays, and on the weekends unless the doctors wished to speak with family members themselves or on a joint basis.

I spoke with the girls that evening and said that dad has to go to the hospital tomorrow and that mom would then be going to a different hospital, probably one farther away, for some time and that she would come home when she got better.

I arrived at the hospital at about 10 a.m. Friday, asked to speak with Ms. Lopez, and asked her about the procedures that would be taking place late that morning or in the afternoon.

She informed me that there would a few hearings that day, as Sandy's was not the only one scheduled. Ms. Lopez also said again that the doctor would recommended that Sandy needed to go full-time to an inpatient long-term facility for further treatments, as the hospital was just a temporary treatment care facility.

I was happy to know that Sandy would be moved to a better facility and that progress was finally at hand.

Sandy's clinician asked if I wished to speak with her, and I said yes.

I then met with my wife in one of the conference rooms.

She was very shocked to see me and asked why I was there as Friday was not a visitation day.

My response was I had a letter that informed me of her hearing today and invited me to participate at it.

Sandy looked at me, became very quiet, and said she did not want me present for her hearing.

I said, "I will be there."

Sandy then got up. She was upset and asked again, "Why are you doing this to me?"

I then left the room as I decided that I would just wait until her hearing was to start and read a book that I had brought with me.

Ms. Lopez came out and told me that I would have to leave the hospital and that there was no point in my staying for Sandy's hearing.

I asked why.

The answer was that Sandy did not want me present at her hearing and had the right to prohibit me from being in attendance.

I looked at Ms. Lopez and said, "Look at this letter from the courts. It says there is a hearing and that I may be present."

Again Ms. Lopez said that my wife had the right to deny my being present at her hearing.

I could not believe my ears. I thought about the newspaper story I'd read and what the man who had lost his son three or four weeks ago must have gone through. I had vowed to myself that I would not allow my family to become another set of victims.

I told the clinician, "I'm staying and will not leave here."

Again she told me that if Sandy didn't want me in the hearing, there was nothing that I could do.

I told her that I was very worried about this situation.

The clinician then said, the following: "Listen, this is not the first time that a patient does this. The doctor is recommending that your wife needs to go to a long-term facility. The judge always follows the doctor recommendations and never overrules the doctor's recommendations." She then again repeated, "There's nothing more you can do here if she does not want you here. Go back home to your children. We will give you a call later and let you know where your wife will be taken to next."

I said, "I will go home and start making some calls to locate a private facility. I may have some problems as it is now lunch time on the Friday before Labor Day weekend, but when I get home I will start."

When I arrived home, I got on the computer and started trying to locate places, which in my belief I would be required to locate for sometime the next week after the Labor Day weekend. I got a list started and made some calls that afternoon, which was difficult as it was now mid-afternoon. Messages were left as no one answered the phones.

At about 2:30 p.m., the phone rang.

I thought the caller would be one of the clinics returning my call. When I answered, it was Ms. Lopez. I had expected her to call later as she'd told me she probably would not get back to me until around 5 p.m.

She told me the judge, Robert J. Brennan, had overruled the doctor who had stated that my wife needed to go to a long-term facility.

All I could think of was that family I'd read about in the newspaper. I asked Ms. Lopez, "How could this happen? You told me that the judge always follow the doctor's recommendations."

She said to me that, in the past ten years, she believed that only once had a judge overruled a doctor's recommendations.

I said, "How could he let her out? She had a fourteen-inch carving knife with her by her daughter's bedside."

There was no answer.

I was informed that Ms. Lopez could only tell me the results of the hearing and that I would have to pick up my wife, Sunday, September 3, which was her court-appointed release date.

A very sinking feeling overcame me, almost helplessness. I was very worried and vowed that if anything happened I would seek my restitution myself. I would not let what had happened in Bernard's Township happen in my household. I had another restless night as I tried to get some sleep. I did not tell the girls that their mom would be home Sunday.

Saturday morning I made a phone call to Scott Noyes, one of my close friends from town. I told him what had transpired. He gave me his condolences, and I asked him if I could leave my shotguns at his home, as even though they had gun locks, I felt it would be best if they were out of our home.

Scott said fine, and I believe that I dropped them off that Saturday.

He asked me if there was anything else that he could do for us.

"Say a prayer," I replied.

Later that morning I spoke with the girls and told them that Mom would be coming home tomorrow.

They asked about the other hospital and I'm not too sure of what I said.

That night, sleeping was difficult as my mind raced over many different thoughts and scenarios: what if? Tomorrow I would have to pick up my ill wife from a mental ward at a hospital where a doctor had recommended her confinement to a long-term facility due to an undiagnosed mental illness. A judge who had no education in the science of mental health was allowed with his infinite wisdom to play God on our family in a country I for so many years had believed in and never once asked a thing of. I believed in the words spoken by a great leader whose life was cut short many years ago: "Ask not what your country can do for you, but what you can do for your country." I wondered why, in our time of need, when I'd never asked a thing of my country, my country was doing this to our fragile household.

Sunday, September 3 arrived, and I left to pick up Sandy with that sinking feeling and worry, not sure of what the future might bring.

I met with Sandy's clinician and again asked, "What do I do now?"

She responded that Sandy must attend outpatient counseling per Judge Brennan's orders and that there was a safety order in place from DYFUS that Sandy must not be left alone with her children. Her outpatient care was to begin Tuesday after the Labor Day holiday and she was to be monitored by DYFUS and the hospital as an outpatient.

I asked, "What if she refuses to go to the hospital?"

The answer was to call DYFUS and the police just like before.

I said, "I am very worried and concerned for everyone's safety at home now."

Kellyn Lopez informed me that the staff and doctors at the hospital were not in approval of Judge Brennan's ruling and handling of Sandy's hearing. She also told me that all the staff felt that Sandy would not comply with her follow up outpatient therapy.

My wife arrived quietly, and we departed the hospital after papers were signed.

I thought about the past events and wondered how in the world this could happen, and vowed again to myself that if something bad happened I would seek justice for my household, no matter how long it took. I was a very concerned and unhappy man. My thought was if anything like what occurred in the next town over occurred in my home, I would need to retrieve my guns and hunt down my prey, Judge Robert J. Brennan.

The Waiting Room
an account by 12-year-old Leslie

I was locked in a tiny gateway room with dad and sister waiting to see my mom for the first time in days. I looked through a small window in the door and noticed the squeaky leather couches, nice tile, colorful walls, cheap pieces of modern art, and fake plants that all tried to hide the fact that this was mental institution. I knew that every other wing in this building had blank walls and cheap flooring.

A nurse emerged from the room, typed in a pass code opening the door and greeted us with a smile. How could she be smiling in a place like this? When we explained that we were here to see Sandy, the woman asked my age. My father answered for me. "12." I stood, Awkward and nervous.

"Do you have a note from your wife's doctor?" she asked my dad in all seriousness. We responded with blank stares. "Without it," she continued, "I'm sorry to say that she cannot enter this wing of St. Claire's." The woman looked at me. Who knew that I needed a permission form to see my own mother? I certainly didn't, and neither did my dad.

By now, the flutters in my stomach turned into a sickly knot. My father asked if I would be alright to stay in the waiting room. I nodded as my mother made her way to the tiny window on the other side of the bolted door.

She looked worn down and sickly, worse than I remembered. It was clear that she was not happy here. Worst of all, she seemed hopeless. As she headed towards us, she committed an apologetic look. I met the gaze, knowing she wouldn't look away.

I couldn't contain myself. Tears built up behind my lids and before I knew it, I exploded with sobs, losing all control of my breath. I couldn't see my mother this way so I trudged out of the gateway room and slumped myself into a waiting room chair (the kind that no matter how many different ways you sit, you can never be comfortable).

I knew what they all were thinking. Dad thought I was scared, Mom was scared, and Jenn was just embarrassed. The nurse probably still had that stupid grin on her face. Gravity pulled harder and harder on my body while the air surrounding pushed ferociously against my face. I dropped my head to my hands for support and focused my eyes downward. I knew that I lost my mom, and had a feeling that she wasn't coming back.

I allowed my mind to trail back in time for the present was too hard to bear. I followed my mind to a series of events that landed my mother in this institution. Flashes of slamming doors, several tears, and horrid memories raced through my mind.

I could hear her trembling voice weeping my name. "Leslie." I could see the shame and confusion in her eyes when they took her away. I recalled that my mother would go several weeks without bathing. The stench would sometimes leak from my mother's discolored turtleneck and worn out jeans. I remembered the slow disappearance of steak knives, dog leashes, and letter openers. Such strange occurrences happened in throughout the summer, but I guess that's how she ended up in here.

My mind brought me back further to a better time, a time when I was known as Munchkin and Leah-Leah-Bean. This was far before my mother ever conjured conspiracies and wrote them down, letting them reside in the cookie jar.

I pictured our days at Castle Park when she'd push me on the zip line and encourage me to plow down the metal slide which roasted from the strong August sun, the days when she would hunt down my splinters and buy me Spongebob ice cream pops. These memories reminded me of the woman she once was. Maybe this place would help return my mother to her original state. Maybe it wasn't so bad after all.

I did not notice when my sobs came to a halt. My dry puffy eyes trailed from the tile and were bleached from the reflection of the florescent lights on the walls. I carefully cracked each individual knuckle and slowly twisted my spine to crack my back. I then lifted myself from that stiff chair, ignoring the dizzy headache that arrived with the sudden rush of blood from my head. I paced through the room in search of a clock but found nothing except dry walls and empty chairs.

I looked around once more with swollen eyes, face cooling. There was nothing for me here so I headed back to my designated chair. I seated myself back down, and patiently anticipated the arrival of my father and sister, ready to leave this waiting room.

September 2006

Having been born and raised in New Jersey, I have always considered the month of September as my favorite. The hot, humid weather that the northeast is noted for in July and August is gone and blue skies abound. It's as if a switch has turned.

September is a time of new beginnings. The new school year arrives, and the weather is wonderful for the next few months. All one has to do is remember the beautiful blue-sky day of September 11, 2001.

I was now placed in a situation, unsure of where, as a family, we were heading. One might say we were in unchartered waters or that this time might be my family's own 9/11.

While Sandy was in the hospital I had been left with all the chores, and the cleanup had been quite a task. I had found knives hidden throughout the house. Letter openers that had been missing were found, as was a set of car keys hidden outside the house. I also found the missing fourteen-inch carving knife hidden under the front seat of the Durango that Sandy had driven.

When I arrived at the hospital that Sunday and met with Kellyn Lopez, she apologized and had a look of concern, but said that there was nothing more the hospital could do as Judge Brennan had overruled the staff and doctor's recommendations.

Sandy was happy to be going home. I noticed how thin she had become, dropping much weight and going from a size six last winter and buying all new clothes in May in a size two, and now they all were too big, all of this occurring in a six-month time frame.

I was very unsure where things were headed and really had no other choice but to try to make the best of things and be sure to monitor her activities in our home.

That Sunday when we arrived home, I took Sandy out to her barn and showed her how clean things were. I explained that I had spent the better part of three full days cleaning out all the garbage that had piled up before her stay at the hospital and I asked her if she would be able to keep up with the barn work.

Sandy responded that she would.

I told her, "Today is Monday, the girls start school on Wednesday and since the court has orders that you cannot be home alone with the girls, we will have to come to a workable solution while you participate in your court-ordered group therapy. Tomorrow is Tuesday, and your sessions start. I'll take the girls out to get their school supplies while you attend your session."

Sandy agreed to do so.

That week I also knew that I had a few other people to speak with regarding the events that had brought our family to this crossroad.

I visited the police department and asked to meet with the chief of police. I had never been in the building before except to vote and discuss a prior issue regarding a neighbor's illegal addition that had caused a water problem on our property. That issue was eventually resolved in our favor.

When I spoke with Chief Gaffney, I said that I wanted to inform him that I had removed my guns from my home and, as required by law, must notify the police of such matters. I realized that he had been present at our home shortly after the first policeman had arrived the day Sandy had been taken to St. Claire's hospital involuntary. I explained my concerns to Chief Gaffney and explained my desire to remove my guns from my home even though all the weapons had safety locks on the triggers.

Chief Gaffney asked me where I had taken the guns.

I explained that Scott Noyes had them at his home.

Chief Gaffney said he knew that Scott lived on a private road right behind the police station in the Municipal Building.

I said, "We can call Scott to verify this if you wish."

Chief Gaffney said that it was not necessary.

I then said, "I am very concerned for my family. You were present and saw the condition of my wife that day, as did other members of your department. Remember your own police officers had to remove a knife and sharp objects from her against her wishes that day and that what got her to the hospital was the fact that she had been sleeping with a carving knife next to my youngest daughter as we'd found out the day she was taken away."

I also explained that DYFUS was to monitor our home and that hopefully things would get back to normal, but if not, I had been instructed that I would need to call his department for assistance again.

Chief Gaffney listened and did not make any comments.

I thanked him for his time and said, "I hope we will not need to bother the police department again. I'm just not sure where, as a family, we are heading to right now."

I then went to both of my daughters' schools to speak with the principals. Leslie was just starting seventh grade and was enrolled at the Harding Township Grammar School, which served kindergarten through eighth grade. Jenny was attending Madison High School. The Harding school is very small, with approximately two classrooms per grade and less than four hundred pupils in attendance. Madison is a very fine high school that's well-ranked within the state of New Jersey.

My first visit was to the middle school, where I asked to speak with Dee Klicker, the now-retired principal and once Jenny's second-grade homeroom teacher. I met her in her office and asked if we could close the door, as I need to share some upsetting family matters at home and arrangements that needed to be made regarding Leslie and her mother. I went over the fact that Sandy had been taken away and released against the hospital's recommendations. I also explained that a safety order had been issued and that Sandy was not allowed unsupervised time alone with Leslie. I did not disclose all the events that ultimately got Sandy into the hospital, as I felt that those were private family matters. I explained that under no circumstances was Sandy allowed to pick up nor take Leslie from school alone, and that I would be picking up my daughter until further notice.

I then said, "Look, I'm flying by the seat of my pants right now and really not too sure what will happen next."

Dee Klicker replied, "Where's the court order?"

I explained that nothing had arrived to our home yet, but if necessary she could call the hospital clinician, who just three days ago had notified me prior to Sandy's release of what was now required of Sandy at the court hearing I was denied the right to attend.

Dee Klicker then replied, "How do I know that's true?"

I replied, "I just told you so."

She responded, "I'm not going to do that."

I could not believe my ears. I thought of my late father and how he'd handled an issue that had happened while I was a boy in ninth grade. At the time I was present with a guidance counselor.

Almost repeating my late father's words I then said to Dee Klicker, "I'm going home and writing everything down that just transpired today, and so help me, if you let Sandy pick Leslie up from school or take her out of school and anything happens to her, I will personally make sure that you will never again work in a school for the rest of your life."

Dee Klicker then blinked and with a look of complete shock at what I'd actually said.

Remembering again my late father's words from so many years ago, I said, "I pay your salary through property taxes I pay this town on property my wife owns. You work for me, not the latter.

This seems to be something most public servants seem to have forgotten today."

Dee Klicker did not respond.

I then added, "I'm going to repeat myself: under no circumstances whatsoever is Sandy to take Leslie away from the school premises."

There was a moment of silence.

Then I said, "Am I understood?"

She looked at me and finally nodded and said yes.

I said, "I am sorry to have had to speak to you this way, but I have very grave concerns for my children and my wife."

My next visit that day was to Madison High School, where I figured I would be subjected to the same response from the principal. This man, however, much to my surprise, was empathetic, extremely helpful, and truly understanding of the dilemma occurring within our household. I explained that I did not have any documents yet, that Jenny's mother had just been released from the hospital Sunday and if necessary, when such documents were to arrive, I would be happy to provide them. I also said that if he had any questions he could call the hospital clinician.

He told me that would not be necessary and whatever the school could do, they would be available at any time and to call whenever necessary.

It turned out that Tuesday, the day before school started, while I was out with the girls picking up school supplies, Sandy did not attend her first scheduled outpatient group therapy session at the hospital.

This noncompliance went on for three days.

Finally Thursday evening I spoke with Sandy privately and gave her an ultimatum, saying, "If you do not attend the sessions by tomorrow, I will call the hospital and police as I was instructed to do by the hospital as per the court's orders." I did not have a copy of any such order, but Sandy's clinician had gone over what was expected of Sandy upon discharge with me present. I also said to

Sandy, "DYFUS will be monitoring our home to make sure you are compliant."

Sandy was guarded and quiet.

In a warning tone, I said, "I will personally call the hospital to make sure that you start you mandatory sessions. Do you understand me?"

Sandy said yes. She again was cautious, guarded and distrustful, to say the least.

I said, "Look, you finally are on medication and hopefully this will correct things for you. As parents with a family, we need to do these things in order to get things back to normal. The girls are back in school, and I will have to pick them up from their after-school sports and activities, as you are not permitted to do so. Hopefully the proper drugs and therapy will make things better for us and, as a family, we will get through this."

My youngest was involved with field hockey on the school team and my oldest was involved with jazz choir and still worked a few afternoons at her job at Dunkin Donuts in Madison.

I went back to work for the first time Wednesday and spoke with my manager about our current situation. I said, "I really need to be home quite a bit right now. I have all sorts of additional duties regarding the children and I will need to be at work for some time on a limited basis." Normally I was in the office by 8:30 a.m. and left sometime after 5 p.m. on a regular basis, but that could not work now.

That week I also received a call from a representative of a state-agency DYFUS who said she had been assigned our case plan and household. Arrangements were made for her to come to the house the next Wednesday at 7 p.m. to go over the case plan and how she would monitor our household with regard to the children's safety.

The next Wednesday our caseworker arrived on time at our home.

I got home early to make sure that the house was clean and everything was in proper order.

Ermene Remy, a young woman in her twenties, introduced herself, sat down with us in the living room, and asked questions of both myself and Sandy. Then she spoke privately with both girls in their rooms as well.

Sandy again tried to dismiss the events that had lead up to her involuntary confinement. She stated that all that was needed was marriage counseling.

I said, "If you want that as well, I will be happy to do so, but you must attend your hospital sessions."

Once again Sandy tried to dismiss all the prior events.

I finally said to Remy, "Sandy did not go to her first three sessions and only did so at my insistence." I also said that that Kellyn Lopez told us together that if Sandy failed to comply that she would be back before the judge again.

Remy said to Sandy, "Your husband is correct." She also said that Sandy must attend all sessions at the hospital and that she would be required to follow up with the hospital as to Sandy's attendance as well.

Before Remy left she made an appointment for 7 p.m. in two weeks' time and said she must stop in every two weeks to monitor Sandy's progress and how the girls were doing.

One more time Sandy tried to brush things off and again insisted that all that was needed was marriage counseling.

While the caseworker was present I said to Sandy, "Look, you are now on medication and this woman must do her job and monitor our home right now. Hopefully we can get through all of this and life can go back to normal."

I wasn't really sure what to do, but at least felt comfortable that there was some structure in place that would prevent any further issues within our household, and if necessary, a way to get my wife back to the hospital where both the doctors and I believed she currently belonged.

By the following week, things started to get out of hand again. Sandy's behavior was somewhat tolerable, but by the evening, things were out of hand. I cannot point to any one item in her behavior, but again was becoming concerned and the knot in my gut kept getting worse each and every day.

I had a discussion with Sandy about having her medications changed or increased as she was starting to repeat herself constantly and seemed to be having more difficulties.

She did not want to have her medications changed.

I spoke with her about this subject a couple of times that week.

Each time, her answer was that she was fine and that any changes were not necessary.

I thought otherwise and had been watching in the morning and evening, making sure Sandy was taking her meds. I had no idea what they were, but was observing that she did take them.

Her children were again withdrawing away from their mother. Who could blame them? I was convinced that she needed more help, but wasn't too sure how to get it for her. Her behavior was getting very odd again, to say the least. One moment she would seem fine and then out of nowhere her mental behavior and personality would completely change. It was as if she had thrown a light switch and then the switch would go off and her behavior would be fine.

After two weeks, I decided to go to the outpatient hospital myself and discuss my concerns with the staff as our DYFUS caseworker was scheduled to arrive that evening.

I left for the hospital early and arrived some time shortly after 8 a.m. I was hoping to find Rosanne Misclone, Sandy's caseworker. She was not in yet; however, her supervisor Dr. Contini was and agreed to speak with me.

Dr. Contini was kind enough to talk with me in his office. I went over all the circumstances that had led to Sandy's involuntary confinement and what I believed needed to be done with an increase of medications or change of medication. I expressed my concerns, saying that Sandy was doing nothing at home and refused to visit any friends. I said I was hoping that perhaps she might look for a part-time job just to get out of the house as I thought it would do her some good.

Dr. Contini said, "Your wife is very ill and may never be able to work again."

I said, "What do you mean?"

He replied, "She is ill and really should not be here. She needs to be in a facility for proper treatment of her current illness."

Up to this point no one had said anything to me regarding the condition of my wife's illness. I had been left out in the dark, but was now determined to make sure she received the help both she and we as a family needed.

I looked at Dr. Contini and said, "Please help me get her to where she needs to be. Our caseworker from DYFUS is arriving tonight and she need to be aware of this immediately."

Dr. Contini agreed, but did not indicate to me he would do so. I thought about the HIPAA laws and the fact that Dr. Contini could not disclose anything to me as most probably Sandy had refused to sign any consent forms here as she had refused in the psych ward as well, something I had now learned the hard way.

I then headed off to work, hoping that after tonight's meeting with our DYFUS worker and a recommendation that she needed to follow up with the hospital, as she had discussed with us on her first visit, that things would finally be moving in the right direction.

Once again things were getting out of control. I arrived home early that afternoon and had to help Sandy get the house ready as she did not straighten up for the visit.

Once the house was clean, I left to pick up Leslie from field hockey and Jenny from work, as Sandy was aware and compliant with the order not to be alone with the children while I was not present in the house. Perhaps Sandy would throw the light switch and start to act very odd while our caseworker was present. I was truly hoping so because then Sandy would be off to a facility where maybe her mental health could be corrected.

That evening, 7 p.m. came and went. No caseworker showed up.

Three phone calls were made and messages left and by 8 p.m., it was pretty apparent our caseworker was not going to show up.

I wondered what the hell was going on. I'd never asked for a thing from my government in my lifetime and now in our time of need, nothing was being done and all I found was my hands tied, making me unable to get my wife and family help.

The next day or perhaps two days later, Ms. Remy finally returned my calls from her missed appointment. She explained that she'd had another case emergency and was unable to make our appointment.

I responded, "What about the emergency going on in our home right now?"

No response was given, and she said she would later call back to reschedule.

Then I told her I had been to the hospital the day of her scheduled visit and had spoken with the supervisor of the hospital, Dr. Contini. I said, " It is imperative that you call him as soon as possible with regards to our current living conditions. Everything is not working."

I cannot express how angry I was after receiving this call, though I knew of the reputation this agency had for rampant mismanagement and waste. One needed only to read the newspapers to find out about the horror stories that had occurred with children under this agency's supervision.

September was coming to a close and nothing was working. Our household was under stress and a government agency that had been assigned to help was nowhere in sight. My thoughts kept going back to that twelve-year-old boy in Basking Ridge whose ill mother in a tragedy had taken her young son's life back in August. I did not know what to do, but I knew that I also had to start spending more time at work or problems would start to arise there. I needed some time to think about what to do next and spent the weekend trying to come up with a game plan.

Monday would be October 2. My production at work had dropped off to nothing and a household I was trying to manage was falling apart before my eyes. I seemed powerless to do anything to stop the freefall. The situation was just crumbling.

The girls were just twelve and fifteen at the time and were withdrawing from their ill mom due to her erratic and odd behavior. Who could blame them? Sandy's behavior was getting worse and it just came from nowhere. It was Dr. Jekyll and Mrs. Hyde when times got bad. We just never knew when Mrs. Hyde would surface.

No Means No Mommy
October 2006

I spoke with my wife about how she was not progressing with her therapy and the fact that her medications were really not working. Sandy said she was fine.

I then said to her that I had gone to see the people at the hospital at the end of September and asked them have a change made in her medications or an increase in the dosage.

We had this conversation at home.

Both girls were holed up in their bedrooms as was now the case every evening after dinner was served. They did not want to be around their ill mother and could not hear this conversation.

Once again Sandy was in denial that anything was wrong. She gave me a look of distrust and said she did not need a change nor would allow a change of her medications.

My answer to her was very clear. I said, "Your own daughters are very upset and leave for school almost daily in tears due to your behavior. This needs to be done for your girls' sake, please."She answered, "I will try to do better."

Things continued. One moment all was fine and the next minute all hell could break loose with Sandy's errant behavior and speech pattern maddening just to listen to and endure.

I told Sandy that I would be leaving for work after the girls left for the school bus and would get home after I'd picked them up from their school activities.

I urged Sandy to visit her friends as she needed to get out of the house and said that staying at home all day was not doing her any good. I went over a major concern that I had with her, which was what she would do once Leslie's field hockey season was over since she was not allowed to be in her own home by herself with her children present. Her youngest daughter would be home shortly after 3:45 p.m. at the end of the month and I could no longer be expected to leave work by 2:30 p.m. to be home as I had done in the entire month of September. I again said, "You must help yourself get through this as our family is starting to fall apart. Your children are withdrawing from you right before your eyes. You are refusing any help, and I do not know what to do." I also stressed that she would need to prepare dinner at a normal time so that when I got back home with the girls by 6 p.m. we could actually eat a meal together at a normal time.

My wife agreed with me and said she would continue to work with her doctors and would agree to have her medications looked at.

I was somewhat relieved, but concerned about where we, as a family, would end up. We were still in uncharted waters, one might say.

I said to Sandy, "Please help yourself because as at some point, we need to have DYFUS, with your doctor's okay, allow you to be home here with your children alone. If we don't, I don't know how long your children and I can go on like this."

Sandy looked me in the eye and promised me that she would do so.

I said, "Thank you. I will do whatever it is I can for you, but will continue to be speaking with your doctors." I believed that they, in turn, would notify DYFUS of Sandy's progress or lack of progress.

About ten days into the month we had to have a family therapy session, as Leslie was having extreme difficulties with her mother. She was taken out of school that day; I believe our appointment was around 10 a.m.

The point of the meeting was to have my youngest daughter discuss her issues with Sandy's therapist so that when Leslie answered her mom, Sandy would not continue to ask her the same question a few moments later as this was now Sandy's behavior pattern.

Sandy would ask a question, receive an answer, and then repeat herself, and her children were having as many problems with this behavior as I was. My wife's behavior was repeating itself again, and Leslie wanted her mother to know that when Sandy asked if she needed any help in the morning before school began and Leslie said, "No, mom," that that meant no mom.

Sandy was treating her youngest as if she were in kindergarten and not soon to become a teenager in seventh grade. She no longer required her moms' help and was very upset with her mom's behavior every morning regarding this issue.

After the session, we all went to lunch and my wife promised her daughter that she would no longer bother her in the morning before school started and would assist only if asked by her daughter.

I again had a talk with Sandy and said, "Look, your children are getting older. One is in seventh grade and one is in tenth grade and before you know it, will be off to college. They no longer are little girls, and you are treating them like five-year-olds. They are pulling back and do not understand what is wrong with their mom and becoming resentful of their mom. Please continue with your doctors and follow their advice and if they suggest a change of medications, please do as they ask."

For a few days after this meeting, things got better, and then they reverted back again. Once again I was speaking with Sandy's therapist and asking her to please reach out to our DYFUS representative.

It was now around mid-October. At this point I was able to handle work and driving after work for the children, but the household duties were getting overwhelming, as Sandy was not even preparing dinner after I had picked up the girls from their school activities. I could not tell what she was doing all day long at home after her therapy sessions, but the house was not getting cleaned and the food shopping was not being done either. There were only two horses out in the barn and even that was going again, judging by the appearance inside of the barn.

Our DYFUS representative finally called me at work; however, I was with a client and told her I would call her back. I did so, but just received her voice mail. I left her a message, asking when she would be back and if she had spoken with the people from the hospital, as things were not good in our home. I did not receive a call back and wondered if she would ever bother to follow up. It had been over a month since her first visit and she had pulled a no-show two weeks later. She did not seem to care or perhaps understand what was going on in our household.

By now my belief was that I had to work with the hospital in charge of Sandy and that I needed to get her back before a judge, and finally have her placed into a facility, as the doctors at St. Clair's hospital had felt was necessary prior to her release by Judge Brennan's orders.

The question remained how to do so.

I was really in the dark as to what my wife's illness was, as I had never even been told of her diagnosis nor what treatments would do for her. My children and I, it seemed, were just left to try to go on as if all was fine. The head of the outpatient hospital had said she really needed to be elsewhere and I was trying to work within a legal system that left us no answers.

Hopefully the hospital would pass on to DYFUS all the issues that were affecting my daughters and our daily lives. Things were out of control again. My true belief was that my wife needed to be placed in an inpatient facility where she would hopefully receive treatment and the chance to find the right medications to control what appeared to be some type of mental illness.

The real question remained how to get her there.

The Whisper

All was truly falling apart at home. I started to believe that it would be necessary for my children to be removed from the home as no progress was being made regarding my wife's behavior. The children did not want to be around their ill mother. They were either in constant arguments with their mom or holed up in their bedrooms when I was home. Again they were asking me to take them away from their home.

A move outside of the township would have required a change of schools and under current circumstances, the girls needed their friends, so I inquired about a house a block away that was about to be rented which would keep both daughters in their current schools. I spoke with the owners about moving in, but still was not too sure what to do. I was hoping to get my wife into a facility, working within the system that was failing my household yet still with the hope that somehow we could get her the help that she truly needed.

The owners said the house would become available by the middle of November if I was interested. Money-wise, this would not be an issue.

It was now the last week of October and the Black River Rod & Gun Club, which I had been a member and officer of for more than ten years, was sponsoring the annual skeet shoot competition. I really wanted to go and get a break from things if just for a couple of hours and I told my wife that I would be attending. Jenny would be dropped off at her job at Dunkin Donuts that morning and I would take Leslie along to my club as Sandy had stated earlier in the week that she did not want to go.

Sunday morning my wife asked me if I was going to the skeet shoot.

I said yes.

She then asked me if it would be alright if she could join us.

I looked at her and wondered what might occur, as she seemed fine in that moment.

She seemed to be okay, was insistent that all was fine and said she did not want to be home alone, so I reluctantly agreed.

We left the house, and I stopped by my friend Scott's home to pick up my two shotguns.

Sandy seemed fine.

We then headed out to the club property about forty-five minutes' drive away for the competition and picnic that follows after all the guys and their guests shoot. The ride out was uneventful.

While we were at the shoot, Sandy's behavior started to become very bizarre again. Mrs. Hyde was coming out again. Shortly after our arrival, Sandy actually became very reclusive. She got a very fearful look on her face and started to look up at the sky and sun while friends started to speak with her.

We did not stay very long that afternoon once lunch had been eaten. It was very apparent to my friends that something was very wrong with my wife. Nothing was said, but the looks on the faces of my friends who'd last seen my wife in April at the club's annual banquet prior to the opening day of the trout fishing season, when all had been fine, were quite surprising, to say the least.

On the ride home all hell broke loose. Sandy kept repeating, "Where are we going?"

I replied that we were going home, driving back to our house in the exact way we'd driven out just in reverse.

Sandy was in the back seat.

My youngest was in the front seat. She decided she did not want to hear her mother much longer and turned up the radio.

Sandy started to reach forward to turn it down.

This pattern went on for some time.

The next thing I knew, Sandy started to reach for the steering wheel and insisted I intended to take her away somewhere.

I kept telling her we were just going home.

She continued to grab at the steering wheel.

We finally got off the highway, and I said, "We are close to home and if you grab the wheel again, I will pull over and drop you off."

Four miles from our home, she did it again and this time, I almost ran off the road. I stopped the car told her to get out. She said no.

I stated that if she did not, I would call the police.

Sandy then got out of the car.

I drove my youngest daughter home and then turned around to pick up my wife. When I reached her, she refused to get back in the car. I followed her for awhile, asking to get back in the car and she refused.

By this time she was about three miles from our home and I knew she would not get back in the car as she insisted I was taking her somewhere far away.

All of this reminded me of the day when she'd jumped out of the car in early August on our trip to our camp with the girls.

After driving about a quarter of a mile, trying to convince her to get back into the car, I came to the conclusion that this effort would be another waste of time. It would take her about forty minutes to get home by foot. If she were late, I would go out again.

Sometime later, when she arrived home, she appeared fine and was apologetic about what had transpired.

I really did not know what to say.

The rest of the afternoon was again uneventful.

Later that evening my good friend Dick Kookogey called my home and spoke to me and asked, "What's going on with Sandy?"

The last time he had seen her was at the annual dinner back in April prior to the opening day of trout fishing. He and his wife Diane had sat next to us at the table during this function. Everything was fine, just months ago.

I gave him the short story and said, "I do not know what to do, Dick, and no one is helping. I cannot get any answers. My children want me to take them out of the house, and if I do so, I'm afraid of what Sandy may do."Dick asked what he could do to help in any way.

I said, "Just say a prayer for us and keep us in your thoughts."

Dick said he would and told me that all the members were very concerned for Sandy after what they had witnessed.

I discussed with Dick a few of the issues that had led us to this point.

He said, "How the hell could that judge let her out over the doctor's recommendation after she was sleeping by her daughter with a carving knife?"

I answered, "I have no idea, but I am very worried and God forbid, if something happens to my children, there will be hell to pay!"

While I was talking to Dick, Sandy came into the downstairs into the den, sat down and asked me what I was discussing with my friend.

I said just a few words about not having had a chance to speak with him while we were at the shoot.

I then told Dick I had to go and asked Sandy if she wished to speak with Dick. I'm not sure what they spoke about as I decided to leave the room so she could talk privately.

A few minutes later she came back upstairs and nothing more was spoken about the day's events.

That evening I cooked dinner as she was having trouble figuring out what to cook.

As I tried to sleep that night my mind kept racing about what to do next. I knew that in just two days' time there was to be a joint meeting of Sandy and her counselor with myself present. This meeting had been set back when Sandy had had her meeting with her counselor and her youngest daughter a few weeks back.

I was determined that by this mandatory joint meeting October 31, I would be able to get help or that once her counselor heard about the last few weeks' issues, she would have to call the DYFUS people and this meeting would finally get my wife the help she needed.

Monday evening I spoke with Sandy regarding her mandatory joint meeting for tomorrow morning.

She informed me that she did not intend to go.

I said, "I received a call today from your counselor as a reminder and I told the woman that I had scheduled my morning off for attendance at this meeting and that you'd told me over the weekend that you'd be going."

I thought, here we go again, but at least if she does not show, I will be able to get her back before a judge due to noncompliance with a court order that I had never seen after her release from the hospital.

That evening I again had to hear for hours why she did not need to see doctor, a repeat of the night prior to her involuntary confinement to St. Clair's hospital.

I said, "You must attend!"

I really got very little sleep that evening and figured that if Sandy did not attend as she stated she wouldn't that our household would finally get help as needed. Anyone who knew my wife could see her mental breakdown; I just could not understand why professionals did not.

Tuesday was Halloween and later in the evening, I would be taking my daughters to their friend's home to go trick-or-treating. After they left for school I again asked Sandy if she would attend her meeting set for 10 a.m.

She gave me no answer.

I then headed to the hospital. It was early, and I arrived at about 8:15 a.m. I spoke with Sandy's counselor, who told me it was very important that Sandy attend. I told her I would be there and would try to convince Sandy to attend.

I also told Sandy's clinician, Roseanne Misclone at Morristown Memorial Hospital, that I did not think that Sandy would attend the meeting.

She told me to go over to the police department and ask for their help.

I then drove over to the police department and asked to see someone. I sat down with the chief of police and I told him that Sandy had an appointment at the hospital and that it was mandatory.

He looked at me and said that there was really nothing he could do.

I said, "You were there the day that they took her away and the hospital told me upon her release by a judge's order that if she were noncompliant, I must inform the police and get her back to the hospital. It was your department's decision to help our family get her there and we need your help again. I do not believe that she will show up today for her session."

For a second time he informed me that there was nothing that they could do.

I decided to go back to our house again to see if I could convince my wife to attend her meeting.

When I arrived home, she again insisted that she did not need to attend, so I left by myself to attend our mandatory joint meeting without my wife.

Once I got to the hospital, Sandy's counselor and I spoke about all the issues. I asked her if anyone had spoken to the people from DYFUS and nothing was said. I discussed all the events that had been going on since our last meeting with my youngest a few weeks ago and said, "I no longer know what to do. My daughters want me to take them away, and I think I really have no other option as nothing is working and no one is listening to our need for help."

Her counselor, Roseanne Misclone, then leaned over and whispered so no one could hear, "Don't leave her. I think she might be suicidal."

For the first time, I had finally been told by a professional what for some time I was beginning to believe might be a reality, and I thought of that man from Basking Ridge who had lost his son and whose wife was also ill.

The counselor whispered this while her door was completely closed.

I asked her what to do and again she whispered the same words.

I left the meeting in a state I cannot really explain. I needed to go into work to let my boss know I would be out again for some time and then head home to get the girls off for the evening.

The counselor had said, "Let's get Sandy back here Thursday, November 2, at 10 a.m. and see if she shows up."

On Halloween in 2006, the ghosts and goblins were in full view. We were living with Mrs. Hyde, but just never knew when she might surface. However, the frequency was now more than Dr. Jekyll.

One other thing disclosed at this meeting was the fact that Sandy really had not been attending all her sessions as required.

I asked if this had been reported to DYFUS and again did not receive an answer because of the wonderful HIPAA law, which protected Sandy's right to privacy and not her family's concern for her health.

It turned out, as I would find out later, that this noncompliance had been going on all along, and that she had not been to a meeting since missing her last one at the end of October. Now I was not even sure if she had medication to take, as her prescriptions were good for only two-week intervals. If she had not run out of her medications yet, she soon would be out and there was a no-refill notice on the bottles.

That evening while the girls were out trick-or-treating, I decided I finally had the ammunition to get Sandy into a hospital, not only for her own sake, but for all of ours. I was sure that once our DYFUS representative Ermene Remy heard from the doctors, Sandy would finally get the chance that she needed to get proper medical help.

Tomorrow morning, November 1, I would have to make some calls. The world was spinning out of control and I felt as a bomber pilot must have during World War II, flying on one engine and low on fuel with the nearest airport beyond his fuel supply and anti-aircraft fire lit up all around.

I kept thinking of the day in August when the police had arrived at our home and Patrolman Gromek had said, "Mr. Dunn, you've done the right thing. Your wife is heading to a fine facility, and she will get the help she needs." I had tried to do everything possible to get my wife the help she needed and I could not comprehend how we, as a family, had arrived at this point. I was determined to get her help and would not rest until she got the help that she needed, and yet my hands seemed to be tied no matter what I tried to do.

The Gales of November

It was now November 1, 2006, and again for the second month in a row disaster seemed to be somewhere. I was just not sure if or when it would strike.

I called our DYFUS representative and left a voicemail message, hoping to get a return phone call. I then headed to my office, as I need to reschedule a few appointments for tomorrow morning. I spoke with my manager, indicating that I was having difficulties at home again. My production was fine, and the month ahead looked to be okay as well. I explained that I might have some additional issues as Leslie's field hockey season had just come to a close and I would have to leave the office no later than 4 p.m., upon the markets' close, as that would allow me to get home a bit earlier.

A discussion about how to handle family matters was made with Sandy. I ask her how we, as a family, were to move forward. Leslie would be arriving at home by 3:45 p.m. after the next weekend as she no longer would have field hockey to attend, and we had a safety issue since Sandy wasn't able to be home alone with the children unattended as per court order. I told her that I could not leave my office at 3 p.m. to be home by 3:45 p.m. as this was no longer working.

Sandy was not responsive.

My solution was that I would try to be home by 4:45 p.m. and Leslie would be required to call me once she arrived home each day. Jenny still had work after school and her after school activities, and she was working every day, as, I believed, she really did not want to be in her mother's presence. My biggest concern was the hour that Leslie would be home alone. Our solution for that was that Sandy had to be out of the house. I really had no other way of making this situation work without taking the girls out of their home.

I asked Sandy, "What else are we to do as a court order requires that you cannot be with your children alone? What do you intend to do or where will you go as field hockey for Leslie ends after this week?"

Sandy had no answer.

The field hockey team's last event was the county championship to be held Saturday, November 4. That meant that once the weekend was over, Sandy leaving the house for that hour in the afternoon could be our only solution.

I begged my wife to attend the family session we had scheduled for the next day and said, "You must attend, and if you do not I will call our DYFUS rep." I did not disclose that I had already done so, leaving a message.

I also spoke to Sandy about my concerns as to how her children were continuing to withdraw from her. I said, "If you do not go back to the hospital, I will take your daughters to a counselor as they, as young children, need to talk with someone about the situation they are living through."

Sandy said she did not want the girls to speak to a counselor.

I replied, "Just go back to the hospital and meet with your group."

I was also concerned about when or if Sandy's medications had run out as her meds were given to her in two-week intervals. From what I had witnessed during the past two months, the medications never really changed my wife's mental condition. If she had missed a number of visits, as her clinician Roseanne had indicated, and all was falling apart again, was she even on medications now? I did not see any at the house. I hoped tomorrow's meeting would provide the answers.

I awoke November 2 after another really sleepless night, hopeful that Sandy would attend today's 10 a.m. joint session that had been rescheduled.

The girls went off to school, and I decided to go once more to my local police department and notify the police that I did not believe that my wife would comply and we might be in need of their services.

I arrived at the station and spoke with Sergeant Nunn. While I was in his office, Lt. Meade walked by and asked what we were discussing. I started to mention Sandy's behavior and her mandatory joint session at the hospital, and he asked me to step into his office and said he would handle things.

I replied, "Okay."

While we were in his office, I explained that nothing was working and Sandy was noncompliant with the outpatient counseling.

Lt. Mead said there really wasn't much they could do.

I told him about my last visit in which Sandy's clinician had told me she might be suicidal.

There was no response.

I said, "My wife was taken against her will to the nut house, released by a judge against her doctor's recommendations and now her outpatient provider is telling me she might be suicidal. My children are begging me to remove them from the house, and I may do so as there is a house around the corner about to be listed for rent. I was instructed by the hospital upon Sandy's release that if she was not compliant that I would have to do what I was now doing, trying to get her back to doctors as she was in need of care.

Lt. Meade's response was again, the same.

As I was about to leave I said to Lt. Meade, "I don't understand why you tell me there is nothing you can do when it was your department back in late August that helped in getting her to the hospital in the first place. What am I to do? Wait till she hangs herself or hurts one of her children?"

No response was given back to me.

I walked away from the municipal building just utterly shocked, wondering how did we get here and why nothing I was trying to do within the system was working.

Off I drove, back to the house to get Sandy to get ready for our meeting.

Needless to say Sandy refused to attend.

I then left by myself, again, to speak once again with Roseanne Misclone at Morristown Memorial Hospital a few miles away.

I arrived at the hospital on time and again spoke with Roseanne about what to do. I said, "Look, I have gone to the police department, as St. Clair's Hospital instructed me to do upon Sandy's discharge from the hospital, and I do not know what else I can do now. I want to remove the girls from the house, but you told me not to do so as Sandy may be suicidal and that I should not leave her. I informed the police of this today, and they will not help me as I was instructed that they would. I'm literally at wit's end. What can I now do?"

Roseanne said, "Go back to the house and get her here and if she does not come, call the police again from the house."

I headed for the house as instructed.

When I got home, I asked Sandy to get into the car and go back with me to the hospital.

Again she refused.

I said, "If you do not, I will call the police."

She grabbed her keys and was about to leave, but I jumped into my car, parked it across the driveway to block her from leaving and called the police again from the end of the driveway.

The police arrived and I told the dispatched officers that Sandy must attend her meeting at the hospital.

Once again I was informed that there really wasn't anything they would do to help.

I pleaded, but the response was again the same.

By now it was after lunchtime and again nothing was done. I was left to be on my own with a wife and family in crisis. I left the house and tried to figure out my next move.

I drove back to the hospital and again spoke with Rosanne who said, "I think you need to see an attorney."

I left and then placed a call to our DYFUS representative Ms. Remy and again got voicemail. I again left a message and stated that things were out of control in our home, children were in peril, and to please call immediately.

I realized I would probably again wait all day for a response, so I decided to take matters up with her supervisor as I was convinced that trying to reach our case manager Remy was just a complete waste of effort. I would have to make calls today to her manager, as well as making calls to try to locate an attorney as Ms. Misclone had instructed. One other issue was to locate a counselor for both girls, as I believed they needed someone to discuss things with. I headed off to work, knowing I had some private matters that had to be answered by the end of the day.

When I arrived at work, I told the staff downstairs that I probably would be unavailable until later in the afternoon. I then went upstairs to our back office, which was located at my hub office in Bloomfield, N.J., and I spoke with Patty, my boss's secretary, and I asked her if I could use his office to make some calls privately, as affairs were crumbling before my eyes at home.

Patty was a good friend who knew of some of the troubles I was going through. She said, "Ron will not be in today. Go ahead, Bill."

I closed the door and went to work making some calls.

I determined that DYFUS had an office in Randolph on Route 10 about twenty-five minutes drive from our home. I called this office and finally got a hold of Ms. Remy's manager Donna Hewitt. I explained that Remy had not been to our home since her first visit on September 13 and had not shown for her follow-up visit set for September 27. I stated that Sandy was noncompliant with her outpatient care, that I was concerned for the safety of my children, and that out of desperation I was reaching out to her for help. I told Ms. Hewitt I'd been informed that Sandy might be suicidal, according to Roseanne Misclone, her outpatient clinician, and that all Ms. Hewitt needed to do was to call Ms. Misclone or speak with Dr. Contini, her supervisor, who was aware of our current situation.

I stated to Ms. Hewitt, "I do not know what to do and your employee does not even return calls back to me. You need to send someone immediately." She responded that she would look into this situation and get someone to our home soon.

I made a number of other calls to try to locate an attorney within Morristown, N.J., as the county courthouse was located there and it was about five miles away from our home. After many calls to different offices I located an attorney who said he handled such matters. An appointment was made for Monday, November 6, in the late afternoon.

I next started to try to locate a counselor for the girls within our healthcare network. Eventually I located a woman who had available time and would meet with the girls next week.

The following day when I arrived home after work I sat down with Sandy and laid out everything on the table. I told her that the girls would be meeting with a counselor, and that I had called DYFUS about her lack of compliance with her outpatient therapy.

I did not disclose that I would be seeing an attorney or mention the issue of suicidal behavior that the hospital had discussed with me. My fear was if I were to speak of these points, they could possibly cause Sandy to hurt herself or possibly someone else.

I picked up the girls that evening. Leslie's field hockey championship game was scheduled for the next day.

I actually got some rest that evening due to exhaustion, both mental and physical. Tomorrow would be the game and hopefully things would be moving in the right direction, or so I thought.

The weekend came and went.

Sandy joined me that Saturday for the field hockey championship at the Harding Township School.

I informed Sandy that the girls would be going to see a counselor Tuesday evening after dinner.

Sandy was upset with my decision.

I continued to tell her, "All you have to do is cooperate with your doctors and to also help yourself."

The girls were completely withdrawn and did not want to spend a minute with her.

Sandy was upset and talking about events from our past.

I responded, "These are all happy memories, but I want us to move forward. You seem unable to comprehend what you are doing to your own family. You truly need medical help and refusing is destroying your own home." I begged and said, "For your children's sake, please go see the doctors immediately."

Monday, November 6, in the late afternoon I visited with an attorney in Morristown. He asked me a number of financial questions and I answered them. I requested that he draft a new will for me as I had finally received the last funds from my mother's estate with the sale of the house, and I had kept these assets separate as we had also done when Sandy had received the house from her mother's estate.

The attorney agreed to do so.

I asked what I should do regarding my issues with Sandy.

He responded, "You may need to divorce her."

I responded, "She is my wife. I love her, and she has never gotten a chance to see if she can recover from whatever mental illness she seems to have. I need to get her back before a judge as she has never ever gotten a chance for any recovery and I have never even been told of any type diagnosis for her current mental state."

He said, "Bill, she may never get better."

I replied that as her husband I needed to provide her the chance for recovery and again asked what should I do.

He responded, "Why you don't go to see the judge who let her out from the hospital?"

I said, "I will do so tomorrow."

Tuesday morning I stopped by the Harding Township Municipal Building, where the police department was located, and requested a copy of the police reports from the first day they'd visited our home back in August as the attorneys I'd consulted had advised me to do.

I was told that the police department did not have the records.

I asked where they were.

I was told the records were up at the county courthouse in Morristown.

That sounded strange to me.

I was asked why I wanted the records.

I replied that I'd seen an attorney yesterday who'd recommended getting copies and seeing the judge personally as this department was refusing to help our family.

I left the police department with no records and headed on to work.

I received a call from a man named John Lynch. He said that he was a DYFUS rep and that he had visited my wife and that she seemed fine.

I asked, "How long you were with her as she can throw a switch regarding her behavior?"

He said about fifteen minutes and repeated that she seemed fine.

I responded, "Stay a while and you will see something is definitely wrong. Why don't you talk with my children and ask them what it like in our household right now?"

Nothing was said about my meeting the prior day with the attorney.

I could not stress enough to him of our current dilemma and my concern regarding the children. I said, "Look, she is not compliant. Why don't you people call her doctors that she is refusing to meet with?"

I got to my office and headed upstairs to speak with my manager. I said, " I need to be out today as I am going to the courthouse in Morristown to ask to meet with Judge Brennan who presided over Sandy's hearing."

I then drove back to Morristown from Bloomfield, parked the car and went to Judge Brennan's office, where I met his secretary. This gal was in her mid-to-late twenties. I briefly explained why I was there and said that a local attorney had advised me to come personally.

The secretary explained that the judge was in court.

I stated that I would wait outside his chamber. There I sat in the hallway in a chair, looking at his open door and his secretary.

The lunch break for his courtroom came and went.

I asked her if she had spoken to him.

She said yes, so I waited again outside on the chair, hoping to plead my family's dilemma.

Once again the door was shut to his office. At about ten minutes before 5 p.m. Judge Robert Brennan's assistant was called into his office. She returned and came to me and said that he was too busy to spend just a few moments with me.

I was so angry I wanted to jump over her desk and break his door down, but I could not as that probably would have placed me in jail for the evening and I had two girls at home to protect. I had sat for hours outside this man's office, the same man who'd had the wisdom to overrule the doctors at a hospital and I'd been turned away. What's next? I thought as I left the courthouse.

I dropped by the office of the attorney who I had met with the evening before and told him of the outcome, and he really did not seem surprised.

My thoughts kept going back to that young boy in Basking Ridge and of what that man must have gone through. I was having grave doubts about my country or state that was failing my household in our hour of need.

I got home, had some dinner, and then left with my daughters for their first session with their counselor, Elizabeth Richards. I brought a book to read. Each of the girls was there for about an hour after I spoke with Elizabeth about our family matters.

Elizabeth then asked to speak with me afterwards and said to bring the girls back in two weeks.

I told her that I was thinking of taking the girls down to the shore to stay at my brother's house over the weekend.

She said she thought it would be a good idea as the girls were under a lot of stress.

I said that I would give my wife an ultimatum: either she goes to visit the doctors or if not, I will take the girls away overnight Saturday and be back Sunday.

Friday I received a call from Sandy's original DYFUS representative Urmene Remy, stating that she would be coming to our home. The meeting was scheduled for next Monday, November 13, at 7 p.m.

That evening I told Sandy of my plans to take the girls to my brother's house the next day and I said, "If you see a doctor in the morning, we will stay home."

Saturday morning all was again crazy in our house. I packed up the van and got ready to take the girls to the beach for a break. The girls wanted to bring Cassey, one of our dogs, with us.

As we tried to get into the van, Sandy's behavior got worse. The next thing I knew she started to try to let the air out of one of the tires on the side of the van. I had to get out of the car and speak with her about this, telling her to stop it. I then got back into the car, and she continued to do so again, this time to a different tire.

Finally, as Sandy was standing in front of the van, blocking the vehicle, I said to Jenny, "Get in the driver's seat, and I will physically move your mom. Drive the car to the end of the driveway and I will run after you and get us out of here."

That was exactly how we left that day. I was just glad to leave, as our home had become an asylum. We got down to the house in Long Branch, had some dinner out, and decided to go see a movie. We saw *Borat* and although the theater was crowded, we could not sit together, and it was a little on the crazy side, it was something we all needed. I hadn't laughed in months, and the girls, while at home, hadn't either. For all of us, it was our first bit of sanity in a long time.

The next day we went out for lunch with my brother John and his longtime girlfriend Kathy and then we returned home Sunday about 4 p.m.

The next day would be the first visit with our DYFUS rep in almost two months. I headed off to work and returned home early to see that the house was in order as Sandy was not functioning and the household chores seemed too overwhelming for her to manage.

I picked up the mail and much to my surprise I found a letter from Morristown Memorial Hospital addressed to Sandy. Before entering the house, I decided to open it. It was dated Nov. 6, 2006, and was written by Sandy's clinician, Roseanne Misclone, indicating that Sandy was not attending her therapy. This was perfect. I got into the house and made a copy that I planned to give to Remy tonight, before Sandy had a chance to see it.

This time Remy arrived on time. She had to check that the house was clean and in proper order.

I stated that I had come home early to straighten things out and all was in proper order with those regards.

Remy asked to speak with the girls, who were holed up in their rooms, and she spoke with each of them privately. I had no idea what was said.

She then came out to speak with Sandy and me in the living room. Much to my surprise, Sandy was not right, and I thought that now a person with the authority would see her behavior and agree with me.

Sandy was rather confused, trying to speak, losing her thoughts, rambling on and really not making any sense of things.

I confronted her about not following up with her therapy and she actually lied to Remy about this behavior.

I then handed Remy the letter I had opened hours earlier indicating Sandy's noncompliance and I told Remy that Sandy had been missing meetings all along.

Sandy was caught in a dilemma and lie and I was convinced that action would finally be taken by DYFUS due to Sandy's lack of actions. I was actually happy to see that she could not compose herself. I asked Ms. Remy if Sandy would be forced back to the courts if she did not see the doctors, and Remy agreed and told Sandy she must attend sessions.

My wife stated that she did not want to see doctors at the hospital, but wanted to select her own as the hospital was too far to drive. It was less than five miles from our home.

Remy stated that if Sandy did not schedule an appointment by Wednesday that "the Division," meaning DYFUS, would be making one for her.

Sandy stated that she would comply and call the hospital tomorrow.

I asked if Remy would follow up on Sandy's progress with the hospital, and she said yes and that she had to.

Ms. Remy left the house and said she would be calling both of us tomorrow, monitoring Sandy's activities from now on extensively, and to expect a call.

My thought was thank God!

The following day, I received Ms. Remy's call and I asked her if she thought Sandy's behavior seemed odd.

She agreed with me.

I said, "Sandy will not attend any meeting you set for her and will continue to lie about her appointments."

Remy agreed that my wife's behavior was not right.

Again I pleaded, "What else do you need from me? You have a document in your possession now from the hospital showing she is noncompliant. Things are out of control again. I'm sure my daughters also said things to you. Please call or just visit Sandy's outpatient counselor and she will confirm this with you. Dr. Contini, the head of the facility, told me back in September that Sandy really should not be here, but rather in a long-term facility."

Remy said she was required to follow up with Sandy's doctors to make sure that Sandy would comply as per DYFUS procedures and if she did not, she would be back before a judge.

I said, "If Sandy does not show up for her scheduled appointment, please notify me immediately."She said she would.

The remainder of the week was again a repeat of the prior weeks. Nothing was working.

Sandy told me that she had been to the doctor's office, and our DYFUS representative presumably had not received any calls to indicate otherwise. The weekend came and went, and again, all was just a mess.

Tuesday evening the girls attended their sessions with their counselor. My oldest really was not happy with this activity, but I truly thought it was necessary and again I was coming to believe that it would be necessary to have them removed from the home if Sandy was not removed.

I also received a call from a family member about the Thanksgiving Day holiday next week. Normally we would head to the town of Sea Girt, N.J., for an extended family celebration for the day. Instead, I was told by a person not directly related to my late aunt Eileen that I should not bring my wife down to the family celebration as I was planning to do.

My thought was that it just might be helpful for Sandy to see all the extended family on this day. I was really torn as to what to do and decided to speak with Sandy once again.

I said, "Look, nothing I do or ask of you seems to be working and you still have not seen a doctor since our meeting with Remy as you tell me something came up and continue to reschedule. I will join you on whatever day you pick and meet with anyone of your choosing and if you go this week to a doctor, we as a family, will visit together the family in Sea Girt next week. If not, I will take the girls down Thursday and return Friday."

Sandy did not know what to say.

I said, "For God's sake, please make an appointment!"

She said she would.

Each night, Sunday, Monday, and Tuesday, I again asked her when we would visit her doctor together and received no answer, so Wednesday evening I told her she had left me no choice as I had told the family member who had called that if Sandy would not meet with a professional that I would be forced to leave her home.

Thanksgiving was not a day of thanks for the Dunn family, though it was really a day that could have been. I took my daughter's down in the early afternoon. All the other extended families had arrived and there I was with my two daughters, trying to make the best of things yet all the while being afraid of what might happen.

That afternoon all the family members spoke to Sandy on the phone, wishing her well and asking her to please see the doctors for own and for her daughters' sake.

The prayers said prior to dinner included one for those who had passed in our family and another for Sandy to get well.

It was good for the girls to get away. The next morning they asked me if we could stay at their Uncle John's house one more night and I decided to do so for their sake.

I called Sandy, told her we would be home Saturday and asked if all was well.

She asked me where we were staying.

I responded, "Johnny's house. You know where we are."

Saturday we arrived home to find my wife in the same condition. Nothing had changed.

Monday, November 27, the girls were again in tears before heading off back to school. Sandy was bothering them, repeating herself, and nothing was working.

I arrived home from work to find Sandy parked just off the end of the driveway on the grass just off the road in front of the house. She had been doing this since the first full week in November. About the only order she followed was the one not to be in the house alone with the children when I was not present.

I had numerous discussions with her about this restriction, saying, "We cannot continue as a family in this manner."

Remy had inquired about this restriction as well and was aware of this arrangement on her visit November 13.

Sandy's pattern was to call shortly after Leslie would arrive home, asking me, "When will you be home?" She was now having physical bouts with her daughters as well, trying to restrain them, grabbing at them, and trying to hold them as if they were infants.

They would shove their mom away as she would not listen to their requests to just leave them alone and they would not listen to her babble on incoherently.

I had to break this up.

Tuesday evening when I arrived home, I noticed that a wood baluster from the floor to the handrail on the landing above the stairwell had a crack in it and was split in half. My thought was that Sandy and Jenny must have had another argument. I asked Sandy if that was so.

Her answer was no.

I then asked her, "What happened to the wood baluster at the top of the stairs as it was not broken this morning when I left for work?"

She said she did not know.

Dinner was not even prepared. It seemed that her mind was gone. She must have called me twenty times that day repeating, "When will you be home?"

The answer was at 4:45 p.m., as I had been all month long.

These calls had started Monday shortly after I had left for work the day before and were really becoming a problem for me at work.

I spoke again with Sandy that evening and asked, "What can I do for you? We cannot continue much longer like this. Do you expect to spend the entire winter out front of our house in a car with the engine running each evening till I come home? You cannot even prepare dinner. Shopping is not being done. What do you do all day long? There are only two horses out in the barn, and

I do not know how they are as I have no time for anything. Are you caring for them properly?"

Wednesday morning was okay. Sandy did not bother the girls, and for the first time in a long time we actually had a normal morning. I went off to work praying for an answer and thinking if I spoke with Sandy every night and reminded her, maybe the morning would be tolerable for her daughters.

By 11 a.m. the phone calls started to come again. Every ten minutes, Sandy would call and ask, "Where are you? When are you coming home?" This went on until 2 p.m., then finally stopped.

I called Remy and told her things were totally out of control. I stated, "Sandy is getting physical now with her daughters and not making any sense. I am afraid. Something terrible will happen soon. She needs to be removed and be back before a judge."

Remy said she would stop by Monday, December 4, at 7 p.m.

I answered, "Bring a court order with you and have her taken back to St. Clair's."

I made this call that afternoon before I left the office and actually spoke with our caseworker, not voicemail. I also asked Remy why, since she knew Sandy had not seen any doctors, her agency hadn't removed my wife from her home, as she'd stated they would during our previous meeting.

Remy gave no answer, but stated she would arrive next Monday evening.

I arrived home at about 4:45 p.m., and Sandy was again out front in her car. She followed me into the house and, much to my surprise, said she had gone shopping and wanted to prepare dinner.

I asked her if she would be able to as many times in the past month I had done this task myself after I came home in the evenings during the week.

Sandy seemed normal this evening. It was about the first time in months I had seen a morning and evening like this on the same day.

We all ate together that evening in the dining room; place settings had been set and it was actually pleasant to have a normal meal as a family together. I could not remember the last time we had actually done so as it had been so long ago.

After dinner the girls went to their rooms, thanking their mom for such a nice meal.

Sandy and I went downstairs to the family room and talked for quite some time.

She spoke for hours in a normal tone and was clear and we discussed our lives together. She talking about how we'd met, all of the trips we'd taken, and the work we'd done on our first home together. She was happy that I had been able to get her farm back in order and that the girls were growing up and would become fine adults one day.

This conservation was unlike anything I had heard Sandy say in months. I will never forget how happy I was that evening, thinking that perhaps a miracle had occurred and perhaps Sandy's mind was coming to a state of health.

Then out of nowhere the voices must have come back. At about 10:30 p.m. and after five-and-a-half hours of normalcy, Sandy went off the deep end again. The light switch had been pulled. She was again making no sense, rambling on.

My prayers had not been answered.

Tomorrow would be November 30, the last day of the month. Christmas was just 25 days away.

What else could happen next?

The Last Day in November

On November 30, 2006, I awoke once again to my wife being completely out of control and my girls again being in tears while I was wondering what could possibly happen next, praying to get through the weekend, and hoping our meeting scheduled for Monday, December 4, with Ms. Remy would be the final straw in placing Sandy where she'd needed to be all along.

The girls left for school.

I told my wife that I had an early appointment, and she wanted to know who the appointment was with.

I told her I need meet with my client Esther Krueger as she need to fill out a form for her Individual Retirement Account distribution for the year.

I headed off to Esther's office in nearby East Hanover, N.J. Esther had been a long-time client and had lost her husband Jerry, a wonderful man, a number of years earlier. She was in her 70s and worked for a marketing company to keep busy, as she was a widow. She had an open office in an area with other reps for the company.

When I arrived, she said to me, "Bill, you look worried and upset."

I said I was.

We then went to a private office.

I said, "Things at home are falling apart," and I gave her a short version of our family's current state of affairs.

Esther asked, "How could a judge let your ill wife out of the hospital?"

I said, "I truly do not know."

Afterwards, I decided to drive over to Heavenly Gate Cemetery, which was only about a mile away from Esther's office.

I went to my grandfather's memorial gravesite. My nana Myrtle Dunn and grandfather William P. Dunn are interned there, as well as my mother Diane, father William P. Dunn III, and Aunt Eileen Slanhoff and Uncle Bud Slanhoff, my father's sister and her husband. The gravesite looked barren that day. It was quiet and the trees were devoid of any leaves as winter was to soon appear.

At the gravesite, I knelt and prayed to God to get my household through the weekend. Hopefully next week things would finally move forward. I never discussed this moment with my family or friends, as it was something I always thought would remain private.

When I'd finished, I left the cemetery and headed to my office.

As I was driving there, my phone rang. Again it was Sandy, inquiring as to where I was and when would I be home.

I answered her and continued on my way to my office.

She continued to call me about every 10 minutes, repeating her behavior of a previous day.

I had a busy schedule, so by early afternoon I finally stopped answering Sandy's calls, which continued to come in.

Shortly after that the phone stopped ringing.

At about 3:45 p.m., my phone rang again. This time the caller was not Sandy, but Leslie calling from our home phone. She was hysterical and in tears. Before I had a chance to say a word, she said, "I think Mommy hurt herself, Daddy."

I immediately knew by her tone of voice that the worst had occurred.

I told her to leave the house and wait for the police. Then I yelled out for someone to call 911 and send the police to our home immediately as I was shaking and could not make the call myself.

I cannot put into words my anxiety or the thoughts that raged through my mind about what Leslie might have walked into.

My manager Ron said, "You cannot drive home in your current state."

I was concerned about how he would get back to the office if he drove me home, but he said Eric from the trust department would follow us.

The drive took forever. I was trying to speak with my daughter and was receiving calls from the first aid squad while in route. The volunteer had not told me what had happened and said only that efforts were being made to help my wife.

The ride took more than an hour due to heavy traffic and numerous calls kept coming into to me; however, nothing had been said of my wife's current state.

When we finally arrived at the house, it was almost dark. An ambulance was in the driveway as were many police cars, all with flashing lights.

I got out of the car hoping that perhaps Sandy might be okay.

I saw Leslie, our youngest. She was crying.

I hugged her and told her that I loved her and that mom loved her, too. We stayed together for a while and then my attention focused on my wife Sandy.

I went to the stairway up to the back of the house. A police officer was there, and as I approached the stairway, he looked away.

When I entered the house, there were a few more police officers and people from the first aid squad inside.

I was told it was too late and that Sandy was gone.

I said, "I want to see her alone."

A number of people told me, "You really do not want see her as she now looks." I was terrified by the thought of what my twelve-year-old daughter had come home to witness.

I went outside to be with Leslie, who was inside an ambulance in tears and I just held her and started to sob myself.

Soon my oldest daughter Jenny arrived as someone had

contacted my sister and she had picked up Jenny from the high school that day.

When Jenny arrived home, she just got out of the car and ran down the street, and someone got her and brought her to Leslie and me. We sat together.

A man in his late 60s arrived and he introduced himself as Wayne Bolton. He said he was a minister from the Presbyterian Church in town and wanted to comfort us.

My good friend Scott Noyes arrived as well and saw us huddled together, now just the three of us. My ill wife and the mother of my daughters was gone, and what could anyone say just hours after a horrible tragedy?

My thoughts were of my daughters, the unknown abyss that lay ahead, how I had failed my children and my ill wife and my prayer at the gravesite that morning. What I had not done to prevent this? I thought I must be a failure to have let things spiral out of control. I remembered the promise I had made to myself when I'd received that call from the hospital saying Sandy was to be discharged, and the vow I had made not to let the horrors the family in Basking Ridge had experienced occur, and yet I had allowed it to happen.

That evening, it was decided that Jenny wanted to stay at her friend's home and I agreed. Leslie and I spent the night at my friend Scott Noyes's home.

We had a very somber night. I went to bed early that evening and lay awake most of the night with Leslie nearby. Sometime in the middle of the night she awoke from her nightmare in tears, saying, "I will never do what Mommy did."

I hugged her and said, "Mommy is with God now. She loves you. I always want you to remember all the happy times. Mommy was very ill. It's my fault that I did not prevent this and that I had failed your mom."

Leslie hugged me and asked if she could stay there with me.

I said, "Fine."

Eventually she drifted off to sleep.

All night long, my mind continued to go over what I had done wrong, failing my family.

Tomorrow I would begin to have to pick up the pieces.

Part 3:
Hocus Pocus

Merry Christmas

Friday, December 1, I got up at my friend Scott Noyes's home and let my daughter Leslie sleep in, figuring she needed the rest.

For me it had been another sleepless night.

Scott had received a call from the Harding Police Department. He spoke with me, saying the police wanted me to come into the municipal building to sign some forms.

I really did not want to go there after what had occurred and the fact that no one had done a thing to help us in our time of crisis. Why should I do a goddamn thing for them now?

Scott, however, convinced me to go.

Had he known of all that had occurred, he may have thought otherwise.

He drove me down to the municipal building and we were seated with the chief of the department Kevin Gaffney, the same man who had been to my house back in August the day I'd called 911 for help.

He would not look me in the eye, but looked down at his desk and said an autopsy need to be performed to determine Sandy's cause of death.

I said, "Why is this necessary? Your department was the first to arrive after a bank employee called 911. It was your employees that removed the noose from her neck prior to the ambulance corps trying to revive her."

I thought of Ed Poneck, the good man I'd known many years ago when I'd parked cars in high school and college and the former chief of this same department. Had he been there that day, would my family's outcome have been different?

Scott suggested that it was necessary to have an autopsy performed, so I signed the document and walked away in disgust.

It was afternoon when I arrived back at the house. I didn't know if the dogs had been out or whether the horses had been cared for the prior evening or this day.

I got out to the barn and it was again a total disaster. There was garbage everywhere. It looked as it had just after Sandy had been taken to St. Claire's Hospital back in August. I started the cleanup and knew it would take some time.

A call was placed to the funeral home as well that day.

Jenny arrived back home Saturday. It was dark outside, and then something very odd happened. I asked Jenny to go out to the barn and show me how the horses were fed in the evening. When she and I got to the barn, the exterior light was on and for the first time in years since the exterior of the barn had been repaired, the interior light in the barn was working. I did not realize this until Jenny pointed this out and said, "Mom has given us a message."

I said, "What are you talking about?"

Jenny said, "Dad, that light has not worked in years and tonight, our first night home after mom passing, it now works."

I got a puzzled look on my face. I thought about what Jenny had said and I realized she was right about the light. Was this a message as my daughter had said?

The rest of the evening was uneventful, and as I drifted off to sleep for the first time in two days, my thoughts kept going back to the light in the barn.

Sunday I told the girls to get dressed and that we would be going to church.

They asked where, and I replied, "The Presbyterian Church in town."

We had not been to service in some time and I thought it was something that was necessary for the girls. When they were very young Sandy had said, "We need to take them to service."

I had been raised Catholic and Sandy Methodist so we'd decided to attend the Presbyterian Church locally for a while. After about six months of attendance, Sandy would say to me that she was busy and that I should take the girls myself, and after about a month of that, I told her that we would either attend as a family or not attend, as I was not going without her, so attending service was dropped.

My thoughts were that we needed to attend and would start today, December 3.

As we walked to the church from the parking lot, I heard the bells and as we started to climb the few steps, I actually almost broke into tears. I managed to climb the stairs up to the balcony where the looks on people's faces said it all.

Walking into church that day was the most difficult thing, mentally, I have ever had to do; however, it would also be the start of a new journey I knew I must take. Perhaps it would be the first light down a long unknown dark tunnel, but it was the first necessary step toward recovery for me that day.

I felt shame, and while in attendance that first morning, I begged God's forgiveness for my failure to my now late-wife and young girls. I listened to Wayne Bolton's sermon, and it was very helpful. He was the same man who had arrived Friday to try to comfort my family.

I took the girls out to lunch that afternoon, and I told them that we would continue to attend service together in the future.

The following Monday, while I was driving from the funeral home to a florist, I received a call from none other than Ermine Remy, our wonderful DYFUS representative.

She was all cheery and said, "Hello, Mr. Dunn. I will be coming at—"

Before she was able to utter another word I said, "Don't bother. Sandy's dead."

I then hung up the phone in disgust.

Sandy's memorial service was held December 6 at 10 a.m. at the New Vernon Presbyterian Church, a short walk from the Harding Township Grammar School that Jenny had attended and where Leslie was in seventh grade.

The church was packed. Would I be able to speak to those present without breaking down?

The jazz choirs from Madison High School were in attendance to sing. Rev. Bolton spoke wonderfully and both of my daughters spoke of their mom.

When it was my turn to speak, as I was the last, I prayed to God to get me through the ordeal in one piece.

I knew what needed to be said.

I walked up to the stand and started to talk. I spoke about Sandy's love for animals and I told the children present that we should remember that we, as people, are God's caretakers of the animals. I told them that Mrs. Dunn had been very ill, and that she would want them to remember her as she was a year or so ago when she would bring cupcakes to school events, and all the wonderful birthday parties they had attended while she was healthy.

I looked at all of Leslie's seventh grade classmates, just young children, and there were tears in their eyes as I spoke.

All of a sudden, as I was about to break down, I leaned on the podium.

It shifted, and I had to grab at it to keep it from falling over. That was a moment sent from heaven for it enabled me to regain my composure and continue with my words.

When I finished, I told the children that Mrs. Dunn was now at peace and to remember all the fun times they'd had when they were younger at our home when she was healthy. I placed my right hand to my mouth, kissed my fingers and touched Sandy's Ash box in a gesture of goodbye and I said, "I will always love you."

As I turned back from my kiss to those in attendance I noticed there were not many dry eyes in the church at that moment and one could hear a pin drop.

I returned to my seat and shortly after that the memorial service was over.

The children were walked back to the grammar school as the entire seventh grade was present and some sixth and eighth grade children were there as well.

The following day we headed up to upstate New York for Sandy's internment. The ride was slow as we encountered a snowstorm just as we got to the Catskills near our old summertime exit, Roscoe, N.Y. We arrived in Genoese, N.Y., around dinnertime.

Friday, December 8, 2006, we headed to the funeral home and then to the cemetery.

It was a very cold, gray, overcast day, which fitted as my somber mood that afternoon.

Afterwards, the girls and I located a headstone to be placed for Sandy nearby, and while we were at the funeral home, I brought Harriet's ashes to be interned as well.

Tomorrow, Saturday, December 9, was Leslie's thirteenth birthday. We decided to head up for the day to Rochester, N.Y., where she found a nice piece of jewelry for her birthday present.

Sunday we drove home back to New Vernon, N.J., to a now-changed household.

The girls went back to school Monday.

I had some work to attend to, cleaning up the barn, which was a mess, and trying to locate all the knives that were missing from the kitchen, similar to what had occurred after Sandy's involuntary confinement in the mental hospital.

At the end of the week I went into work. It was the day of the office Christmas party. Everyone was surprised to see me, and our regional manager was present that day. They all said, "Why don't you just go back home?"

My thoughts were that my home and everything I had worked

for were gone. I tried to show a pleasant face and got home early that day, passing on the evening party at a local restaurant.

Christmas was a little over a week away, so I got some shopping done for the girls and decided that a trip would do us all some good.

Christmas Eve, 2006, I took the girls out for dinner at The Old Mill in Bernardsville, the same place Sandy and I had been taking them the last few years on Christmas Eve. I decided this year would be the last time I would take them there. Memories of past happy days filled my head that evening, and tomorrow would be our first Christmas morning without their mother.

The girls opened their gifts and then their stockings.

I said, "You missed one item at the bottom. Look again in your stocking."

They did and found plane tickets.

I said, "Start packing as we fly out tomorrow at 7 a.m. for St. Thomas."

They packed their bags that afternoon. We headed to Philly for an overnight stay and then a direct flight to the Caribbean.

We arrived at Sapphire Beach Resort by early afternoon the next day. The view was incredible. Off in the distance, St. Johns and other exotic islands lay within view. We had left the cold and winter and a different house behind to visit a tropical paradise.

I was glad we took the trip, as it was good to leave the house behind for a few days. We were scheduled to return January 1 so the girls would be home in time for school.

One evening I took a walk by myself about 10 p.m. I sat down by the water at the end of the swimming pool area and looked out at a perfect balmy evening with a full moon overhead and it just hit me. I started to cry, and did so for hours by myself as I tried to comprehend what had happened and why.

The more I thought, the angrier I got. I decided that when I got home I needed to do some digging. I could not understand how an agency could not even show up and why, when I reached out for help to my local police, they turned their backs on us. Something was amiss and I needed to know what it was or whether it was just a lousy set of circumstances that had brought disaster to our once tranquil home.

January 1 we flew back home to a cold New Jersey winter and a new unknown way of life for the three of us.

Happy New Year 2007, Right?

The girls returned to school, where I felt sure they were both subject to the rumor mill that was sweeping all around our family as they were victims of their late mother's suicide. I just hoped and prayed for the best.

I now had my routine down pat for Monday through Friday. The alarm clock still went off as usual at 5:45 a.m. I got my coffee made, turned on the Bloomberg TV channel to digest the overseas markets and financial headlines, and made sure the girls were up by 6:30 a.m. to catch the school bus.

Once the girls were on the bus, I headed out to the barn to do the barn chores. First, the animals would get their a.m. grains, and once they were finished, the horses and Bud, the world's largest sheep who thought he was just a small furrier horse, would be let out into one of the pastures.

Then I would do my daily a.m. run or jog of three miles. Upon returning home I went back into the barn, mucked the stalls, and placed the hay, grain, and fresh water for the evening. These tasks took about ten or fifteen minutes and were also my cool-down time from running.

Once the barn chores were finished, it was into the house, shower, put the dogs into the utility room, and then off to work by 8:30 a.m.

That first week I received a call one evening from Harriet's and Sandy's good friend Leslie Bocchino, who lived down at the Jersey

Shore in Fair Haven in a very nice home. Leslie had been a friend of Harriet's and had known Sandy while she was growing up in Harding Township. Years back, Leslie and her past husband had resided in town for many years and had been at our wedding in 1989. Leslie's house was also used to host Sandy's surprise bridal shower, which I dropped her off for so many years ago.

Leslie and I talked for about three hours and she listened as I relayed the events.

When I'd finished, Leslie said, "Bill, Sandy, at the end, was a paranoid schizophrenic."

I said, "What are you talking about?"

Leslie told me that as a young woman, she'd received an under-graduate degree in psychology and master's in psychology from Berkeley. She'd been studying for her doctorate degree and had wanted to become a licensed psychologist. During the last year before she received her final degree, she and her husband had their first child, a son. The moment she'd looked into his eyes as a mother all thoughts of her chosen career path had changed in a flash. Financially, all was great, and though she knew her decision went against all she had learned at college, it was her choice and she knew she'd made the right choice.

I asked Leslie, "Why didn't I see this coming?"

Leslie said, "You have been the glue that held everything together and with all the responsibilities--work, family matters, illnesses, and unwinding your late mother's estate after fifty-plus years. You are very fortunate that Sandy did not hurt you or your daughters."

I said, "I do not think that Sandy would be capable of that."

Leslie said, "A paranoid schizophrenic is one of the most dangerous people walking today. One moment they are fine and the next, out of nowhere, all hell breaks loose. Everything you have described to me fits that pattern. You did all that was humanly possible under the circumstances. That judge should be discharged for what he did to your family and never be allowed to sit behind a bench ever again." She offered to help us in any manner and at any time if we ever needed a favor or helping word.

I got off the phone and thought again about why and when these answers would unravel and how to go about finding the answers. The more I thought about Leslie's comment about what Judge Robert Brennan had done to my family, the angrier I got.

The most dangerous animal in the jungle is man. The most dangerous man is the man who has no fear of his own mortality and nothing left to lose. For myself, I was that man; however, if I took the path I wanted to, my children would have been lost, and therefore, I did not take that path to hunt down my prey. If what had occurred to the man in Basking Ridge with his son had taken place in my home, I would have ended up in a jail cell. Judge Brennan is a very lucky man that November 30, 2006, Sandy, my ill wife, chose to take her own life and not take her children with her.

A few days later, the first weekend after the girls went back to school, I found one of Sandy's empty prescription bottles in the house. Out of curiosity I decided to do a Google search of this drug. What did I find? Geodon is a drug described as an antipsychotic medicine prescribed for schizophrenia.

My God, I thought, Leslie was right.

How in the hell could that judge overrule doctors and let a woman out of the psych ward if she were being treated for schizophrenia? This should be a crime as Leslie had said to me over the phone that day. It made no sense at all. I cannot describe my anger, nor shall I call it the hatred, I had for this man and what his decision had placed my twelve-year-old daughter in position to witness that last day of November 2006. As far as I was concerned this man had stolen the remainder of her childhood from her; or, shall I say, robbed her of her innocence that day back in September of 2006, because of his refusal to even take five minutes from his day as I begged for his help in early November only to hear the words, "Judge Brennan is too busy and has no time for you."

The following week, Tuesday, January 9, late in the afternoon,

Leslie was helping me move the animals' grain and bagged wood shavings for their bedding from the garage, where they were delivered once a month, to the barn. As it was starting to get dark, a car arrived and turned down our driveway. The driveway was about three hundred fifty feet from the house to the road, so we did not get many unexpected visitors and I did not recognize this car, a sedan of some type. My guess was that someone was lost, saw us and wanted directions, which happened every once in a while.

The car came to a stop, and as my back was turned ready to move a wheelbarrow full of supplies to the barn, a voice came from the passenger window. It was none other than Ermene Remy. I turned and saw another woman had been driving.

Ms. Remy said, "Mr. Dunn, we need to talk with you now."

My response was just seven words: "You need to leave my home now." Not wanting to utter another word, I did not yell, but was firm in voice and started to push the wheelbarrow towards the barn.

I heard her voice again as she repeated, "But Mr. Dunn, we need to talk with you right now."

Again I turned, walked a few paces towards the vehicle and repeated my same seven words, making sure not to sound threatening. "You need to leave my home now."

I then turned again to return to my work at hand.

Leslie was watching.

I thought that would be the end of it. It was not.

Ms. Remy said, "Mr. Dunn, we need to talk with you so we can close out your family's file."

The anger and rage was inside me, but instead of giving in, I calmly walked to the open passenger window and said, "I find it reprehensible that you now have the audacity to show up to our home unannounced when you could not make the time to appear for your scheduled appointments nor return phone calls in our family's time of need. I have asked you now three times to leave my home now. Please go now and never return or I will go inside a make a call and have you removed for trespassing."

I was so angry it was all I could do—I wanted to go inside, grab my shotgun, and tell them "get the hell out of here." Had I done so, they probably would have filed charges against me and gotten a court order to remove my children from our home, so instead I turned round went back to the wheelbarrow. As I went to the barn to store the supplies, I heard the car start up.

That evening after the chores were done and children were fed and in bed, I thought about all that had transpired and the fact that these supposed public servants, whose salaries I had been forced to support through an income tax paid to the state of New Jersey, had no working clue. In the real world, in which I work, there is a thing called accountability; however, these people seemed to have no clue of that word. My thoughts were that they were soon to find out what accountability was. The real question was with whom and where did that accountability lie?

The following weekend I had a long conversation with my good friend Matthew Donovan. We had meet in 2003 at a new hire trainee seminar in St. Cloud, Minn. We both were working as new investment advisors, and as such new hires were required to attend a five-day workshop. Matt grew up in Wayne, N.J., and I in Florham Park, and we found we had mutual friends and interests such as golf, trout fishing, and hunting, though for myself, it's just upland game birds like pheasants and quail. Matt had relocated to Chestertown, MD. We had always spoken and gotten together periodically.

Matt said, "Bill, this should not have happened."

I replied, "I know, but really do not know where to turn. I have until January 29, 2007, the end of this month, to file suit.

Matt said, "Don't you have two years to sort this out?"

I responded, "When you decide to take on a government entity in New Jersey, a tort claim notice must be filed within sixty days. Otherwise, you have lost your window of opportunity."

Matt said, "I think you're wrong. I'm going to call Bill Vosper, my old neighbor up in Blairstown. He's an attorney. He will know."

A few days later Matthew called me back and said, "You're right, Bill. You only have sixty days. Do you know who to call?"

I said, "Matt, I really never had a need for an attorney and the last time I used one was for a pre-marriage agreement on the house and the closing of the house."

Matt said, "Bill Vosper wants you to call him and wanted to know why you hadn't."

The real reason I had not was probably embarrassment, as Bill knew Sandy and me. He also had a farm and raised hay for sale, and while Sandy was well we had stopped by and made some purchases from him. I still had not come to terms with what had actually occurred, and I was, one could say, a beaten down man looking for an answer.

It was now the middle of January, and I spoke with Bill Vosper by phone. He was extremely sympathetic to our family's crisis and said, "Billy, this should never have happened."

He then said, "You will need an attorney outside of your home county as most attorneys in Morris County will not want to file a case within the Morris County courthouse, since a standing judge ruled letting your wife out of St. Claire's pysch ward."Bill then told me he had made a call to an attorney he knew up in Sussex County who would like to sit in with him and me on a preliminary consultation regarding a possible lawsuit against the state and or any other government entity. Bill explained to me that this was not his area of law, but he believed he could assist and might need another attorney to assist in such a legal matter.

I agreed and a date was set a few days later. My thought was that perhaps something would finally move in the right direction, and perhaps now I might get some sleep, as I really was not getting much.

I met with Bill Vosper and the fellow he had chosen on the appointed day, feeling that now someone would be on my side. I met them up in Blairstown at the appointed time.

Bill Vosper told me the other attorney had been the Sussex County prosecutor and had handled psychiatric cases for his county up in Sussex County.

Questions were asked of me, such as why I did not seek counsel and why I did not go to the police? I said that I had. The attorney grilled me as if I was a criminal, and I kept a stern face and answered all his questions. My belief was that he did not believe a word that I said.

At the end of the meeting I walked away and said to myself, "So this is how it's going to be: me against the world. Nobody seems to give a shit, and we are to accept that that's just the way things are."

I remembered my late dad who'd said, "Always tell the truth and never back away from a fight." God rest his soul, I'm not backing down. I kept my composure, now knowing what I was up against. It was not just City Hall. It was the state, and no one wanted to take that fight on but me.

A day later Bill Vosper called me and apologized to me for the behavior of the attorney he had brought in.

I said, "Bill, it's not your fault. No one ever wants to fight the government, especially the state, to boot." I would have a few more sleepless nights.

Earlier in my life I had been very active with a nonprofit organization called Trout Unlimited, and every year I'd attended the Somerset Fly-Fishing Show. It always runs the same time every year, during the third weekend in January. This year I knew I would run into some people who would now know of our loss of my late wife Sandy. For me, it was a sort of winter reunion to see my old fishing buddies.

My day was always the same, the first day of the show on Friday. I decided to go that day and, as fate would have, it was a good choice. Many people gave me their condolences. I really did not want to go into the details and instead decided to defer the questions.

Late that afternoon I ran into John H., a member of the Central

Jersey chapter who had fished a number of times with both Sandy and me up in the Catskills. He was a police officer in Edison, N.J., and lived out in western New Jersey in Hunterdon County.

John inquired about Sandy and the girls, as he knew we were not spending that much time upstate and he asked how the farm and horse thing was going for us.

I said, "I have some very sad news to tell you, John. Sandy passed away this fall."He asked, "How?"

I said, "Let's step outside somewhere so we can talk privately."

We found a table in the adjacent restaurant at the hotel at the complex and I told him a short version of the story.

He said, "Bill, I'm a police officer, and when I get summoned to an incident like what you described, I have to file reports. Something is wrong here, and I think your local police department in Harding is involved somehow. I know of a very good attorney and I want you to call him Monday. I will call him tomorrow personally for you."

John then handed me his business card from the Edison police force with a name Victor Rotolo and his phone number and said, "I know when he hears this story, he will want to help you and your children find the answers you need to find."

I left the show wondering if perhaps divine providence had just been sent from heaven.

The weekend was filled with the usual activities, including football playoffs and church Sunday morning. While in attendance, I wondered if I would come across another attorney like the last, but felt that this process was no longer in my hands, but God's.

Monday morning I called Victor Rotolo.

He said he'd expected my call and asked me to meet with him the following day.

The meeting was set.

I really did not know what to think of what would occur after the last meeting up in Sussex.

The Rotolo Law office was located in Hunterdon County,

outside of Morris County. John H. had said that I would need an attorney outside my own county, which was correct.

I really did not get much sleep Monday evening, and I awoke the following day hesitant, but hopeful that if this man heard of my family's loss, he would have a different opinion than the last man I'd spoken with.

I arrived Tuesday on time and hoped that someone would listen. I was not really sure as to the outcome, but I knew that time was running out as January 29 was next Monday.

I meet with Victor Rotolo in his private office. After a formal introduction, he got out a pen and paper and asked me to go over the details of Sandy's behavior.

I started on the story.

His look at times was absolute disbelief.

At one point I said, "I just don't understand what happened and why. I remember last Mother's Day my wife and daughters were riding horses on the new ring on the property and I was feeling that I was the luckiest man in the world while watching them from the deck and cooking a Mother's Day meal, and then seven months later having to bury her." I broke down and started to cry.

Victor got up from his chair, gave me a tissue, placed his arm over my shoulder and said, "This never should have happened to your household and family. I would like to represent your family." He then went on to tell me of numerous cases that he had taken that no one wanted and prevailed.

I looked him in the eye, thanked God above for providing this man to appear from nowhere, signed the necessary documents, and left his office feeling that I had done the right thing. I'm a guy who always goes by his gut, and my gut said this man was up for the task. My line was cast by a fly-fishing show. Where this would take us or myself I did not know, but perhaps some questions would find an answer.

That evening when I got home, I informed the girls that I'd met a man who was an lawyer and a good man, an honest man, and that a lawsuit would be filed on their mother's passing. I said, "He believes an injustice was done to our home. I do not know how long all this will take, but this is a matter that must be done."

I'm not too sure what the girls thought at that time. Perhaps they thought I was crazy myself, but I truly did not want to hear the system failed us. I wanted to know the names that had failed and why. Up to this point, I had kept my mouth quiet about things due to embarrassment, humiliation, and the belief that somehow I had failed as a husband and father for my children. Perhaps I had not. Things were now out of my control, perhaps I was wrong and everyone had done their jobs.

One thing was certain: the truth was going to come out.

Happy Birthday

January 29, 2007, had just passed and Victor Rotolo had called to inform me that he had filed tort claim notices and suits on all parties involved with Sandy's passing: DYFUS, the Harding Township Police Department, St. Claire's and Morristown Memorial Hospital. He'd also included the public defender who'd apparently handled Sandy's hearing.

I asked about Judge Brennan, and Victor informed me that judges are immune from a lawsuit within the state of New Jersey.

I responded, "So he gets to play God Almighty and has no repercussion whatsoever. Well, one day a man like that will his find his punishment."

My birthday was a few days away, and I realized I was at the halfway point in my life, I was alone and the woman I'd chosen to spend my life with was gone.

February 3rd arrived. I was now 50 years old, a widowed father with two teenage daughters, two horses, one sheep, three dogs, and finally one Guinea pig and a six-acre facility that was still not finished off as it needed to be.

My girls said, "Let's go out for dinner."

I asked, "Where?"

They said, "Charlie Browns down by Hickory Tree Plaza over in Chatham."

I thought, why not? I really do not want to cook on my birthday.

Later that evening we arrived at Charlie Browns and to my surprise my daughters, with the help of Sally Curtiss, had arranged a surprise party.

Sometime shortly after my birthday, I received a call from Victor and he said, "Bill, I have my smoking gun for this case if we ever get to court."

I asked what he had.

He said, "I have a copy of Leslie's 911 call from the house upon finding her mother."

I said, "I thought she called me first that day."

He responded, "No she made a call first to the police department. Whoever is involved in a suit will never want a jury to hear her call, and Bill, you do not want to hear it either, trust me."

I asked if I could come down and hear her tape, and he said, "For your sake, I think it's best left to a later time and date."

It was now early March and I received a call from my good friend Scott Noyes, the world's best left-handed fly fisherman.

He asked how things were going.

I replied, "About as good as one can expect."

He said, "Bill, there is something I need to tell you."

I asked what.

He replied, "You need to know something. The rumor mill around town here says that you and Sandy were filing for divorce."

I replied, "What are you talking about?"

Scott said that people from the first aid squad, local volunteer fire department, and even some within the local police department were circulating this rumor.

I said, "Scott, that is absolutely bullshit, and you know it."

He replied that he knew it, but that was what he'd found out by asking a few questions of some people from town, and as he did he'd kept his mouth shut.

I said, "Who started this?"

He replied, "You will find out soon enough, but here are a few."

My thought was how in the world could this be?

I said, "I did not fabricate anything to anyone, but to the contrary, kept reaching out for help."

Scott said, "I know you did, but wanted to personally tell you this as I knew eventually you would find out and as your friend I felt obligated to do so."

It was a new piece to a puzzle that was still unfolding.

What else could possibly have occurred?

In late March, Jenny said to me that a girl from town, who'd been in ninth grade with her at Madison High School, had asked her if we would be interested in leasing Jack, Sandy's horse. We had a discussion and decided that if she was a competent enough rider, that this might be suitable. Jenny informed this girl, who also lived in New Vernon, that we may be receptive, but did not inform her that we would do so and told her that she should stop by the house with her mom and see our facility and we would discuss possible arrangements. Jenny did not know of this girl's riding abilities, but we thought if she were capable of handling Jack, after seeing her ride, we would make our decision.

This girl and mother arrived on a Saturday a few weeks later and after watching her ride, Jenny and I determined that we did not feel comfortable with her riding abilities, and decided together not to have this girl lease Jack on our facility, as we did not want her to possibly get hurt at our place. I later called this girl's mom and told her we had decided for the time being not to lease any of our horses. I did not inform this girl's mother as to why.

My first day away from the girls was sometime at the end of April or beginning of May. The camper needed to be opened up, and the drive up to Roscoe that first time was a somber one, as all along the way there were memories of happy times with my now late-wife and then as a family together with the girls.

That evening I called the girls, as I was too emotionally drained to make the two-hour drive back. Instead I had a sleepless evening and left at 4:45 a.m. to make sure the girls were up in time and ready for school. My thoughts were to just put the unit up for sale, but the girls said, "Dad, you love being up there in the spring and summer. You can afford it. Just keep it for yourself," and so I decided to do so for another year.

In late February I had to put Callie, our black lab mix, down. She was a wonderful dog that Sandy had adopted years ago. We had Callie almost fifteen years.

My thoughts were of Leslie and what would I do once school ended. I decided that year that from Memorial Day till Labor Day I would take every Friday off. But this plan would still leave the girls alone all day. Jenny would be sixteen in August, but Leslie was only thirteen and heading into eighth grade next year. I needed to do something for Leslie besides field hockey camp, which did not start till August.

My solution was another dog. This time I searched out a breed that was what I was looking for, but also a good family dog. The breed I choose was an Irish Field Setter. There are two such breeders in the country and one was nearby in Reading, PA.

In early April, we made a drive out to see the facility and selected a puppy with green eyes and a white patch on his chest. The puppy was only four weeks old and arrangements were made to pick him up in another six-to-eight weeks. My thoughts were that a puppy would help Leslie while she was home through the summer and I had always wanted a field dog for my bird hunting up at the Black River Rod and Gun Club, which I had been a member of for ten years.

Summer was flying by. Leslie was nurturing our new puppy Danneyboy, and it was time for our trip upstate. Sandy's grave stone was there, and it was necessary to visit. My thought was how I would hold up.

We made the drive and arrived late that afternoon. The girls were tired, and I was concerned about how I would be tomorrow with my girls. I informed the girls I wanted to go to mom's gravesite by myself and left them at the hotel.

I drove to the site, and as I pulled up to the entrance all the emotions of the past year's events hit me. As I got close to Sandy's gravesite, the tears came and my body shook with emotions. I sat at the gravesite and talked to both Sandy and her parents. I apologized to Sandy's late dad for my failure as her husband as I had not kept that promise that I had made to him upon his internment so many years ago.

I was gone for an hour and a half. When I had finally cried all my tears out and gained my composure, it was time to place that yellow rose on Sandy's grave, and tomorrow I would hold up with her daughters present. I left that evening looking to the west and the beautiful sunset and thinking how lovely and tranquil the view was. I now understood why Sandy's parents had chosen the site so far from their home in New Jersey.

The following morning we went back to the gravesite. The girls placed their flowers and I was able to hold my composure. We visited with some distant relatives for a couple of days and then headed up to Niagara Falls, staying on the Canadian side for a few days, and then headed back home as school was about to start.

Summer came and went. The girls were back in school, Leslie in eighth grade and Jenny in eleventh. We attended church service regularly. Jenny joined the church choir, and the girls and I met with their counselor every two weeks.

I was becoming rather tired of telling the counselor the same thing. I said that I slept well, which I did not, and that I wished someone would take out Judge Brennan.

I received a call from Victor Rotolo saying there would be a hearing at the end of the month as their law firm had requested documents from all listed parties, but one entity had refused and a judge would have to rule if we were to have the documents.

I asked who had refused.

Victor replied DYFUS and said a judge would determine if we were allowed their notes and records.

I told Victor, "If he rules against us, you might be defending me for a crime as of yet not committed."

Victor said, "You cannot say that."

I responded, "It could be a speeding ticket I'm referring about."

Victor said, "You're fairly smart, Bill, aren't you?"

I responded, "That's your call."

I attended the hearing with Victor up in the Superior court-house in Morristown that September day.

Victor said, "Bill, not all judges are assholes like that one who let Sandy out of the hospital that day. Many are good men and women and this man today I know and believe will allow us the DYFUS records."

The whole process took about six hours. Esther Bakonyi from the Department of the Attorney General argued that DYFUS records were private and cannot be released as policy prohibits release of any of their documents.

My guess was that Judge John J. Harper had anticipated her argument as he had three or four law books at his seat and all had tabs and with each argument he cited counters.

In the end he ruled in our favor, stating that if DYFUS had nothing to fear then their records would indicate such and there would be no reason to file anything further, reducing the caseload for the courts. I remember leaving the court that day wondering how anything actually gets done in our legal system at such a snail's pace. Chalk one up for the good guys. DYFUS was now required to mail all documents within ten days, as I believe the judge had ruled.

After Victor and I parted company that afternoon, I decided to take a walk to the elevator. We were in the same building where I had shown up, almost ten months prior, when I'd visited Judge Brennan's office in early November 2006.

I got off the elevator, walked around the sixth floor, and finally located Judge Brennan's courtroom. I could hear voices and grabbed hold of the door handle. As I started to open the door my mind went fast-forward and had some thoughts. I despised this man more than the terrorist who'd attacked my country on September 11, 2001. To me, this man was my family's most wanted terrorist. If I opened that door that late afternoon and saw this man, what would the future hold? If I saw him and his family some-where, say, in a restaurant, happy, I would never be able to contain myself. I was afraid of what I might do so I let go of that door that day. This simple act was another step towards my recovery.

I received a call from Victor in early December. We played phone tag. His message said the call wasn't important, but he would post me later on this one. The New Year was beckoning, and my hope was that maybe sometime next year we would be in a court of law.

2008, The Second Message

It was now a new year. The holidays were over, and the girls were back at school. For me, work was going fine, and yet life seemed empty and void. I had stopped seeing a counselor, though the girls continued to do so every two weeks, and I still had no answers as to what had actually occurred to our household.

Victor and I played phone tag, until one afternoon he called me to inform me that he had dropped one of the lawsuits he'd filed. It had been against the public defender who had been present for Sandy's hearing while she was in St. Clair's psych ward.

I asked him why, and he said the woman who'd been Sandy's public defender had committed suicide. Victor thought it ironic that she had done so almost a year to the date of Sandy's passing.

When he asked me my thoughts, I said I wished it had been the damn Judge Brennan instead.

I had an appointment with a woman named Catherine, who was my accountant Brian Corcoran's aunt. The appointment had been postponed a few times and was to take place Monday, April 28. Brian had called me because he wanted a safe investment for his aunt. She had received a large check from her divorce and her children would be asking for money.

The night before the appointment I did not sleep very well. On the day, I arrived at the bank branch up in Randolph. I did not cover this territory; however, it was more convenient for Catherine, who lived nearby. I arrived and met Catherine, and she had brought a friend named Gloria Weichand.

Gloria was a redhead with blue eyes just like Sandy, but Gloria had short-cropped hair. She was in her mid-to-late-fifties, I thought, and Catherine was about ten years her senior.

During the appointment Gloria kept asking me personal questions and I responded.

By the end of the appointment I figured that nothing was to come of the meeting because Gloria just kept asking a lot of questions.

I was wrong. A large amount of money was placed.

Gloria said that she had not been able to sleep the prior evening. She'd been thinking that her best friend in the world was about to meet a stranger with most of her life savings and she been getting a message that she needed to be there for her "Aunt Catherine," as she called her friend and my accountant Brian's aunt.

I had done investments for Brian's mother in the past and all had performed well. The new investment was made and at the end of the appointment, I came back from the copying machine and gave Catherine copies of all the documents she'd signed.

Gloria looked at me and said, "Bill, I need to speak with you about something."

I said, "It's getting late. I have to get this paperwork in and if you want to speak with me about your own finances that can be done another day."

Gloria asked if we could go into another room where the door could be closed, and I directed her to a conference room behind a closed door at the bank.

Gloria and I sat down. Catherine was present, too.

Gloria said, "Bill, do you know what a medium is?"

I looked at her and said no.

She replied, "Your late wife Sandy was standing behind you during the entire appointment as you were speaking to the two of us and she kept pointing her finger and waving her arms and repeating 'tell him, tell him.'"

Gloria explained that she had had this blessing for almost thirty-plus years and that her husband was a deacon in the Catholic Church.

I asked her what Sandy had to say.

"First off," Gloria said, "your wife says you cry every night alone late in bed and that it was not your fault, but the 'voices' that told her to do what she did. She says that you, Bill, were her true love."

Gloria continued until the tears welled up inside me, and I broke down and started to cry. Gloria finished by saying, "Sandy says that you told a friend recently that you never went out with a redhead before her, that you fell in love with one, but would never go out with another. She wants you to know that might not be the case for you and to keep an open mind."

I finally said to Gloria, "I did not expect this, but can I take your number as I would like to call you at another point if possible?"

Gloria agreed and provided me with her phone number.

As I left to head back to my Bloomfield office, I thought what just happened to me? The things Gloria had said could have come only from someone who had gone to her grave. There was no way that Gloria could have made this up even if she tried to. The things said could have come only from someone from beyond.

Gloria told me Sandy had not gone to the light yet as she was worried about us and was waiting to go. Gloria also told me that Barry, our son, was with Sandy together that afternoon and he had also been waiting for his mom. Gloria was not sure when he had passed or what had happened to him.

I replied that Sandy had had an abortion before she'd met me. She had gotten pregnant and was not sure what she should do and had a talk with her mom Harriet and it was decided to terminate the baby. This had always been a difficult issue for Sandy as she had been adopted. We never spoke of it after she told me.

I drove back to the bank and as I arrived my friend Brian Lange, who also worked as an advisor, was walking out and heading towards his car and saw me. Brian looked at me and said, "Bill, are you all right? You look like you've seen a ghost."

I responded, "Brian, I just talked with one. Let's go next door for a soda. I have something to tell you."

We went next door and I proceeded to tell him what had just happened.

He looked at me with shock and bewilderment.

I said, "Brian, remember a week ago, when we had sushi across the street, and I told you I had never dated a redhead, but fell in love with one?"

He said, "Yes I do remember, Bill."

I said, "Gloria repeated that from my late wife Sandy about an hour ago verbatim and now you are the first person I see once I have left her back in Randolph."

Brian said, "Spooky."

I replied, "Hocus-Pocus."

I told Brian, "There was no way that message had come from this world but from the other side. Up into this point in my life if I had not just gone through this, I would never have believed it, but now I'm not sure what to believe anymore."

I then headed back up to the office to drop off the paperwork and then home to some real questions that I could not answer.

The Blue Dress

A few days later, I had no appointments in the afternoon so I went trout fishing. It was May 1, 2008. The afternoon was beautiful, with the temperature in the 70s. The birds were singing when I left the office.

Spring was early that year and the trees were just starting to bloom, so I headed to the Black River to the club where I had been a member for more than ten years. I caught and released a few trout that afternoon.

While I was fishing that day, a fawn, maybe a few days old, walked right into the river and headed right to me, unafraid even though I was probably the first human this small, frail, newborn animal had ever seen. The mother deer was nowhere to be found. The fawn actually walked right up to me, and I lowered my hand and it put its nose to my hand to smell my scent. A few moments later its mother appeared, looked at her offspring, and started to snort at me and paw at the ground with her foot. The fawn left the river and both deer ran away.

I decided to go to the cabin and just take in the sunshine for a few moments. I closed my eyes and could hear the birds singing. I thought of the special blessing that had just taken place with the fawn. I looked up and felt the warmth of the sun on my face and closed eyelids. That moment I said a prayer, "Sandy, I want you to cross over now. I want you to be with God. Go to the light now. Somehow I know things will be fine."

For the first time in almost one and a half years I started to feel some form of peace inside.

In the second week of May, I decided to call Gloria. It was Friday afternoon.

I picked up the phone and before I dialed, I heard a voice on the line.

It was Gloria.

I was a little startled, but after the first encounter, I figured it was divine intervention.

I had a fairly long conversation with Gloria.

She asked how I was doing.

I replied that for the first time in a long time I was not in tears late in bed every night and I wanted to thank her for speaking with me that day.

I learned that Gloria had been asked to attend a conference in London for a school that studies the paranormal and teaches those such as herself with said abilities. She had been asked to teach as a guest for the upcoming summer schedule. She told me that Sandy had visited her while she'd been in a group session and she had a message for me.

I asked what the message was.

Gloria replied, "Leslie needs to get the blue strapless dress for the dance."

I replied that Leslie had no dance to attend that I knew of.

Gloria said, "Sandy wants you to make sure Leslie gets the blue strapless dress."

I got off the phone happy with our conversation, but a little confused.

A week later Leslie informed me that she needed to get a knee-length white dress for her eighth grade graduation and that she would wear that dress to a dance in a few weeks' time as well.

I asked Leslie if this event was the graduation dance.

She said, "No, Dad, it's for the cotillion dance that I signed up for last October."

I had forgotten about the dance as I had written the check months ago. It was a formal event for young girls and hosted at a formal catering hall.

I said, "Do you want to get the dress now?"

Leslie said, "No, let's go another day."

About a week later I needed to cut the grass. It was Monday, about 5:15 p.m., and I asked Leslie if she would help me as we had two large riding mowers. I gave her a nice allowance so if I needed her she always agreed to do so. All one had to do was sit and steer. I did the perimeters of both the front and back and when those were done I came in and asked Leslie to help me.

She said she would be right out.

About fifteen minutes later she still was not outside and the other mower was out in the backyard running. I went in to check on her.

She was quiet, and I asked why she was not outside to help me as I had asked her to do so.

Leslie said she was very upset.

I asked what had happened at school to make her so.

She said it was nothing like that, but graduation was coming up and the teacher had asked all the students to bring some pictures of their family from home.

I was not aware of this project, and Leslie told me she had gone through all the old photo albums of home the night before Sunday. It had been a difficult day for her.

I said, "Look, honey, we all have those days, but I recently meet someone who changed my thoughts about what has happened. I now think of all the great times we all had while Mommy was healthy and normal. Mom wants you to remember those days and not the end days. Do me a favor: go up to your room, take some time and remember your happiest memory of Mom and then when you feel better, if you don't mind helping me with the grass, I would appreciate it. If we get it done, we should go to the mall and get your dress after we have dinner tonight somewhere, if that's okay with you."

About ten minutes later, Leslie said all was fine and she would help me with the grass. I informed her we would be getting two dresses as this event was to be her first formal dance and she should be in attendance as a young lady that evening.

We went to the Livingston Mall, had diner at Applebee's, and then went to Macy's junior miss department. We walked down the aisles and the next thing I saw was my daughter looking at a blue dress. It wasn't strapless. It had short sleeves, but it was a light shade of blue. My thought was my God, what's next?

A moment later Leslie looked up at the wall and there, hanging for all to see, was a beautiful pink dress. The blue dress went back to its place, and I thought so much for Gloria's message.

I followed Leslie over to the other area. She was holding up the dress and asked what I thought of it.

I said, "If this is what you want, then go try it on."

Leslie proceeded to the dressing room. She was in there for about fifteen minutes and had asked the attendant to bring in the same dress in other sizes.

I finally said, "Leslie, will you please come out so I can see you in the pretty pink dress."

She came around the corner and I was in shock. Instead of a pink dress as I'd thought, she was standing before me in a sky blue strapless dress, the exact dress Gloria had told me Sandy wanted her to get.

Leslie said, "Daddy, what do you think?"

With tears in my eyes I said, "Wonderful. Why don't you have the girls help you with some shoes and the knee-length graduation dress next?" I turned to walk away to gain my composure.

We left the store that evening with two dresses, one a knee-length white dress and the other the sky blue chiffon strapless dress.

My head was now totally baffled as to what might happen next.

Leslie went to that dance just as her late mother had wanted her to. Next year she would be starting high school. I was wondering how this sequence of events could possibly have occurred.

The Friday after the dance I decided to call Gloria again, and once again as I picked up the phone she was there. This time she told me Sandy came to her in a group session. For the first time in her life, Gloria'd seen a departed one in color, and it was Sandy.

I said, "Let me ask you a question, Gloria. How could Sandy possibly know Leslie would pick a blue strapless dress three weeks prior to the events?"

Gloria responded, "They can go backward and forward, and Sandy is now riding horses with your late dad."

Gloria knew that we had a horse farm in New Vernon, but she never knew that my father rode as a young man and at the age of sixteen won the Mclay Cup back in 1942, the year after William Steinkrauss, former Olympian and equestrian champion had won it.

Gloria told me that Sandy and my dad were doing show events together. Gloria went on to describe the vision of Sandy and said that the girls were there as well. The vision she described was that of a picture that I had of all three of them taken at the wedding in August 2005. An object Gloria said she could not quite make out was the lighthouse.

I said, "I have that picture of her and the girls."

Gloria said, "You're right. I just did not know what they were standing in front of."

Gloria then said, "I have two other messages from Sandy. She wants you to stop worrying and find someone else. You have to let her go now." I asked, "Has she gone to the light yet?"

Gloria said she did not know.

Gloria then added, "Sandy says you will win the lawsuit."

I had not discussed this topic with Gloria prior to this call.

I decided that this call would be my last, as I did not want to hear any more messages from my late wife. I thanked Gloria for taking the time to speak again with me that day.

Time Passages
2008

Victor had been sending me copies of all incoming mail and outgoing correspondences regarding the girls' case.

It took the state agency DYFUS more than six months to comply with the judge's order back in September to provide all field notes and documents regarding their involvement with our case. That was not the ten days as ordered. If I'd done that, I would have been hauled off to jail for failure to comply.

When the Rotolo Law Group received the notes and documents, many irregularities appeared. Shortly after my initial meeting, I had been asked to provide a timeline of the sequence of events that summer and fall of 2006 to the Rotolo Law Group, and my timeline was very accurate. When I received DYFUS' information, I was outraged as to what had been written. I called Woody, the girls' attorney who had been assigned the case, about it.

He responded not to worry.

I was starting to heal, but with every new piece to the puzzle it was becoming clear that more than one party was involved and where, as a matter of law, could the blame be placed?

It was now the summer of 2008 and it was becoming clear that no one wanted responsibility for what had happened and that each party would blame the others for mistakes that had been made.

In August, Jenny, who had been involved with the arts, both

singing and painting, got involved in a karaoke contest down at the Jersey shore. She was going there every week and continued to make the cut off. The finals were being held at a local tavern and a number of us showed up for the finalist that evening.

I was there with Leslie, my sister, my brother John, and Cathy, and we sat down to the evening final event wondering if my six-teen-year-old would win. Cathy told me she'd invited a friend, Vern, who was going to stop by and join us as well. She said that they were longtime friends, and I thought nothing of it.

A little later Vern joined us. He was a man in his mid-sixties about six feet tall and was pleasant when introduced to all of us by Cathy. As fate would have it Vern sat down next to me.

Jenny sang and the rest of the contestants did as well.

We were all having dinner when Vern asked me, "Where do you live, Bill?"

I responded, "A place that most have never heard of as it's a small town up in northern New Jersey. The township is Harding and our ZIP code is New Vernon. There is no ski resort there as many would think of Vernon Township, where the old Playboy Club and ski area in New Jersey is located."

It turned out that Vern was the chief of police in the town next to my late grandmother's town of Sea Girt, Spring Lake, a beautiful full-time and summertime beach community. Spring Lake is, in my opinion, one of the prettiest places on the New Jersey coastline, home to many wealthy homes.

Vern said, "I know of New Vernon."

I said, "How?"

He answered that his very good friend was the chief of police Kevin Gaffney and he knew this man.

I told Vern that we had been residents since 1988, that my wife passed away a few years back and that I was a single dad with a six-acre horse facility in town.

He asked me if I knew of Gaffney.

I responded, "Yes, I do."

Vern replied, saying how wonderful Kevin was and how good of a job he did up there in my township.

I sat there and nodded yes like a bobblehead doll behind the backseat of a car.

Vern must have gone on for twenty minutes about Gaffney until I excused myself to the men's room, saying I needed to go when I really did not.

Fortunately, when I got back to my seat the contestants had started to sing again, and while I finished my dinner I thought I had handled things correctly as this man really did not want to hear my personal thoughts about his good friend. He might not like to hear what I really thought.

It turned out that night that my daughter, who can sing beautifully, won the contest and beat a few local professional singers, winning five hundred dollars.

The owner of the pub stopped by our table, figured out I was her dad and asked who she sang for.

I replied, "She's only sixteen and will be seventeen very shortly."

We left that evening and headed home. I said to Jenny, "Spend your money wisely, but get yourself something special. You earned it!"

The summer came to a close and many things were now coming into a clearer picture of the events of now almost two years ago.

School had started. It was late September, and my good friend from the Black River Rod and Gun Club Sheldon Kay gave me a call.

Sheldon said, "Bill, have you seen the article in the *Star Ledger* about the large suit just won against DYFUS?"

I replied no.

Sheldon said, "You need to read the article."

I got a copy of the paper and read that a young college-aged woman had come back to her mother's home from college and found her mother, sister, and father all dead in her parents' home. The parents had been separated due to the father's mental health, and the mother had taken him back, even as a court order was in place prohibiting him from the home. This college-aged daughter had called DYFUS repeatedly, warning them of the situation. Nothing was done, and the end result was the father killed his wife, daughter, and then himself only to be found by this young girl arriving home for the weekend to visit.

I gave Victor Rotolo a call the next morning.

He informed me that he had already spoken to this girl's attorney, discussed our case and asked him to provide copies of DYFUS' manuals that Victor was still unable to obtain as DYFUS refused his request.

A few months later Victor informed me that his law firm's belief was that even though many parties had screwed up, the greatest fault lay with DYFUS, and that the other suits should be dropped. Otherwise, this state agency could try to place the blame elsewhere.

I reluctantly agreed and asked, "What do we need to do now?"

Victor replied, "I will file suit shortly."

The holidays were soon in sight. Another year was ahead and still no firm court dates had been set. The wheels of justice can turn very slowly when tackling a government entity.

Just before the new year I received another call from Victor, who said that we needed to hire an outside expert witness to go over this case. He said that he had located the right man, Richard J. Gelles, Ph.D., the Dean who headed the Joanne and Raymond Welsh Chair of Child Welfare and Family Violence in the School of Social Policy and Practice at the University of Pennsylvania out of Philadelphia. His resume was extensive, and he'd also worked for the U.S. House of Representatives in 1996 on legislation that ultimately became The Adoption and Safe Families Act of 1997 (PL 105-89).

In Dr. Gelles report, which was to follow later, he had been asked to respond to the following questions:

1. Did the DYFUS Defendants have a duty to ensure the safety, permanency and well-being of J. and L. Dunn?

2. Did the DYFUS Defendants breach their duty to ensure the safety and well-being of J. and L. Dunn?

3. If the answer to Question #2 is "yes," did the DYFUS Defendants act in an objectively reasonable manner when breaching their duty to ensure the safety and well-being of the Dunn children?

4. If the answer to question # 3 is "no," did the DYFUS Defendants' unreasonable failure to ensure the safety and well-being of the Dunn children cause harm to J. and L. Dunn?

Here are the final three paragraphs from Dr. Gelles' summary, which was twenty pages:

"With the exception of the fact that a caseworker prepared an inaccurate and inconsistent Safety Assessment, DYFUS had a clear and accurate picture of the mental status of Mrs. Dunn and the emotional toll Mrs. Dunn's psychotic condition was taking on her two daughters. The Division knew Mr. Dunn worked full-time and that he and her mental health providers had deep concerns about his wife. Given the risks in the household and goal of safety and well-being of the children, the Division made the correct decision to open the case for supervision.

"And yet, with a goal of safety and well-being, and the known risks and Mrs. Dunn's expected lack of compliance with such treatment or medication, the Division failed to meet the standard of care and intervene such that the children would be protected from Mrs. Dunn. When Mrs. Dunn failed to comply, on multiple occasions, with appointments, and knowing that Mr. Dunn was working outside his home full-time, the Division nevertheless failed to take reasonable action to remove either the children or Mrs. Dunn from the household. This action meant that DYFUS was not following its own recommendations and thus was failing to fulfill its own standard of care.

"In conclusion, and to a reasonable degree of scientific knowledge, I conclude that DYFUS and its agents/supervisors Lichter, Remy and Hewitt knew what the standard of care was in the case of the case of the Dunn family and failed to meet that standard in its response to and supervision of the case. I further conclude that the DYFUS Defendants' actions and/or omissions with respect to the handling of the Dunn case were not objectively reasonable under the circumstances."

We had our case.

It was just be a matter of time till said day would arrive, God willing.

More Messages

It was now 2009, and I now knew all the facts for the girls' case. It was determined that the girls had a suit, and I wanted no appearance of my trying to receive any monetary compensation myself as it might appear that I, too, wanted something from the state. My only wish was that someday those who'd failed to do their jobs would be held accountable, as I had worked all my life in the real world, not the make-believe land of the supposed public servant.

One of my former coworkers was in prison and for good cause. Brian Anderson was sentenced for embezzling millions of dollars of elderly clients' money. My thought was that what the DYFUS workers had done was a similar crime and that they should also lose their jobs. I had told Victor Rotolo on more than one occasion that if the state pays money to my children and these incompetent workers remain in their position perhaps another family will suffer. To me it was not about money, but righting an injustice brought to my family by the supposed public servants of New Jersey.

I decided to take a trip to Florida to visit my brother and left the first week of May. It was time for me to start thinking about a new location to live, as the Garden State of my youth, which my late wife had called "the Guard Rail State" since the late-1990s and I was now calling "the Garbage State," had become an intolerable place for me to live. I had decided a long time ago it was time to leave.

With all the circumstances surrounding and coming to light over Sandy's passing, I no longer wished to pay the state another penny. Every time I received a paycheck or bought something, I was supporting the State of Sue Lousey and it's wonderful public workforce. I had had it, and most of my friends had the same opinions of where the state was heading. The state was now the most expensive to live in and the infrastructure, traffic, and crowding had made it a place most people who are wealthy can afford to leave once the last child is out of high school.

While I was in Florida, my brother John and I hung out at the beach, took it easy, and one day went fishing in John's small boat, which he calls "the Johnny Rocket." The day we went fishing, John's friend Guy decided to join us. We all hopped into Guy's large pickup truck and towed John's boat to a canal between the intercoastal and the "mosquito lagoon," as it is called, just north of Cape Canaveral. John assured us he had fished this place before and would guarantee we would catch fish.

When we got to the ramp to drop off the boat there must have been at least twenty manatees in the water. We had to be careful leaving the area as these animals are protected. We motored off into the canal to my brother's secret spot to land some fish. Much to my surprise, the spot was so secret that the fish failed to find it that day.

Still, the weather was perfect so, after a cold and long winter, I didn't care if we didn't catch anything. We were there about two hours and then a manatee came to the back of the boat where I was sitting with my rod in hand. The manatee just sat there and looked at me and did not leave the boat. After about ten minutes I looked into this creature's brown eyes and started to scratch its nose. After a few minutes I stopped and thought the manatee would swim off, but did not, so for about an hour I had the pleasure to speak to and rub the nose and face of this gentle giant.

We got home late that afternoon and sat down and discussed

the day, and then a thought came to me: today was May 6, 2009, twenty years to the day since I had married my now late wife.

I said, "John, it's another message from Sandy. Perhaps this is where I should move to: a place where the weather is always pleasant."

Later that evening we had another talk, and I found out that Cathy, John's better half, had received a call earlier that year from none other than Vern, her longtime friend and the same man I had sat next to last summer at Jenny's final singing contest. John had been at the house when the call came in. Cathy had been a little flustered and said to whomever she was talking to "I don't think this is something we should be talking about."

John had asked her who she was talking to and she'd responded, "Vern and he is talking to me about Billy's late wife Sandy."

John then said, "Let me talk with Vern."

Vern then started to tell my brother that I should know that his good friend, none other than Kevin Gaffney, was very sorry about what had happened.

John responded, "Vern, if you knew what that man and his department did to my brother's family, you would not call him your friend. I never want to have a discussion about this matter ever again. I'm sorry, but it's something you should not have called to say. Why doesn't that man apologize himself to my brother?"

I came back from Florida refreshed, and I called the Rotolo Law Group about what had happened.

Woody, the girl's attorney, said, "This guy is afraid that he may also be named and is just trying to figure out a way to cover his ass."

I had yet to see the police reports, and I wondered why Gaffney might be concerned. I asked Woody to please send me copies of all police records that the Harding Department had on this matter.

Over the past few years I had been working on the facility that we lived on. I'd completely replaced the fence and installed a bridge out in the back so the horses could be lead through the backyard instead of across the front to get to the new side pasture. The exterior of the barn looked nice; however, the interior was just the original and now old and tired. I decided that to make the place a showplace, the interior needed a complete upgrade and this project was something beyond my scope to do myself. I located a man through a friend and started the project in late July. I ordered all new cast aluminum, new hardware to the tune of about eight thousand dollars, and had the contractor Peter install all new doors. The stalls were of Southern Yellow Pine. They started the work, and by the third Thursday of August, 2009, had finished the four stalls. Peter said they would stain and paint the remainder, and I replied that I would do that starting the next day. He said okay and that he would stop by next week to pick up his final check.

I awoke early that morning and placed the horses outside. It would take me two full days to apply the two coats of marine grade-finish that were needed. By dinnertime Friday I had finished the first coat, and tomorrow's second coat would go on much quicker. If I started by 5 a.m., I just might finish the Hunter Green trim paint that was needed as well and that matched the hardware I'd ordered earlier.

I went to sleep early that night and awoke as the alarm went off at 5 a.m. As expected, by 7 p.m. I had finished the job. It looked fantastic.

When we had dinner that evening, I showed the girls how things looked. The horses would need to spend another evening outside in the pastures.

It was just about dark when I went back to the barn. I had a beer in my hand and I remembered the first "light" that now, three years later, still worked as if it always had. I said to Sandy, "I know that you can see this. I wish it had been done for you before you left this earth, but I know you are smiling down from heaven above with approval. It's soon time for me to leave this place, but I know it would be both your wish and your late parents' wish that this place remains a horse facility and by my words to all of you, it will remain so. You have my word."

By 10 p.m. I headed off to bed and for some reason tossed and turned all night long. Perhaps I was worried about the last two days' work or the fact that this weekend would be three years to the day Sandy had been taken from her home in a straitjacket. All night long I watched the idiot box, closing my eyes, but I just could not get to sleep.

At about 3 a.m., my eyes were closed and I could hear the TV in the background. The next thing I could feel a breath of air going to my left ear and a heart beating on top of my chest. The TV noise faded and all I could see was a bright white light.

I said, "It's you Sandy."

As I was about to open my eyes she said, "Keep them closed," so I did.

We spoke for some time.

I said, "You've gone to the light, haven't you?"

She said, "Yes and it is a wonderful place."

I said, "Can you take me with you now, please?"

She said, "It not your time to go. You have unfinished business to take care of."

We continued to talk until she said, "It's now time for me to go. You will see me again one day when it's your time."

I told her, "I loved you" and I said I was sorry she had to go away.

She told me she'd always loved me and when I'd joined her one day I would understand.

With that the light started to fade and I could hear the TV again.

I was so at peace I did not want to leave the light.

For the remainder of the morning I lay there and tried to figure out if it was a dream or an actual life-changing experience, and I kept coming to the conclusion that something wonderful had just happened and I wasn't dreaming.

That Sunday morning we, as a family, had been scheduled to

host the coffee and doughnuts after service. Our pastor was away and Gordon Ward, who ran the youth ministry, would be leading the service that morning.

Gordon, who is the author of a few books, gave a sermon that morning. The subject matter was sometimes bad things happen to good people.

After the coffee hour, I asked him if I could speak with him privately. We went upstairs to a private room and I told him of last night's experience saying, "I think it was real, but perhaps I was dreaming."

He said, "You were graced by an angel last night and others have also. You are not alone on this matter." He spoke to me of others that he personally knew who had had some type of life-changing experience.

I left the church that day in, one might say, a different place, trying to comprehend the past three years and all that had transpired. Life sometimes can be a mystery.

That fall I decided to have Peter, the contractor, come back to finish off the remainder of the barn. I removed two stalls and added an enclosed tack room with an air-conditioner so the leather would remain fresh, a cedar-lined closet for all the blankets, and shelving for ointments for the animals. Peter did a good job adding the pine to the walls; I also added a workshop for myself.

The private horse facility was probably the finest within an hour of Manhattan.

Jenny was a senior in high school and Leslie was entering her first year in high school.

Once the girls' case was filed by the Rotolo Law Group, I had some very serious doubts as no other then Judge Brennan, who had been responsible for discharging my late wife from the hospital overruling her doctors, had somehow been assigned our case.

At some point in time if we passed what is referred to as summary judgment, in which your attorney must ask the court's permission to file suit, then Judge Brennan may or may not allow this to take place.

I expressed my concerns to the girls' attorney, and he said, "Bill, perhaps he feels badly about what had occurred. He keeps signing off to any requests we have or extensions we ask for."

I said to Woody, "I never want to see that man and when it comes down to the wire, he must excuse himself as a conflict of interest may occur. I don't trust the man at all. After all, it was his decision that started all of this."

The year 2010 was about to arrive, and I still had a feeling a cover up would occur.

A Final Message from Beyond

One place holds my fondest memories of a past when all was happy within our household. The place is called Alder Lake. I can truly say that my happiest times with my family occurred there a long time ago when the girls were young. It was a magical place that very few ever visited in the mid-to-late-1990s.

In the summer of 2010, I decided to sell my camper, as I had decided that there were too many memories up there and I knew a change was necessary. My last trip to Roscoe occurred in late May that year, just before "bug week" when all the mayflies and caddis hatches occur in great quantities. I had decided that I would head up to the camper, take the last items left in the unit I wished to keep, and fish a few days.

I had two guests arrive that week. After the last fellow left, I decided that I would pack the remainder of the belongings that I wished to keep and then drive to a favorite place where I once used to fish together with a redhead many times and years ago.

I arrived at the location, sat down, and just looked out. Many memories came to mind that late morning. I had decided that I would fish one last time here and then drive, instead of home, up to Livonia and Sandy's headstone as I did not think I would do so again for some time. The ride up was only three hours from where I sat, and I thought one more day away would be good for me.

I was on the West Branch of the Delaware in a place I had fished many times, but I had not been here once since 2006. The river was quiet, and I noticed that out along the far bank one fish had started feeding, I had no idea how large the fish was as the river was well over one hundred yards across from my seat on this side of the river bank. I got my waders on, rigged up my fly rod, grabbed my fly box, and started to cross towards the far bank. The current was swift but manageable and about hip deep.

The sky was a beautiful shade of springtime blue and white clouds dotted the sky. It was a beautiful spring day, and the odors of a nearby cow field hung in the air. It was about late morning and when I finally got within casting distance of this fish, I still could not tell its size as it was just dimpling the surface. I saw some bugs on the water and "matched the hatch," as they say. The fly that day was none other than a Sandy Blue Dun. I thought to myself how interesting it was that I'd arrived here on what would probably be my last fishing trip to this region for who knew how long, and perhaps Bo of the Beverkill would be with me somehow while I was here.

I tied one of my own hand-tied versions of this pattern to my leader (Sandy Blue Dun), looked up to the sky and said a little prayer to myself, hoping that the future would be better. This would be my last trip, I thought, to the region as the camper was to be sold next week. I cast out to the rising fish and on the second or third cast a dimple occurred and the fly disappeared. I set the hook and the next thing I knew the line went screaming off the reel.

The fish was big—very big. I played the fish for some time. My leader was light, about 6x or three-and-a-half pounds test. The fish would come near, see me, and the line would again disappear off my reel. This played out a number of times and each time the fish's run was a little shorter than the last.

I finally beached the fish. It was a brown trout, twenty-six inches in length, measured by a tape that I had attached to the side of my fly rod years ago, starting just at the cork handle. I did not have a camera, but I thought to myself that in all my years up here, this fish was the largest brown trout I'd ever landed. I revived this creature, watched his gills open and close repeatedly and when he was ready, I let go and he slowly swam off back to his world.

It turned out that this hatch had just started and was now in full swing. Fish were popping everywhere. It was Monday, and I had the place to myself and could have probably caught many more. Instead I got up, walked back into the river and continued to wade back to my car.

In trout fishing, the largest fish generally has the prime holding place in any section of a river or stream, and most probably the fish I had just landed was this case. I could have fished longer, but I thought why? This was my last outing here and somehow I had just landed the largest wild brown trout of my life. I had caught many fish longer than twenty inches in my day up here. Perhaps I'd hooked a few this large in more than thirty years, but I'd never beached one of this size. Somehow I knew someone up there over the rainbow had brought me to this day.

Was it Bo of the Beverkill?

I think it was.

I decided it was time to leave, so I got in the car and drove up to Livonia, stopping in town to buy some flowers. I arrived at the gravesite and my prayer that day was good. I spoke to Peter, Harriet, and Sandy. I did not need to ask their forgiveness this time. I just wanted to thank them for sharing their lives with me. It was not necessary for me to stay long this time, but I was happy I had made this journey. I decided to head home, back to their home, the farm that they had all shared and left for me to care for. I knew they were all at peace and all three were "with the light."

Two years later, in the summer of 2012, my good friend and old neighbor Marybeth asked me to accompany her to a party up in the Catskills near my old stomping grounds. I hemmed and hawed about this invitation, thinking of my last visit to the region, which I'd wanted to be my last. The party was for her sister's husband, all her family was to be present and her parents had rented a place in Margaretville where everyone would be staying.

I finally said to myself, "Why not?"

On the ride up we decided that I would show Marybeth Alder Lake, as it was located just south of Margaretville, accessible by some rough roads through the mountains.

We stopped in Livingston Manor and had lunch at the Robin Hood diner. I had been there a few times before with my late wife and children. We then proceeded through the mountain roads up to Alder Lake. I had not been there in a long time as I'd gone back only one time in the spring of 2007, and at that time the old Mansion had been torn down.

We pulled into the parking lot under a shaded tree. The sunroof was opened up just a tiny bit to keep the car cooler for our return. The lot was packed, and the spot we pulled into was the only available. Many thoughts raced through my mind as we left the car. I was unsure what we would see. Had anything changed?

We walked down to the lake and it was as beautiful as the first day when I'd taken my family there that fall afternoon. There was not a breath of wind and the mirror that day of the peaks reflecting had been broken. However, there was one very big change and it was not the color of the foliage. The area was now full of people, perhaps as many as two hundred. Some were swimming or canoeing, young and old, families grilling just as we had so many years ago. There were tents at the rough sites and best of all, no garbage. People were respectful of this place and my heart was filled with happiness at seeing all those present doing what our family had done more than fifteen years ago when we'd had this place to ourselves.

Marybeth and I walked around a bit. I pointed to Balsam Mountain in the distance and the area where the old apple orchard was and the lake intake stream just beyond. When we got to the dam, I showed her the remnants of the caretaker's cottage and where the old hatchery once stood. They are almost gone by decay now. The reflection I was hoping to see had changed, but the change made my heart full of happiness seeing all those people enjoying what once upon a time was our own private memory, now something for all to embrace.

We then headed back to the car. I was driving and Marybeth was in the passenger seat.

As I started the engine what looked like a black leaf fell down through the small opening in the sunroof.

I placed my hand down to shift the car.

The leaf moved, then it stood up and its black wings began to open up.

Marybeth and I both looked down and saw this happening at the same time.

As the wings opened the colors appeared, a red to orange band at the end of the wings and bright dots of the same hue were present, the same color as Sandy's hair.

Marybeth and I had seen this type of butterfly at her home one day. It had appeared as we were talking of Sandy, and Marybeth had said that day that it was a message.

This time Marybeth's mouth just opened and she was speechless. The butterfly flew right towards her and next to the window where it remained, fluttering its wings as it was trapped behind the glass window.

I looked over to the window and pressed the button to lower it as I said, "Be free and I am now free."

Epilogue
My Final Words

When Marybeth and I left Alder Lake that summer day in 2012, we went over the mountain on the back roads I had traveled before many times a long time ago. As we headed over the mountain to Margaretville and the party for Marybeth's family, my thoughts were happy for that special blessing that had just occurred from nowhere. I have not been back to either place since then and will not go, as I want those two memories of both the trout and the butterfly to be my last of the area. I am grateful for the days I spent there so many times.

On the ride back that Sunday, we drove through many of the old places that my family and I once had frequented so many years ago. To me, they looked tired and old somehow. I cannot really say why. Perhaps I had changed. In fact, I know I have changed. It's hard to go back sometimes, and time marches forward.

Many will wonder why I decided to write this biography of my life with my late wife Sandy.

My answer is quite simple.

Sandy would want her story told. She was a kind compassionate gal, who did not have a mean bone in her body. She was a giver and not a taker and she taught me the difference. I am a better man because she chose to share her life with me and I learned to also be a better person and giver as well.

If Sandy were alive today, she would say, "Write this, Bill, and if just one family is spared from the hardships and grief that both you and the girls had to endure then my passing would not be in vain," and so this is my reason to do so. Maybe this was what she meant when she came to me and gave me the gift of the light.

As of this writing, I have reached 57 years of age. This manuscript has been a long journey, started in the late fall of 2010 on the day of Sandy's passing. It is currently 2014, almost four years later, and soon the anniversary of her death will approach.

In the beginning, the words were very difficult as I still had sadness and anger inside me. I have since come to understand that she would not be happy if I did not let it go, and as such I've done so and will remember her words that night: "It's not your time yet. You have more unfinished business to attend to. One day you will join me and then will understand."

I have come to understand that she is right and that my time, someday, will bring myself to cross over to the light. There I will join her and all those who have left this world, both friends and family members. As Gloria said to me that day, "They just go to a different place. Sandy now is riding show horses again with your dad as he was unable due to his health problems later in life."

I now have very different beliefs since the events that occurred after Sandy's passing. I guess one might say I now am very spiritual in my religious beliefs. Faith is a personal issue. As long as you have it, one should be respectful, and if you have no faith, the Bill of Rights gives you that right. One day, we all, at our passing, have that question before us.

For myself, I have my answer.

In the summer of 2012, our day of judgment was to occur. The date was set for August 15, 2012, and Woody, the girls' attorney, was scheduled to file his motion before Judge Robert Brennan in Superior Court at the county courthouse up in Morristown.

Just a few days before, I received a call from Woody saying that our date had been canceled. My guess was it would take another year.

Apparently what happened was that I got my wish and Judge Brennan withdrew himself from the case.

Woody always told me the judge probably felt bad about what had occurred.

I never believed that and he'd just signed his name to all the extensions.

The documents presented were approximately four-inches thick as I have the copy, which I have never read. Once again the wheels of justice would drag on. In my opinion this was the only honorable thing that Judge Brennan did for our household.

After I received Woody's call, I spoke with Scott Noyes about what had transpired.

He said, "Bill, don't worry about it. Sandy told you that you will prevail."

I had forgotten about the conversation in which Gloria had told me those same words, and I said now it was out of my hands.

It turned out that our new judgment day was to be a month later.

I still had a nagging feeling a cover-up would occur.

This time I was wrong.

On September 15, 2012, Woody prevailed and summary judgment went to the girls' favor. We would get our day in court. The only question was when. I was to find out that we had to go before an arbitrator by law. The date was set for November 15, 2012.

In October 2012, I decided to join Leslie for parents' weekend at the university she was attending. We were to go to the football game. I arrived a day early and had an appointment with the undergraduate dean. I needed to speak with the school about the court date that the Rotolo Law group felt would occur sometime in the springtime. Leslie would be required to attend as well as her older sister Jenny. I explained to the dean the circumstances of the girls' late mom's passing, avoiding all the details, just saying we had prevailed over the hardest hurdle and showing him the document for our arbitration date.

The dean was very sympathetic and said the school would do whatever was necessary to help if a case were to occur during the spring session.

I responded that we might be able to get a postponement, but I did not know if this was possible. I also told the dean that November 15, 2012, was a date that I would attend as by law the girls' attorney must meet with an arbitrator and I felt it was necessary for me to be present as well. I really did not want to attend, but I knew that I must. I wanted justice for my family and those responsible held accountable in a court of law.

The dean wished us well, and I told him I would advise him of the direction in which we'd move.

I flew back from Florida to New Jersey on November 14, 2012, the day before our arbitration date. I had a telephone conference with Victor Rotolo and received some news that did not make me happy. Victor knew that all I ever wanted the whole time was for those who were named in the suit to be held accountable just as those the government prosecutes in the real world. Basically, I wanted a few to lose their jobs. I felt they had destroyed our home and might do so again to another family, and I wanted them fired and barred from ever having the chance to harm another family again.

Victor said, "Bill, I have never wanted to tell you this as I have known all along your position. These people will never lose their jobs for what happened to your family. What happened to your household is one of the worst things I have had to handle and you have done what one in ten thousand, no, let me say, one in twenty-five thousand could not do."

I said, "Look, we have these guys right between the crosshairs."

He said, "Yes, we do."

He then added that if we received an award that was large enough, it should be taken.

"If you go to court, you may not win," he said.

I said, "I believe that we will prevail."

Victor responded that a judge could throw out any bit of evidence he wished to.

I replied, "I will call *The New York Times* and ask them to follow the case."

"It doesn't matter," Victor said.

I said, "We could have a polygraph test done on the defendants."

Then I found out that in a civil case against a government body such tests are inadmissible.

The truth is the game of law is rigged when you're taking on your government.

Victor added, "If we go to court and do win in favor of the girls, then the state would appeal the verdict. In reality, it could be another five-to-seven years before this matter will be resolved."

I could not believe what I was hearing.

Victor also added that the state was losing millions each year; judges were very aware that the governor was not happy with all the losses; judges were held unaccountable, as I knew, and they could rule any way with the thought of their own reappointments over that of my family's injustice.

I remained quiet.

Victor asked me to control myself tomorrow at the arbitration, which I had waited six years for. He added, "You won, Bill. They will be forced to pay compensation to your girls."

I thought about what he said and realized he might be right. I actually did sleep well that evening.

November 15, 2012, found me back in the Morristown superior courthouse, this time with an arbitrator.

Woody and Esther Bakonyi from the Department of the Attorney General's office were present.

I was seated outside as they spoke behind a closed door for about twenty minutes in a small office near a courtroom.

The door opened, and I was asked if I wished to speak.

I said, "Yes, I would like to do so."

The arbitrator introduced himself and expressed his

condolences for my family's loss. He then went on with a short explanation of why the arbitration was necessary and he asked me a few questions, reminding me that I was under oath.

I answered truthfully, and I remember my last words: "I used to believe in my country, and I have never once asked a thing from it. The one time I sought out help from it, this was what occurred. I used to believe that the truth was important, but I no longer know what to believe anymore. All I've ever wanted was for those responsible to be held accountable and now, six years later, this is what it all comes down to."

I held back my tears and left the room.

Woody later said I did well.

I just spoke the truth.

My late father said, "Billy, always tell the truth," and so I have done to the best of my ability.

When Leslie was just a little girl, about four years old, she went through the fibbing stage. She would tell a fib, and I would ask her, "Leslie, are you telling the truth?"

She would look up to me and say, "Why, yes, Daddy."

I would repeat this question as I knew she was fibbing.

We would play this game until finally she would start to cry and admit she was fibbing.

I would send her to her room and say, "You must now sit on your bed for ten minutes without any toys." Ten minutes is an eternity to a four-year-old.

So this is my family's story. After a short twenty-minute synopsis of the events I have presented in these pages, the arbitrator said he would issue his decision no later than the next day.

The settlement was about as large as he was able to award, I believe; however, he ruled that the defendant DYFUS was only fifty percent responsible and I personally bore the other fifty percent.

My belief was that another local entity was responsible for the other fifty percent.

I will let readers decide for themselves who that may be.

For myself, I have my own thoughts.

I learned of this ruling a few days later as I flew out the following morning to my new home far away the day his decision was to be rendered.

Once an arbitrator makes a decision it is final. Both parties have thirty days to decide whether or not to appeal. For me, this time period was very difficult. My late wife had been dead more than six years and everything my daughters had had to endure was worth just twenty minutes of my government's time. There was no accountability and as far as I was concerned, no justice at all.

I had until December 15, 2012, to make a decision and I really wanted to pursue the appeal. My oldest Jenny wanted this as well. My concern was for Leslie. I really did not know if she could handle a trial and losing three or four weeks or possibly a semester from her university studies if a court date could not be set according to her school schedule next spring. I also thought about how a trial would bring back everything she'd lived through and in a public forum.

What was best?

In the end I decided that it was in both girls' best interest to accept the award. It was not now about what was best for me, but for the girls. Sandy taught me that to make someone happy is to place their needs before your own. She lived by that example and taught me this lesson.

I personally spent about $20,000 on the lawsuit. I was responsible for such charges as expert witness fees, psychological interviews by doctors for both girls, and also stenographer fees. All money awarded as fees would reduce the award to the girls by the amount I'd personally spent and would be returned to me. In the end I told the Rotolo Law firm I didn't want the monies and to let the girls have everything. For myself, this was the best $20,000 I have ever spent. My daughters to this day do not even know I did this for them.

A girl whose room was near Leslie's on her dorm floor had taken pills a number of times and wound up in the hospital twice that first semester. Just before Leslie's midterms her second semester, this tragedy occurred for the third time. The same day Leslie also learned a childhood schoolmate with whom she'd attended kindergarten through high school had also taken their own life in a suicide while away at college.

Leslie called me, hysterical in tears, and the next day I was at her university speaking with the dean again. I informed the dean that arbitration had been reached and after witnessing this situation I knew that I had made the right decision for Leslie and Jenny. Leslie was moved to another location, as she did not need to rehash the possibility of a suicide again for the second time in her young life.

I have been to New Jersey only a few times since my departure and have come to peace with myself now. If I am blessed, I may live to a ripe old age. That one is out of my hands, but all my great grandparents broke a c-note, 100, so who knows.

If I were asked whether I would do anything different today from what occurred during the summer and fall of 2006, I would have to answer yes.

The only regret I have is that after I received a call from a relative I did not take my ill wife to the Thanksgiving celebration for the family down in Sea Girt, N.J. Maybe we should have stayed home, but I left Sandy home that day and that is my sin I will carry to my grave. I have a saying that I can pick my nose and pick my friends, but I cannot pick my relatives; however, I can pick the relatives I choose to spend my time with and now do so today. By speaking with good friends, I have learned this type of choice is actually very common. Sometimes one can turn their cheeks only so often and must turn their back.

Once I realized Sandy was ill I did try to the best of my abilities to get help for both Sandy and my girls. I thank God above that

I had the financial resources to do so as so many do not, and I can go to my grave with the knowledge of what really occurred the summer and fall of 2006.

I cannot tell anyone that my late wife would have recovered from her illness as Dr. Contini said that morning she was a very ill woman and might never recover. Perhaps in the end she may have died the same way. One will never know. Sandy was never given the chance for recovery due to the actions of the public dis-servants of the state of New Jersey. I know "dis-servants" is not a real word, but I believe it should be added to the English diction-ary just as selfie has been. I will not mention who I believe fits this description, but will let the readers decide for themselves whether public servants or public dis-servants served our household in 2006. I have my own opinions.

I have tried to provide a complete picture of our lives together. I cannot explain the sequence of events or why they occurred, but have come to accept them and now believe that it was God's call-ing to take Sandy from this earth that last day of November 2006. I also believe that it is God's calling to compel me to write this manuscript so that others may benefit, and perhaps somehow our elected leaders will be compelled to take a hard look into a law passed back in the fall of 1996.

This law today is now known as "HIPAA," the Health Insurance Portability and Accountability Act. As well-intentioned as it may have been, it does not work in the cases of those suffering a mental illness. Under this act the patient has privacy rules that prohibit any communication from doctors once the person reaches adult-hood, age eighteen, without the patient's consent. That means spouses or parents, if the child becomes eighteen while living in the parents' home, are left clueless as to what the patient is being treated for, what medications have been prescribed, and what the effects of those medicines are. Since the passage of this Federal law there seems to have been a rise in the number of attacks of the public at large from those suffering from mental illnesses. Perhaps there is a correlation. My personal belief is that I am correct on this issue.

I sometimes reflect on the visit I received that evening in August 2009 with the completion of the interior of the barn. I still to this day believe that what I experienced was truly a blessing. I kept my marriage vows and can truly say that I loved, honored, cherished, and remained faithful till death did us part. Perhaps that is why from beyond I received the blessing of the "light" and I guess that is why Sandy said to me that evening, "When you join me one day you will understand, Bill."

Many years later I asked Leslie how she came to find the blue dress. The answer was that when she went into the dressing room with the two pink dresses to try on there happened to be a blue dress hanging in the dressing room all by itself. After trying on the first two dresses she asked the attendant to bring her the last one that might fit in her size. It did not fit, so she decided to just try on the blue dress that was hanging up in the dressing room by itself.

I believe it was the only one of its kind in the store that day as I never saw another while I was in Macy's waiting for Leslie. I learned this from her at Christmas break in December 2014. Some may just say it was chance or coincidence. Gordon Ward, author of a book called "Tracing Infinity," uses the term "Godincidence." I prefer to think that Gordon is correct.

For those who might have questions of the medium Gloria, who I met by an act of a Godincidence, as Gordon writes, her full name is Gloria Weichand. I believe Gloria was sent by a spirit that day, by divine intervention or by God's hand and not just as a coincidence as some may believe. Gloria is an International Spiritual Medium. She has been seen in television appearances, interviewed by Tom Brokaw on NBC Nightly News and made numerous appearances on The Rosie O'Donnell Show, where she received funds to open her own Gloria's Place of Hope House, and Oprah Winfrey's Oxygen. Gloria is the recipient of the "Woman of the Year Award" from *Glamour Magazine*; Parent of the Month by *Parents Magazine* and also been the subject of a feature article in *People* magazine. She is also the recipient of the NYU Medical Center's yearly Humanitarian Award. Gloria runs The Spiritual Education Center & Sanctuary in the Pocono Mountains region of Pennsylvania.

I made two calls to Gloria after my last conversation with her in June 2008. I called her one year to the day after our first meeting, April 28, 2009, and thanked her and said, "I think I'm going to make it by whoever's hand that day meant for us to meet. If not for that chance Godincidence, I may never have survived and I realize today that all of this was meant to be."

In the summer of 2013, my youngest daughter, while visiting the area, made a call to Gloria, who took the time to schedule Leslie for an individual session. Leslie wanted a few answers and her mom came through and gave them to her. She also received some words from her grandfather, my dad, that day. I had suggested before she left on the trip that perhaps it was time for her to reach out to her mom and Leslie decided to do so. I asked her only if it was helpful, and Leslie said yes.

My last phone call to Gloria occurred in December 2014 just prior to Leslie's arriving for her break between fall and spring semesters. I called Gloria, telling her that I had written a book and asking if I could use her full name.

She said yes.

I then learned that she had a website, which I looked at just after Leslie returned to class in January of the New Year. I'd had no idea that this woman I had met by happenstance through an appointment by my accountant Brian Corcoran in 2008 had such credentials. Hocus-Pocus is for real, at least from my point of view. If not for this chance meeting, I do not believe our family's outcome would be the same. I did not search Gloria out; somehow she was meant to find me. Don't ask me how or why. That, when I leave this world, will be answered.

Most who know me well think of me as a good man. I am

because of a lady I met one evening. Her maiden name was Sandy Fushi. She had stunning red hair and the most beautiful blue eyes I ever saw. One enchanted evening across a crowded room our eyes locked. I will be forever grateful for that chance meeting. I got to pick up my Cinderella's glass slipper.

I was a very happy man for a long time and fortunate that she chose me to spend her life with.

Some may think not so due to this world's ending.

To those, I would say, "There is another world, and from beyond I have been blessed to have been there but for a short time in the light."

I have no fears of my own mortality and for those who do the last gift that Sandy shared from beyond is the gift of the light.

To any who may read this, Sandy's gift to all of you is the gift of the light to be shared.

May God bless all.

Best Wishes,

Bill

Appendices

The Sins of ZIP Code 07976

Sometime in March 2007, my good friend Scott Noyes had called and given me news of the rumor mill of my supposed divorce, circulated by some within the local first aid squad, fire department, and police department. Apparently this gossip was real as I later found out. In the summer of that same year, an incident came to light via the mother of one of Leslie's closest friends—the girl whose mother had wanted to lease Sandy's horse Jack.

In late July or early August 2007, both my daughters, victims of their late mother's suicide, and I were the subject of the rumor mill of a small town where most of the mothers did not work and were what one might call "trophy wives."

After church one morning Gwen Claytor stopped me and said, "Bill, I need to talk with you about something that happened last night." Gwen informed me that she and her husband had been at a party and a woman who had a few too many drinks had openly made comments about myself and my late wife. Gwen told me that she interrupted this woman, stating that she knew us very well and the woman should not be speaking of this subject and that all she was saying was untrue. Gwen informed me of what this woman said.

I thanked her and said I would handle this matter myself. I did a slow burn on the drive home from church that day. I had work to take care of on the farm that day, and while I worked I continued to think about how to make this call without losing my temper.

It was Sunday evening, and I waited till after 8 p.m. to make my call. I called this home, and the mother answered. I introduced myself as the man she'd met last March as the owner of Jack, Sandy's horse, who she had wished to lease on our facility for her daughter. My guess was that she thought I was about to ask her if she wanted to lease a horse.

I informed her that I had received a call from a friend about a party that both she and her husband had attended last night. I then proceeded to inform her as well that if I ever heard another word that she had to say about my family or late wife that I would have no problem filing a lawsuit for slander. I told her a lawsuit had been filed in Superior Court naming as defendants a state agency DYFUS, the Harding Township Police Department, two hospitals, and a public defender. I also told her that if she thought I was kidding that tomorrow I would contact the Rotolo Law firm with regards to this matter and that a suit for slander would be a much simpler matter than taking on government agencies.

As she started to speak, I said I am not through and I added one more comment.

This woman's husband was a member of the New Vernon fire department and a lifelong resident of New Vernon, and his parents had lived just up the road from us off of Pleasantville Road. I added that she and her husband should be extremely sympathetic of our family's loss, as her own husband's sister had committed suicide about twenty years ago in his parents' home, and from what I knew in the same manner in which Sandy had passed. I then added, "Is there anything you now wish to tell me?"

A moment of silence passed and then she apologized for her comments the prior evening.

I said, "Thank you," and added, "Why don't you call all your friends and inform them of the fact the an attorney has been retained and spread the truth and not a falsehood and slander about my family's loss?"

Again there was a pause.

I again asked, "Do you understand what I have just said?"

She again apologized and asked for our family's forgiveness.

I accepted her apology.

My late father was an accomplished horseman as a child, and at one point in the early 1960s he decided to change careers. Dad had always loved horses and a stable became available for sale. After many years away, traveling for his job while his children were small, he purchased the West Orange Riding Club in 1961.

An attorney named Mr. Colquhoun boarded his horses at Dad's facility when the family lived in Glen Ridge. Mr. Colquhoun's young son Brian grew up and became a horse vet, and we were reintroduced many years later. Brian Colquhoun was our horse vet, selected by Sandy. He was a good man and a very good vet as well.

Brian told me I had really turned the place around. He said it was always a lovely place, full of potential, and that he was very happy to see what I had done. He would stop by twice a year for shots as necessary, and after Sandy's passing, I was always present.

On one of his visits he said, "Bill, we have known one another a long time. Your dad and mine were friends as well, and I need to tell you of some things said by the local horse people around here."

I said, "Brian, I have heard that I beat my children and late wife, that we moved here because we had no money and that I was living by necessity and not to assist with my late wife's wishes and more than just that. Many things have been said by people who've never even met me, but I decided to just shut up. My late mother always said, 'If you don't like someone, don't spend time with them or worry about them' and I live by those smart words. I really don't care to hear any more and for those who have comments, shame on them."

Later I found out that people in town were saying that Sandy had been sniffing. Years later, an old friend informed me of this one as well. Sandy's friend, who had been in St. Claire's Hospital at the same time as Sandy, had been doing so.

I didn't even know what sniffing was. Sniffing happens to be inhaling chemical fumes from cleaning products. Sandy underwent a physical and blood draws while she was in the hospital and all came back clear. She was just a woman who became mentally ill. Mental illness knows no boundaries, not race, color, nor creed. It is an illness just like that of cancer. The only difference is a social taboo associated with this illness.

The following summer of 2007, Jenny had a girlfriend named Qlane who she had met attending Madison High School. Qlane resided with her single mom in an apartment in Madison. It turned out that when Sandy and Qlane's mother had met, they'd had something in common. They'd ridden horses as young girls against each other in the 4-H circuit back in the late 60s and 70s. It was a small world, one might say, and they'd met again after their daughters had become friends in high school.

One day Jenny asked me if it would be all right if Qlane came over and rode with her.

I said, "Sure, and ask her mom if, afterwards when you are through riding, they would both care to join us out back on the deck overlooking the place for dinner since she will have to pick her up anyway."

The day arrived for the trail ride. The girls got on the horses, and Qlane's mother Diana decided to stay for the afternoon. It was a nice summer day, not too hot, humidity was low and who would not care to spend an afternoon on a nice small horse facility?

Diana worked for a doctor's office in West Orange. It was an OB-GYN facility.

We got to talking and I gave her a brief overview of what had occurred.

She said she was very sorry for us and that if we needed any help I should feel free to call.

I said, "Thank you," but I knew I would not do so as she was also a single parent and time is so precious as a single parent.

Diana said that Sandy had told her that we had money problems.

I said, "Diana, I can come up with seven digits within three business days if necessary by liquidating stocks and other investments I have.

Diana gave me a puzzled look and my guess was that she did not understand what I had said, so I said, "Six digits starts at $100,000, and if you wish, I can go downstairs and get the files as I have all paper records of my bank accounts and securities positions in binders by account."

Her mouth dropped.

I added that I cut my grass myself and did the work on the property because I enjoyed it, not because I could not write a check for it. I also told her that people within the town who did not even know me said the same thing about a man they had never met. I explained that I worked in finance, understood financial markets, had a degree in economics, and had spent my first twenty-plus years on Wall St. in the U.S. government primary dealers bond markets.

The girls finished their trail ride that afternoon, and we all had a nice dinner out back that evening.

I could go on all day long about who and what, but what I came to find out about this gossip over the course of a few years was that Scott Noyes was correct during our initial phone call back in March 2007. There were many, especially a nearby couple I will just refer to as "the Olds." Apparently Mrs. Old had many things to say. I have not named anyone by name, and unfortunately, I wish we could just call this fiction, however; unfortunately, I cannot.

Public Servants?

There was a time, long ago when I was a child growing up in America, when good men and women took jobs in the public sector and truly cared for their employers, the taxpayers. I cannot say when the perception changed. My guess is sometime in the late 1990s, but there certainly has been a change. It seems that today in America the public servants are the taxpayer in the private workforce, men and women who can lose their jobs due to technological innovation, demographic shifts or other market forces a new modern twenty-first century economy can bring in the private sector. Meanwhile their counterparts in the public sector have no idea nor clue of these same market forces today.

Here are some numbers from the USDEBTCLOCK.org from September 2014:

U.S. population: 319 million

U.S. workforce: 146 million

U.S. income tax payers: 117 million

U.S. self-employed: 8 million

U.S. federal workforce: 4 million

U.S. state and local workforce: 20 million

If there are 146 million people in the workforce and only 117 million paying taxes, that means 29 million are the working poor whose taxes are returned in a refund after they file a Federal tax return. If 117 million people are paying taxes and 24 million work in the public sector, then 93 million, a ratio of 4 to 1, is supporting the public workforce in America today.

Some may want to include the tax-paying public employees. I do not include these workers, and the ratio will then move to about 5 to 1.

For most Americans today, distrust of the U.S. House of Representatives and U.S. Senate is at an all-time high. Both legislative bodies enjoy a fifteen percent approval rating. Perhaps it may move up some, but one gets the point. The consensus is that both parties are to blame, and I agree. I will not side with one party over another party as neither represents my beliefs. My guess is that one could call me a Constitutionalist or Libertarian.

In 2009 I decided to start dating a bit. As I had very little time and did not hang out in bars, this desire left the Internet as a new choice. I did get out some and was selective. One woman I meet for dinner one evening tipped me off as to why we no longer have faith in our elected supposed representatives in Washington.

This woman's name was Debbie. She resided up in Bergen County, the next county north of Morris. We met at a nice steak house up in her neck of the woods. She was an attorney by trade; however, she had left the law profession. She told me she was currently traveling back and forth to Washington, D.C., and that her new career path was as a paid professional lobbyist.

I asked her who she represented and her reply was whatever group was willing to pay her.

I did not want to give my opinions, but I thought it would be interesting to hear her point of view about how Washington, D.C., works.

It turned out that her ex took care of their son during the week while she was away, and she had her son most weekends. She seemed pleasant and was attractive; however, later in the evening she said something that got to me.

We all hear how it works in D.C., how our Congress is bought and sold, but to hear it first hand from someone on the inside was another thing. We started to talk about a piece of legislation that was due to come to a vote in a few weeks. I do not remember the bill, but I recall that most polls in America said the voting base was not in favor of passage of this particular bill.

I said, "Debbie, look, this thing is dead on arrival. Nobody wants this passed from what I can see."

Debbie said, "It's already passed."

I answered, "It's three weeks away and the voters don't want it."

Debbie said, "We already bought enough votes. It will pass."

I thanked her for the pleasant or—how shall I say?—informative evening about how our so-called elected elite in D.C. operate.

Sure enough, the bill passed a few weeks later just as Debbie had said it would.

I did not go out with this gal again as my thoughts were of that wonderful law HIPAA, which also passed this same Congress. I thought of the burden this law put upon my household.

I understood that she was just doing her job.

Perhaps one day our elected leaders will be required to read the laws that they pass. Most of the time bills pass both houses with only ten to fifteen elected leaders seated within the chambers. If our laws required a quorum with at least two-thirds present in person when a vote was to be taken, something might actually get done for the betterment of our nation. But alas, that it just naïve wishful thinking. It would also be a good idea if our so-called leaders were subject to the very laws that are passed, as are the masses, but the elected leaders sometimes exempt themselves.

If anyone believes I am wrong about this matter, just go to YouTube and search out what the former Speaker of the House said prior to passage of the largest legislative bill ever passed. Nancy Pelosi said, "We had to pass the bill so you can find out what's in it."

My guess is that now that it has passed we are finding out what's in it.

One item in it is a special tax for those working in what I call "the real world." Those with what our elected officials call a "Cadillac health plan" will be subject to a tax as if they were receiving income. How it is that all the public employees within the United States, most of whom pay nothing toward their own health care, are not subject to the same? Most public employees have the most generous health care in the country. They don't have a Cadillac plan, but rather a red Ferrari plan.

It is estimated that today in Washington, D.C., approximately eighty-five percent of an elected official's time is spent raising money for Political Action Committees (PACs). Today they can have two PACs, one for their reelection and another to play with.

In the times of Rome, the Roman Senate utilized a system called "tribute" in which votes were bought and sold to the highest bidder. Today Washington has taken to its finest art form, perfecting the game legally by the legislation passed within its own walls to protect itself.

Both parties are to blame. Power corrupts, and one only need look no farther than to Democratic former Gov. Rod Blagojevich of Illinois, Republican former Gov. Bob McDonnell of Virginia, or the latest Republican former Gov. John Rowland of Connecticut. The corruption starts at local levels, but has been perfected to its current status by the masters of the universe in Washington, D.C. if anyone disagrees, I have a bridge in Brooklyn that I own personally for sale.

Here are some statistics from my former home state New Jersey, or as I prefer to call it today "Sue Lousy." Sandy and I had discussed what we saw as a state in transition by the late 1990s. What we saw has now come to pass and we did not like what was coming. In 2010 The Star-Ledger published an article about the current state of affairs within the state and how the current Gov. Chris Christie was trying to bring some change within the state.

The article said in the decade that ended December 31, 2009, the state had continued to lose jobs. There were many reasons why; however, the most alarming was the fact that during this decade the private workforce had shrunk by 250,000 jobs. The only reason that New Jersey had positive job growth was the public work force had increased by 260,000 jobs, for a total of net job growth of 10,000 jobs from 2000 to 2010.

At the time of the article there were approximately 3.2 million jobs within the state. Almost 600,000 were in the public workforce covered by an underfunded pension, short about $45 billion, and its health care plan with another $57 billion shortfall. The governor was trying to pass legislation to stem the red ink within the pension system, including a small percentage contribution from those currently working towards their own pension. Today the shortfall and impasse is still present and growing.

The article also stated that while Gov. Jon Corzine was in office, $90 billion of net wealth fled the state for greener pastures. That trend continues to this day. The real problem today is the fact that only in the public workforce do people expect to retire with almost or close to their peak earnings for the remainder of their lives. In the private workforce this benefit is not available.

I voted for Chris Christie in 2009 and believe he truly cares about his state, but the public employees now number about 540,000 and current retirees collecting a pension number about 475,000, supported by approximately 2.6 million private job holders. If 540,000 plus 475,000 equals 1,015,000 and just half are currently married, then 1,522,500 votes are stacked against this man, who won the state a second time.

Guess what, public servants? The jig is up. Those in the private workforce no longer care for those who are over-paid, doing the same position for one-and-a-half times the current wages in the real world.

I will say no more.

These numbers are public, and the state currently spends fourteen percent of all revenue toward its pension system, about four times the national average. An article, "Pensions that ate Jersey," appeared in *New York Post* June 1, 2014. The Star-Ledger ran an article September 26, 2004, in which I read that the shortfall had now reached $90 billion. This was a doubling in just four years. There will be a day of reckoning for the public employees of New Jersey covered by an underfunded pension system. It's not if, but when.

Numbers don't lie. People do. Math is a pure science, and because of these numbers there is less for roads, bridges, and other necessary expenditures that the state needs. Perhaps a few less in the public workforce is necessary.

All of my good friends who have lived there feel the same and are now leaving the state with the highest cost of living in the nation. When you lose the affluent, the jobs go with them. This is being played out throughout the Midwest and Northeast and those leaving are heading toward more favorable climates and business-friendly states.

I could write more, but why?

I no longer reside there.

It appears that the only time that a government employee is fired or leaves a post prematurely within the confines of the public workforce is when a witch hunt arrives from the opposite party of the said witch's party and blood is in the air.

I will cite two recent examples, both occurring in New Jersey within the last ten years:

The most recent involves the current Gov. Chris Christie and the Bridgegate fallout. Bridget Ann Kelly, a governor's aide, was found at fault and fired from her position as deputy chief of staff by Gov. Christie, and rightly so. She will probably disappear and at some point resurface as a lobbyist within the state.

The other would be the former Gov. of New Jersey, none other than Jim McGreevey. This man's sin was not that he is gay. Who cares today? His real sin was the fact that he hired his male lover or prostitute to be the state's homeland czar to protect the citizens of New Jersey from terrorists, a post created out of thin air after the

September 11, 2001, attacks. The salary paid to Golan Cipen was $110,000 for performing services for the governor and the taxpayers. This amount is the exact salary that McGreevey receives today as director of employment for Jersey City.

I'm sure that both of these former state employees are entitled to a pension under the laws of New Jersey. Too bad McGreevey is not asked to pay his employers back for "services," the salary paid Cipen. As such he should be required to make restitution as my old former co-worker Brian Anderson, who stole from his clients as well and served jail time to boot. Anderson lost everything from what I understand, including his pension after he stole, and the firm had to make restitution for the remainder of losses incurred. When it comes to the public domain, it becomes the taxpayer's burden. So much for justice in America.

In Washington, a one-term Congressman upon losing his or her seat can find work as a lobbyist. It is estimated that lobbyist's starting salaries begin at about $1 million. These guys and gals know the ropes and how the game is played. Is it any wonder that during the Great Recession, the country experienced housing declines and the only areas not to do so were the high-net worth suburban areas surrounding Washington, D.C.? Why was that?

In the 2012 Presidential election and final debate, a closing speech was given by both candidates. Mitt Romney spoke first and President Obama finished. Obama went right to his political base, the public employees making up 24 million strong. He pointed his finger at the audience, as he loves to do, and said, "We need to hire more teachers, firemen and police."

I totally whole-heartedly agreed with the President.

Unfortunately, he forgot to add that we must have the ability to dismiss the incompetent before we are able to replace them. Please do not take this point the wrong way. There are many fine public employees today working for the public good. If you talk with them, they will roll their eyes about some within their ranks. Most of us in the real world get it, and these people have no clue.

It does not matter if a public servant is in the upper echelon in Washington, D.C., such as the recent matter surrounding none other than Lois Lerner, head of the Internal Revenue Service. On March 5, 2014, Lois Lerner, while under testimony to the House, invoked her right to none other than the Fifth Amendment privilege against self-incrimination. Months later her e-mails apparently disappeared.

My guess is that Lois Lerner has a bridge in Brooklyn for sale as well. The simplest way to uncover the truth about the IRS denying Tea Party groups' tax-exempt status is to place the agents responsible, who denied the tax-exempt in the first place, on an unpaid leave of absence. Then explain to those agents that if they were responsible, they will be fired and lose any pension built permanently. However, if they were instructed to do so by a superior and were to provide the proof, they may return to their job and benefits earned. One could continue up the chain of command and eventually the truth would be found. It is basically the same way police departments get to the drug kingpin. They start at the bottom and work their way up.

The reason this process does not occur is that both parties, Democrat and Republican alike, like the system just as it is. It does not matter whether one is looking at the local, state, or federal level. The only time there is a firing today is, as I stated earlier, when a political witch hunt occurs.

A Court Hearing

I will now write of the facts that were uncovered once the Rotolo Law firm got involved. These facts start with Sandy's hearing, which I was told I could not attend as Sandy did not want me present. It turned out that her hearing took place late that afternoon with Judge Robert Brennan presiding. Apparently Sandy requested an attorney to be present to represent her. She had the right to a public defender and requested it. She was not stupid, just sick with an unknown mental illness.

Based on the transcripts which the Rotolo Law firm provided to me in 2008, here is what transpired in about five minutes: The doctors present stated that the patient (Sandy) was in complete denial of her mental health problems as all are when placed involuntary to the psych ward of the hospital. The doctors then laid out before the court police reports and the initial contact reports from the DYFUS representative Nick Mangold. These reports had the incidents that lead up to Sandy's confinement to St. Clair's hospital, including jumping from a car and Sandy's youngest daughter telling DYFUS that she awoke with her mother holding a fourteen-inch carving knife just inches from her mattress where she'd been asleep on the floor that one Monday morning.

Not all of the events were listed in the police reports from that day, but they were somewhat accurate with the exception of one fact: the reports indicate that the police asked Sandy questions about my behavior, such as whether I'd hurt her, when it was I who'd made the call asking for help. Sandy's public defender, who I will not name as to protect her family as another set of victims of a suicide, argued that none of the information could be used as there were no witness present to validate police reports or documents from DYFUS.

In their discharge summary, the hospital workers at St. Clair's stated, "We feel the patient continued to represent a danger to herself and to others and that commitment should be continued. The court felt otherwise after her court hearing, ordering her to be released within 48 hours."

Judge Brennan ruled that the police and DYFUS documents were to be considered inadmissible evidence in his court of law. Sandy's public defender cited these reports as hearsay and Judge Brennen supported this view in his court. These conclusions are from the court transcripts of that hearing the Friday before Labor Day weekend in 2006.

I really cannot understand how this man was allowed the power to let a suicidal woman, according to hospital records, with children back into her home after she was been found to be sleeping inches away from her twelve-year-old daughter with a fourteen-inch carving knife as Leslie had reported to a DYFUS representative. If this is justice, my hope is that one day one of Judge Brennan's peers bestows the same fate and his family becomes a victim of a mentally incompetent person.

My guess is that Sandy's entire hearing lasted about five minutes, and this man overruled competent professionals learned in a chosen field with degrees. My guess is also that our story is repeated time and again, as all one has to do is read the news with regards to all the school shootings across the country. The most recent of these incidents just occurred in Santa Barbara, California. This time around six students died, three by gunshot and three by knife wounds. The common theme of all of these tragic deaths of innocent victims continues to be mental health. I wonder in all of these cases whether the courts took the recommendations of doctors seriously. In the case of the Virginia Tech shootings, the judge did not.

For the life of me I cannot understand how a judge is allowed to overrule doctors' recommendations; however, this is the way things are done in America today. Anyone with common sense would have ruled otherwise. Judge Brennan, according to Sandy's discharge summary, jokingly stated, "If this were a book it would be published" and also made statements that while in the hospital Sandy wondered if she was in a reality show.

Judge Brennan, I want the world to know of your decision that day. Hopefully you will take that decision with you to your grave! I am very thankful that I decided that day in September 2007, after our request to obtain DYFUS records, that I let go of the door handle to your courtroom. I have never seen you nor wish to ever in the future as well. It is said, Judge Brennan, that the pen is mightier than the sword. I have chosen my pen instead of my sword to slay this dragon from my past.

I have added to this short chapter the discharge summary from St. Claire's hospital and have highlighted a few words. My true hope, Judge Brennan, is that one day an amendment could be added to our existing HIPAA laws. Under that change I would urge that when children are present in a household and professional doctors with degrees from universities recommend that a patient that is considered a threat to themselves and the public that these recommendations are final. My name for such a law would be "SAD-Brennan" in memory of my late wife Sandra Ann Dunn.

PATIENT NAME: DUNN, SANDRA	**ADMISSION DATE:**	08/18/2006
MR#: 2381783	**DISCHARGE DATE:**	09/03/2006
ATTENDING MD: Michael H. Bell, MD	**PT ACCOUNT#:**	6913552

HISTORY OF PRESENT ILLNESS: This is a 47-year-old, white female who was originally brought to the hospital by the police after her husband had called the Psychiatric Emergency Services hotline because she was becoming increasingly delusional and paranoid. The police reportedly had to remove two pocket knives, a screwdriver, and a skewer, and she was reportedly holding them in an offensive nature. Over the past two weeks prior to admission, the admitting psychiatrist noted increasing sleep difficulty, bizarre behavior, at times sleeping in front of her daughters doors. She also was holding a steak knife when she was sleeping there. About a week prior to admission, she reportedly saw a plane fly over the house and she believed that it was going to land on her house and take her away. About two weeks ago, she was reported to have jumped out of the family car which was going at about 25 miles per hour. Her family had to coach her for three hours to get her back into the car. She also reportedly stated that she was going to die and was not leaving the house for the past two days prior to admission.

FAMILY HISTORY: She was adopted. Her father died in 1986. Her mother died in 2003.

SOCIAL HISTORY: She reportedly was an average student in school. She went to college for four years and then worked for an ad agency. She has two daughters.

She was described on admission as being a petite, blond female. She appeared her stated age. She was cooperative. She was circumstantial in her thinking. She had minimal insight regarding her behavior. She minimized her delusional thoughts. She stated that it was just a joke. She did not explain why she was carrying a knife and sleeping outside of her daughter's bedroom. She justified carrying the screwdriver, stating it was the only way she could open her daughter's bedroom door. She denied hallucinations. There was report from the Psychiatric Emergency Services that she might have been responding to internal stimuli. Insight and judgment were impaired.

Initial impression was psychotic disorder, NOS, and the admitting psychiatrist noted thoughts of starting the patient on Geodon.

HOSPITAL COURSE: Early on she continued to have very poor insight and judgment. I saw the patient for the first time on August 21, 2006. She was refusing to take her Geodon but finally took her first dose the night before. She was not complaining of any side effects from the medication. She continued to laugh inappropriately and made statements like she wondered if this was a reality show that was going on in the hospital at the present time. She also jokingly stated that if this was a book that it would be published, referring to her chart where all the details were available. She was somewhat paranoid. She admitted to having problems with her job prior to coming in and tapered down problems with her husband who she claimed had a history of drinking, etcetera. She was denying suicidal or homicidal ideation. The plan was to continue the patient on the Geodon. Geodon was increased and the patient was complaining of some fatigue. She tended to be quite paranoid, anxious, and obsessive. She had difficulty signing the release of information forms so that we could talk with her husband. In fact, she refused to do it for so long that finally the husband had left with her daughters for the Labor Day holiday. Still the patient was resistant to signing release of information. This type of paranoid continued throughout her stay. The patient also knew one of the other female patients from the outside and both of them were quite similar in their paranoia and suspiciousness of medications, and people's motives. The patient finally gave verbal consent for the clinician to contact her husband who, as we noted, was

continued...

DISCHARGE SUMMARY

atient: DUNN, SANDRA
MR #: 002381783

continued...

away in the North Carolina area on Labor Day vacation. There was consideration given to adding an antidepressant. The patient was denying suicidal ideation. The patient ultimately was started on the Prozac. The patient appeared to have difficulty adjusting to change and other problems.

We felt that the patient continued to represent a danger to herself and others, and that commitment should be continued. The Court felt otherwise after her court hearing, ordering her to be released within 48 hours. Her husband had come to visit her that day but it was a very tumultuous meeting according to the clinician and the husband had left. She did not want him to come into court. She was concerned about what he might say. We spoke to her about the possibility of going to our CARES Program, a supervised short-term residential program, before going home but she refused that. DYFS had become involved because of her behavior at home including breaking the doors to get into her daughter's rooms and that they did not want her to be at home alone with her children, and this was made clear to her prior to her discharge as ordered by the Courts.

DISCHARGE MEDICATIONS: At the time of discharge, her Prozac was 20 mg a day and Geodon 60 mg 2 capsules at bedtime for a total of 120 mg.

FOLLOW UP INSTRUCTIONS: Follow-up was to be at the Morristown Memorial Hospital Partial Hospital Program.

DISCHARGE DIAGNOSES: AXIS I: 1.   Psychotic disorder, not otherwise specified.
                                    2.   Rule out major depression with psychotic features.
                          AXIS II: Deferred.
                          AXIS III: Clear.
                          AXIS IV: Support system problems.
                          AXIS V: 15, 50.

DISPOSITION: The patient was discharged on September 3, 2006, by the psychiatrist covering for the weekend as ordered by the judge who had ordered the release to take place within 48 hours of the court hearing.

_____
Michael H. Bell, MD

CC:
DD: 10/17/2006
DT: 10/18/2006

NJPR MTS MHB/jf
JOB #: 500165

DISCHARGE SUMMARY

DYFUS, a State Agency: Destruction of Youth and a Family Thank You for the Service

In September 2007 the Rotolo Law firm got a court order requiring DYFUS to turn over all documents relating to the possible case. It took this agency many months to comply with this order. Finally, the agency did provide copies of all handwritten notes by the first field agents who had visited the house. Later, transcripts were obtained of typewritten reports by none other than Eremene Remy. I have included some of her reports at the end of this chapter. All reports were signed and dated November 29, 2006, just one day before my late wife took her life. It seems a bit odd to me that one the day before Sandy's death, Remy was able to spend hours writing reports. Her October 18, 2006, report that she reached out and called is correct; however, I called back a number of times, left messages on her voicemail and never received any calls back. The Rotolo Law firm had to subpoena all phone records and was allowed to get them only from my cell phone or home to this agent.

Remy's November 8, 2006, report states that the police reported that "dad calls to get an edge on his divorce."

Apparently when Mr. Lynch showed up to visit for ten minutes after I had called out of desperation, Remy's manager sent this man over that day, which originally I believed happened the following week. In Mr. Lynch's notes, the Harding Township police department stated that Mrs. Dunn was fine and that she and I were filing for divorce.

I never said a thing to the police department about a divorce. I did say to Lt. Mead that morning that I did not understand why he could not help our family, that it was his department that got Sandy into the nut house, that I had recently been informed that she may be suicidal and that Lt. Mead had said there was nothing they could do.

My response at the time was "What am I to do now? Wait till she hangs herself?"

Four weeks later to the day those spoken words came true.

Remy's November 8, 2006, report says that she spoke with Mr. Dunn and I supposedly wanted to file for a divorce. I said no such statement. I had seen an attorney previously and been advised to ask the judge for help. Judge Brennen denied seeing me. I never was seeking a divorce from my late wife. All I was trying to do was get medical help for her, and I never informed Remy of any such meeting regarding an attorney. I also never advised anyone in the Harding Police Department of those words as my last visit to the police department took place November 2, 2006. I had not seen an attorney then either, as it was not until the second meeting after I left the Harding Township police Department and then went back to see Rosanne Misclone on November 2, 2006, that I was told, "You may need to see an attorney." The Harding Township police were not contacted again until later when my young daughter found her mother November 30, 2006. All of this information is from the typed reports, which were signed off November 29, 2006.

Shortly after the New Year, January 11, 2007, two days after Remy and her supervisor appeared unannounced in our driveway, the following was signed off on from her phone call to me trying to confirm her appointment for December 4, 2006. "Worker asked how did that happen and He (I) stated that she overdosed herself with medication. All of the information has been reported to supervisor and caseworker supervisor." I never said such a thing and when I received this call I said, "She's dead. Don't bother coming," and hung up on Remy. My daughters were in the car with me at the time as we were almost at the Hanover florist to locate flowers for Sandy's service, and I felt it would be too much from me to say more over the phone with the girls present just four days after their mother's passing.

I received a few other calls after that, but when I recognized who was calling, Remy, I just would not answer nor did I return any of her calls. I felt why should I? This agency went on to its other business at hand of whatever it does and had absolutely no care nor any reason to think that its actions would become accountable, like most public servants in my former state.

When employees of this agency were deposed for questioning by E. Carr "Woody" Cornog, III, Esq. many years later, the term I have used to describe investment clients who tell an advisor one thing and a few months later seem to not remember what was discussed, "selective memory loss," came into play.

Esther E. Bakonyi was the D. A.G. representative on this case supporting the state DYFUS defendants. During questioning, every time Woody asked a question of the defendants, Bakonyi would object. Not once in a while, but on every question. The standard answer given by the defendants was "I don't remember. It was a long time ago."

Remy was asked, "What happened to all the field notes?" and she said, "They have been shredded."

To which Woody asked, "Is it standard to shred documents when a lawsuit is filed in a case?"

Bakonyi objected on this matter as well.

Remy replied that it was standard policy as she thought it was.

Fortunately, the Rotolo Law firm had all such copies of documents, which would at a later point in time come forward in a trial, if we were someday to pass summary judgment, which currently was in Judge Brennan's hands, of all people.

The Rotolo Law firm informed me as everything came to light and also provided me with copies of all documents they received regarding the case.

The field agents did not even show up for a scheduled recorded disposition date. They never even bothered to advise Woody that they would not be present. If an individual had done that for a court-appointed hearing or deposition, a warrant would have been issued for that person's arrest.

I remember Woody telling me, "We have them. They have cut and pasted some records and when the time comes it will not look so good for this government agency."

Falsehoods, slanders, and outright lies were written by this agency, perhaps to try to cover up any misdeeds or cover their asses. If the members of this agency had done their job, they would have known that it was impossible for Sandy to overdose on her medications, as she had none. If Sandy had not been to outpatient therapy in almost six weeks and her prescriptions were only refilled in two-week intervals, how could she possibly overdose on meds?

The day Remy arrived, November 13, 2006, I gave her a copy of a letter dated November 6, 2006, from Rosanna Miscione, Sandy's clinical worker at Morristown Memorial Hospital, stating that Sandy had not been going to her therapy. This agent for DYFUS just needed to get a copy of the police report or autopsy to know the cause of her death. My guess is she was just too lazy to even do that while trying to cover her tracks.

Apparently Mr. Lynch did call the Harding Township Police Department before his arrival at the house that day. He did not call me, however, until the following week. I cannot say who he spoke to by phone that day at the police department as his field notes do not indicate who he talked with or who said I was trying "to get an edge" on my supposed divorce, a falsehood.

I also cannot say from the police report which police officers told Mr. Lynch that "dad calls the police to get an edge on his divorce."

Apparently when Mr. Lynch arrived, he had police present at our home, but according to the report filed that day, the two officers are listed as Earl Hyde and David Achenbach. Perhaps someone should ask them who told this state agency that I was filing for divorce. I have attached the three police reports and included the first report from the day Sandy was involuntary taken from her home.

The report from the first day shows that her behavior did a one-hundred-and-eighty degree turnaround once a car arrived with a license plate that read "State Government" on it.

She was not stupid just ill.

Of the two visits that I made speaking with Chief Gaffney regarding our household, no report exists. I do not know why, but would deflect that one to him as he is now retired and collecting a rather large pension.

On November 2, 2006, I went to see Roseanne Misclone prior to Sandy's joint session with myself earlier. Roseanne then instructed me to go to the Harding Township Police Department, which I did only to ask for help and be turned away. I returned home to pick up my wife, she refused to attend her session, so I went alone at 10 a.m. and was told by Roseanne to go home and get Sandy and that if she refused, to call the police a second time.

Sandy stated she needed to go somewhere else and that was when I blocked the driveway and called the police department once again as instructed to do. Police arrived and said again there was nothing they could do. I then headed back to the hospital, met with Roseanne and told her the police would not assist as she'd told me they must and asked her, "What am I to do now?"

Roseanne then said, "I think you need to call an attorney."

I headed off to work, called Remy's supervisor, then located an attorney locally and was to meet with him Monday, November 6, 2006. That was followed up with my trying to visit all day with Judge Robert Brennan Tuesday, November 7, 2006.

For the life of me I have no idea who, or more importantly

why, someone within the Harding Township Police Department informed an employee of DYFUS that Sandy was fine and I was trying to get the upper hand in my supposed divorce. I guess that question should be directed to retired Chief Kevin Gaffney or one of his subordinates.

I made a total of four visits to the police department. For two of those visits no report exists. Both of those visits were with Chief Kevin Gaffney, one in September to notify him of the removal of my guns from our home and the second was on October 31, 2006. My third visit was November 2, 6006, and my last was November 7, 2006, when I was trying to obtain copies of the reports. I have attached three police reports and have not included the report of the day of Sandy's death.

HEALTH

Rosanna Miscione, MSW, LCSW
ABH - IOP
T: 973 971-4773
F: 973 290-7614fax
email

Atlantic Rehabilitation Institute
P.O. Box 1978
95 Mount Kemble Avenue
Morristown, NJ 07962-1978

Morristown
Memorial
Hospital

◢

Overlook
Hospital

◢

Goryeb
Children's
Hospital

◢

Carol G. Simon
Cancer Center

◢

Gagnon Heart
Hospital

◢

Atlantic
Neuroscience
Institute

◢

Mountainside
Hospital

November 6, 2006

Ms. Sandra Dunn
24 Miller Road
New Vernon, NJ 07976

Dear Sandi,

I hope this letter finds you and your family doing well.

This letter is to confirm that you have not attended IOP since October 27, 2006 and you did not attend the couple's session scheduled for October 31, 2006. It is difficult to provide you with appropriate services under these circumstances. If you do not contact us within ten days of this letter, it will be assumed that you are not interested in services at this time.

Take good care of yourself.

Very truly yours,

Rosanna D Miscione, MSW LCSW

Rosanna D. Miscione, MSW, LCSW
ABH-IOP Social Worker

RDM/ck

DYFS 26-52 (Rev. 08/2002)

CONTACT SHEET

Case Name : Dunn				Case Number : KC388531
MVR	MVR by External Agency	Date of Contact	Date of Entry	Type of Contact (Phone, in Person, Written) / Place (Office, Home, etc.)
☐	☐	11/08/2006	11/08/2006	In person DYFS Office

Participants (Name, Relationship)

Supervisor updated Uremene Remy on the status of the case. Mr. Dunn had called to report that mom was not going to therapy and needed to be stabilized on her medication. Supervisor had John Lynch go out to the home on Thursday November 2, 2006. He reported that he had contacted the police also. Mr. Lynch reported that mom was not in need of mobile crisis. The police was there and did not think mom needed to be assessed. The police reported that dad calls the police to get a edge on his divorce. The children are not being left alone with mom. Mr. Lynch went over the case plan with mom. Ms. Remy is to follow up with dad and also contact mom's therapist and psychiatrist for updates. Worker to reconference with supervisor.

Supervisor's Initials : _____ | Date:_____

Participants (Name, Relationship)

Worker reached out to Mr. Dunn regarding the schedule appointment which was scheduled for 12/4/06. Worker spoke with Mr. Dunn and WOrker noticed that Mr. Dunn voice was very low. WOrker then asked if he was ok and he reported that Sandra Dunn committed Suicide over the weekend and he was in the process of making funeral arrangement. WOrker asked how did that happen and he stated that she overdose herself with medication. All of the information has been reported to supervisor and caseworker supervisor.

Case Manager's Signature : _____ | Date: 1/11/07

Supervisor's Initials : ___DL___ | Date: 1/11/07

HARDING TWP POLICE DEPARTMENT
21 Blue Mill Rd, Harding Township, NJ 07976
(973) 455-0500

INITIAL GENERAL COMPLAINT REPORT

Case Number: 2006-010144   **GC Type:** ASSIST - ALL OTHERS   **Date/Time:** 8/18/2006 15:57
Dispatch Location: 24 MILLER RD   **Call Status:** CLOSED   **Created by:** Daniel Irons

Officer(s) Dispatched	Dispatched Time	Assigned Time	Arrival Time	Cleared Time
MICHAEL GROMEK	8/18/2006 15:57	8/18/2006 15:57	8/18/2006 15:59	8/18/2006 19:44
DANIEL IRONS	8/18/2006 15:57	8/18/2006 15:57	8/18/2006 15:59	8/18/2006 19:00

Caller Name	Address	Phone Number
ST. CLAIRE'S HOSPITAL	25 POCONO ROAD, DENVILLE, NJ	973-625-6150

Assisting Agencies

New Vernon First Aid Squad

PARTIES INVOLVED INFORMATION

Type	Name	Address	Home Phone
VICTIM	SANDRA DUNN	24 MILLER ROAD, HARDING TWP, NJ, 07976	973-966-6155
COMPLAINANT	ST. CLAIRE'S HOSPITAL	25 POCONO ROAD, DENVILLE, NJ, 07834	973-625-6150

INITIAL NARRATIVE

IN THE AFTERNOON HOURS OF AUGUST 18TH, 2006 AT APPROXIMATLEY 1557 HOURS, WE WERE DISPATCHED BY ST. CLAIRE'S HOSPITAL TO 24 MILLER ROAD. OUR OBJECTIVE FOR THIS CALL WAS TO TRY AND RESOLVE THE SITUATION IN AN ORDERLY FASHION BY TRYING TO CONVINCE SANDRA DUNN TO ADMIT HERSELF INTO A HOSPITAL, TO BE EVALUATED BY A MENTAL HEALTH PROFESSIONAL. WHEN WE ARRIVED, IT WAS CLEAR TO US THAT SANDRA DUNN WAS IN THE SAME STATE OF MIND AS WHEN WE LEFT HER EARLIER IN THE DAY. SANDRA APPEARED TO BE DISORIENTED AND PREOCCUPIED. ONCE AGAIN, WE TRIED TO REASON WITH HER REGARDING GETTING HELP AT A HOSPITAL. SANDRA BELIEVED WE WERE "SENDING HER TO BEIRUT". SANDRA STRESSED TO US THAT SHE DID NOT WANT TO GO "OVERSEAS" AND WAS "AFRAID". WHILE ATTEMPTING TO CALM SANDRA, IT TOOK US AT LEAST 30-45 MINUTES TO GET SANDRA TO SIT DOWN. SANDRA WAS NOT COMPLIANT WITH ANY OF THE ORDERS WE WERE GIVING HER IN TRYING TO PREVENT THE SITUATION FROM BECOMING PHYSICAL. WHILE ON THE BACK STEPS TO THE SECOND FLOOR DECK, SANDRA REMOVED A SMALL SHARP POINTED METAL OBJECT FROM HER RIGHT FRONT POCKET OR PURSE AND BEGAN TO MOVE TOWARD SGT. IRONS AND WILLIAM DUNN, HER HUSBAND. AT THIS POINT I WAS BEHIND SANDRA AND GRABBED HER WRIST UNTIL THE METAL OBJECT WAS REMOVED FROM HER HAND. AFTER THIS, A SMALL POCKET KNIFE AND SCREWDRIVER WERE TAKEN AWAY FROM SANDRA. IT WAS OBVIOUS THAT SANDRA WAS NOT GOING TO ADMIT HERSELF TO A MEDICAL INSTITUTION FOR AN EVALUATION. SANDRA APPEARED PREOCCUPIED AND DISTRACTED THE ENTIRE TIME WE WERE TRYING TO GET HER TO CALM DOWN. SHE APPEARED PARANOID. SANDRA COULD NOT REMEMBER WHAT HAS HAPPENED FROM MINUTE TO MINUTE, REPEATING HERSELF FREQUENTLY AND FORGETTING WHO SHE WAS TALKING TO. SANDRA AGREED THAT SHE NEEDED HELP BUT DID NOT WANT TO GO TO THE HOSPITAL TO RECEIVE TREATMENT. CINDY DUNN AS WELL AS WILLIAM DUNN, STATED THAT SANDRA HAD BEEN ACTING "WEIRD" AND "CRAZY" FOR ABOUT SIX MONTHS. REFERENCES WERE MADE TO SANDRA SLEEPING WITH A STEAK KNIFE AND ATTEMPTING TO JUMP OUT OF MOVING VEHICLES IN THE RECENT PAST. JENNIFER AND LESLIE BOTH AGREED WITH CINDY AND WITNESSED THE EVENTS. AS I WAS WAITING WITH ANDRA NEAR THE GARAGE, A SILVER VEHICLE PULLED UP IN THE DUNN DRIVEWAY. SANDRA WALKED OVER TO SEE WHO IT WAS. WHEN SHE SAW THE LICENSE PLATE ON THE VEHICLE, SHE SAID "STATE GOVERNMENT". FROM THIS POINT ON IT WAS AS IF I WAS TALKING WITH A TOTALLY DIFFERENT WOMAN. SANDRA IMMEDIATLY CALMED DOWN AND SAT IN A CHAIR ON THE REAR DECK. ALL OF THE PLEADING TO SEE HER HUSBAND, CRYING AND INATTENTIVENESS CEASED. SANDRA APPEARED TO BE A TOTALLY DIFFERENT PERSON. DUE TO THE FACT THAT THE NEW JERSEY DIVISION OF YOUTH AND FAMILY SERVICES HAD TO BE CONTACTED BECAUSE OF THE PRESENCE OF A CHILD DURING THE FIRST CALL OF THE DAY, NICK MANGOLD (973-927-0931 XT. 249) RESPONDED TO THE SCENE AT APPROXIMATLEY 1735 HOURS. MANGOLD BEGAN HIS INVESTIGATION. AT APPROXIMATLEY 1745 HOURS, DOROTHY GERGELY (973-625-6150), A SCREENER FROM ST. CLAIRE'S HOSPITAL ARRIVED ON SCENE. AFTER CONCLUDING HER INVESTIGATION / EVALUATION AND SPEAKING WITH HER SUPERVISOR, GERGELY SIGNED A SCREENING OUTREACH AUTHORIZATION FOR POLICE TRANSPORT FORM. SANDRA WAS NOW TO BE TAKEN TO ST. CLAIRE'S HOSPITAL BY THE NEW VERNON VOLUNTEER FIRST AID SQUAD ALONG WITH MYSELF. MANGOLD CONCLUDED HIS INVESTIGATION AND BELIEVED THE CHILDREN WOULD BE IN GOOD HANDS IF LEFT WITH THE HUSBAND. MANGOLD ALSO TOLD US THAT HE WOULD ATTEMPT TO GET A COURT ORDER FOR SANDRA TO GO TO THE HOSPITAL FOR AN EVALUATION IF THE SCREENER DIDN'T AUTHORIZE A POLICE TRANSPORT. THROUGHOUT THE TRANSPORT, SANDRA BELIEVED WE WERE TAKING HER SOMEWHERE "BAD". AS WE ARRIVED AT THE HOSPITAL, SANDRA BEGGED US NOT TO TAKE HER ON THE ROOF. WE ADVISED HER THAT SHE WAS NOT GOING TO BE ON THE ROOF. DURING ONE OF OUR MANY ATTEMPTS TO CALM HER DOWN. TRANSPORT WAS COMPLETED WITHOUT INCIDENT.

HARDING TWP POLICE DEPARTMENT
21 Blue Mill Rd, Harding Township, NJ 07976
(973) 455-0500

INITIAL GENERAL COMPLAINT REPORT

Case Number: 2006-012881   **GC Type:** INFORMATION RECEIVED - UNCLASSIFIABLE **Date/Time:** 11/2/2006 16:13
Dispatch Location: 24 MILLER RD   **Call Status:** CLOSED   **Created by:** Michael Meade

Officer(s) Dispatched	Dispatched Time	Assigned Time	Arrival Time	Cleared Time
MICHAEL MEADE	11/2/2006 16:13	11/2/2006 16:13	11/2/2006 16:13	11/2/2006 16:14

Caller Name	Address	Phone Number

Assisting Agencies

PARTIES INVOLVED INFORMATION

Type	Name	Address	Home Phone
COMPLAINANT	WILLIAM DUNN	24 MILLER RD, HARDING TWP, NJ, 07976	973-966-6155
OTHER	SANDRA DUNN	24 MILLER ROAD, NEW VERNON, NJ, 07976	973-966-6155

INITIAL NARRATIVE

MR. DUNN WAS IN HEADQUARTERS TALKING TO SGT. NUNN UPON MY ARRIVAL AT WORK THIS MORNING. HE CAME INTO HEADQUATERS TO ADVISE US THAT HIS WIFE HAD AN APPOINTMENT WITH A DOCTOR THIS MORNING AT 1000 HOURS AND HE DIDN'T THINK SHE WAS GOING TO KEEP THE APPOINTMENT THAT HE FELT WAS VERY IMPORTANT AS THEY WERE TO CHANGE HER MEDICINE. HE WENT ON TO SAY SINCE THE INCIDENT THAT THEY HAD AROUND LABOR DAY THING HAD NOT IMPROVED WITH HER CONDITION. AN EXAMPLE HE GAVE WAS THAT SHE WOULD NOT STOP ARGUING AND WAVING HER HAND AROUND ON A TRIP HOME ONE DAY AND AFTER THEY EXITED ROUTE #287 HE MADE HER GET OUT OF THE CAR AND WALK HOME FROM AT&T COMPLEX RIGHT OFF THE HIGHWAY. HE ALSO STATED THAT HE WAS THINKING ABOUT RENTING THE FRAZIER PROPERTY ON WOODLAND ROAD IN GREEN VILLAGE AND MOVE WITH THE KIDS AND GET OUT OF THE HOUSE AND LET HER HANG HERSELF. SEVERAL REFERENCES IN HIS CONVERSATION HE REFERRED TO HER STAY AT ST. CLAIRES HOSPITAL AS THE "NUT HOUSE." I WAS TAKEN BACK BY SEVERAL OF THESE REMARKS. HE WAS ADVISED THAT IF HE NEEDED ASSIST TO CALL.

HARDING TWP POLICE DEPARTMENT
21 Blue Mill Rd, Harding Township, NJ 07976
(973) 455-0500

INITIAL GENERAL COMPLAINT REPORT

Case Number: 2006-012873

GC Type: DISORDERLY CONDUCT - FAMILY DISTURBANCE - NO ASSAULT

Date/Time: 11/2/2006 10:02

Dispatch Location: 24 MILLER RD

Call Status: CLOSED

Created by: David Achenbach

Officer(s) Dispatched	Dispatched Time	Assigned Time	Arrival Time	Cleared Time
DAVID ACHENBACH	11/2/2006 10:02	11/2/2006 10:02	11/2/2006 10:06	11/2/2006 10:42
EARL HYDE	11/2/2006 10:02	11/2/2006 10:02	11/2/2006 10:06	11/2/2006 10:42

Caller Name	Address	Phone Number
WILLIAM DUNN	24 MILLER RD, HARDING TWP, NJ	

Assisting Agencies

PARTIES INVOLVED INFORMATION

Type	Name	Address	Home Phone
COMPLAINANT	WILLIAM DUNN	24 MILLER RD, HARDING TWP, NJ, 07976	973-966-6155
ACTOR	SANDRA DUNN	24 MILLER ROAD, HARDING TWP, NJ, 07976	973-966-6155

INITIAL NARRATIVE

PATROLS RESPONDED TO 24 MILLER ROAD ON A REPORT OF A DOMESTIC IN PROGRESS. UPON ARRIVAL I OBSERVED A WHITE FEMALE, IDENTIFIED AS MRS. SANDRA DUNN, STANDING AT THE END OF THE DRIVEWAY. THE END OF THE DRIVEWAY WAS BEING BLOCKED BY A VEHICLE WITH A WHITE MALE SITTING IN THE DRIVER'S SEAT, IDENTIFIED AS MR. WILLIAM DUNN. I APPROACHED MRS. DUNN AND ASKED HER WHAT HAD TAKEN PLACE TODAY. SHE SPOKE IN A VERY CALM MANNER AND ADVISED ME THAT HER HUSBAND WANTS HER TO GO AND SEE HER DOCTOR TODAY. MRS. DUNN STATED SHE PREFERRED TO GO TOMORROW AND SHE WOULD LIKE TO MAKE SOME DECISIONS FOR HERSELF. SHE FURTHER STATED THAT SHE AND HER HUSBAND HAVE BEEN HAVING MARITAL ISSUES WHICH SHE WOULD LIKE THEM TO GET COUNSELING FOR, HOWEVER, HER HUSBAND IS UNWILLING. MRS. DUNN STATED THAT THERE WAS NO PHYSICAL ALTERCATION BETWEEN THE TWO PARTIES NOR WERE THERE ANY THREATS MADE OF ANY KIND. MRS. DUNN APPEARED VERY CALM AND IN NO WAY DID SHE APPEAR TO BE A THREAT TO HERSELF OR ANY THIRD PARTY. AS I SPOKE WITH MRS. DUNN, SGT. HYDE SPOKE WITH MR. DUNN. MR. DUNN REQUESTED PATROLS REMOVE MRS. DUNN FROM THE PREMISES AND FORCE HER TO SEE HER DOCTOR TODAY. SGT. HYDE ADVISED MR. DUNN THAT WE DID NOT HAVE THE AUTHORITY TO TAKE SUCH ACTION AS MRS. DUNN APPEARED TO BE MENTALLY STABLE AT THIS TIME AND SHE DID NOT WISH TO SEE HER DOCTOR TODAY. MR. DUNN THEN LEFT THE AREA IN HIS VEHICLE. SGT. HYDE ADVISED ME THAT NO ACT OF DOMESTIC VIOLENCE TRANSPIRED TODAY, AS PER HIS DISCUSSION WITH MR. DUNN, AND THERE WAS NO NEED FOR A VICTIM NOTIFICATION FORM TO BE FILLED OUT. NO FURTHER ACTION BY PATROL. AT 1330 HRS. MR. JOHN LYNCH FROM D.Y.F.S. ARRIVED AT HARDING TWP. POLICE HEADQUARTERS AND ADVISED SAME, THAT HE RECEIVED A CALL FROM MR. DUNN AND WOULD LIKE PATROL TO RESPOND TO THE RESIDENCE WITH HIM. I SGT. HYDE, ADVISED MR. LYNCH OF PATROLS FINDINGS AND RESPONDED TO THE DUNN RESIDENCE TO SPEAK TO MRS. DUNN. AFTER MR. LYNCH SPOKE TO MRS. DUNN, WE LEFT THE RESIDENCE AND MR. LYNCH STATED HE WOULD FOLLOW UP WITH RECOMMENDED ASSISTANCE. MR. JOHN LYNCH CAN BE REACHED AT 800-392-9518 IF NEEDED.

Mental Health in America: The Whispered Unspoken Taboo and Truths

Within America today, there is a taboo associated with mental illness. It is something that those not personally affected can't comprehend. My daughters and I were victims of that taboo.

No one can even comprehend what the families of the loved ones suffering from these illnesses go through. Mental illness knows no boundaries. It cares not for gender, race, nor creed and can strike at any time without warning. It is an illness the patient would never wish to receive, like any other illness, and families' lives can be ruined by it.

In the fall of 2013 a state senator from Virginia, Creigh Deeds, and his family suffered from just the same fate with their late son Gus. Sen. Deeds now wears the scars from Gus's knife slashing to prove that and, trust me, the scars within this man's heart are the deepest.

"I really don't want Gus to be defined by his illness," Deeds, 56, said. "I don't want Gus to be defined by what happened on the nineteen of November 2013. It's clear the system failed Gus. It killed Gus." These are quotes from Sen. Deeds himself when he appeared on *60 Minutes* on a Sunday in January 2014.

It turned out that Gus was diagnosed as bipolar and on that particular day Sen. Deeds had gotten a court order to take his son to the emergency room. The rest is public knowledge. Sen. Deeds was lucky to get a court order to get his son to the emergency room. Most never can get that same court order. I wondered whether he would have gotten that the same court order had he been a common man like myself.

In my opinion, the hospital that discharged this young man with an illness bears responsibility. It turned out that a bed was unavailable at the hospital, so this young man was discharged by the hospital after six hours. A bed at a nearby hospital was available; however, Gus was not taken to the nearby hospital. Why are the pleas of the family members who have firsthand knowledge of what is going on ignored? The answer lies in laws passed and endorsed by none other than the U.S. Congress. These laws aren't read by those voting and instead are written by lobbyists who wish to protect their employers from any responsibilities.

The National Institute of Mental Health has some figures about mental disorders today in America. It is estimated that twenty-six percent of Americans aged eighteen and older suffer from a diagnosable mental disorder in a given year; however, the main burden of illness is concentrated in a much smaller group, just six percent of the population or about one in seventeen who suffer from serious mental illness.

The following numbers come from this institute:

Mood Disorder: 20.9 million or about 9.5%

Major Depressive Disorder: 14.8 million or about 6.7%

Dysthymic Disorder: 3.3 million or about 1.5%

Bipolar Disorder: 5.7 million or about 2.6%

Schizophrenia: 2.4 million or about 1.1%

Many suffer from more than one disorder at the same time.

There were 33,300 suicide victims in 2006, the year when Sandy was a victim herself. Ninety percent have a diagnosable mental disorder, most commonly a depressive disorder or substance abuse disorder. For my late wife it was an undiagnosed mental disorder as we, as a family, were never allowed to be told by doctors of Sandy's condition due to the HIPAA laws.

America has many problems today and for most today, mental health seems like a non-event. Most take their health for granted and never even consider mental health as anything to worry about. I can tell you firsthand that until I'd lived through the last seven months with my late-wife I, too, was guilty of ignorance as well; however, now that I have lived through the horrors of a mental illness, I truly count my blessings for good health and a sound mind.

It is my personal belief that, unfortunately, nothing will change to address our nation under siege from these illnesses. The victims and their families are left to try to manage in an unmanageable system to get help and the odds are stacked up against them. Under normal conditions or "thinking processes" if a patient goes to the doctor and gets a prescription, it is followed. Unfortunately, due to the fact that patients suffering from a mental illness are not in their right mind to begin with, one can throw out any thoughts of normalcy.

I hope that one day the elected elite in Washington, D.C., will address these issues, but truly believe that the only way this perhaps can happen is if their immediate families become victim's themselves. School shootings will continue and the same at theaters and shopping areas throughout this nation. Every time an incident occurs, the anti-gun advocates scream, "It's the gun." The truth of the matter is that it is the deranged person that most of the time has a mental health disorder. Many times the families of this ill person have tried to reached out for help, but been denied that help due to the laws in place from Washington, D.C.

Every day that I wake up, I wonder if there will be another headline about another horror story of an innocent family victimized from the horrors of those suffering from mental health-related illnesses. It seems to make the national headlines quite frequently, and for some reason, is more common today than when I was younger. My belief is that the current laws provide the answer.

Today is September 20, 2014, and so far, as of this early morning, no such headline appears over the news wire services, and thank God for that. I truly hope and pray every morning to awake with the same headlines, but unfortunately, I know that this will not be the case. Sometime before the year is out another tragedy will occur. I do not know where or when, but I am sure that it will occur, just as I am sure that the sun will rise in the morning and set at nighttime.

I have but one wish, which is that if another horror story is to occur, that those elected officials who never bother to read the laws they pass are the next set of victims. If a shooting occurs at the special private schools that the children of our privileged dignitaries in D.C. attend and their families become victims themselves, then and only then will laws be changed. I truly hope that this never occurs, but do believe that it is the only way Washington, with blood on its own hands, will truly understand what it has done to the rest of its citizens.

A few years ago a Congresswoman named Gabby Gifford became the victim of a young man with a mental health sickness. One could just look at this man's eyes and see all was not well. Officials at the college he was attending were concerned with this man's behavior before he dropped out of college. Jared Loughner, 24, had a history of psychiatric disorders for some time. In all, thirteen people were seriously injured and six killed, including a small girl at a supermarket parking lot on that tragic eighth day of January 2011.

At this man's sentencing, while Gabby Gifford looked on, the prosecutor declared that he would never have the ability to pick up a gun again in his lifetime. Jared Loughner was sentenced to seven life terms and 140 years behind bars.

The unfortunate truth about this horrible act was that many had pointed out that this man was not right; however, the laws in place today prevent individuals such as this from getting any help. Jared Loughner, as well as those he hurt or killed, are all unfortunate victims as are all their families.

I could have provided additional documents, but feel that enough has been presented to provide an accurate detail of the events that took place from the summer and fall of 2006. Many incidents of that time period have been left out, as I believe they are too personal to share and not necessary and wish them to remain private family matters.

While hospitalized, Sandy told doctors she was meant to die when she turned 47 years of age. No explanation by her was given to her doctors, according to hospital records. My guess is that this belief was due to the "voices" she was hearing. Dorothy Gergly, who St. Clair's dispatched to the house in August 2006, said Sandy was hearing voices, and Gloria Weichand gave me that same message from beyond in April 2008, saying it was the voices that told Sandy to take her own life in November 2006. Years later, Jenny informed me that the night of her fifteen birthday, her mother had said she would not join us for dinner as her dad was going to have her poisoned at the restaurant that evening. Only God above and the voices inside Sandy's mind can know what she heard.

There are no lobbyists to represent the patients and their families and, as a nation, we are in need of laws drafted that will allow families knowledge of a patient's medical condition. I hope sharing our story can enlighten some and perhaps bring about that change.

THE ROTOLO LAW FIRM

A PROFESSIONAL CORPORATION

502 ROUTE 22 WEST, SUITE 3
THE ROTOLO BUILDING
LEBANON, NEW JERSEY 08833
Phone - (908) 534-7900
Fax - (908) 534-7743

E-Mail – VROTOLO@ROTOLOLAWFIRM.COM
Website – WWW.ROTOLOLAWFIRM.COM

VICTOR A. ROTOLO
Certified By The Supreme Court Of
New Jersey As A Civil Trial Attorney

E. CARR CORNOG III

DANIEL B. TUNE
Member of NJ & NY Bar

RYAN E. MELSKY

HYUN J. LEE
Member of NJ & NY Bar

WILLIAM E. REUTELHUBER
Of Counsel

HAEKYOUNG SUH
Of Counsel

CYNTHIA A. ROTOLO
Of Counsel

January 30, 2012 *Should Be 2013*

Esther E. Bakonyi, D.A.G.
Hughes Justice Complex, P.O. Box 116
25 Market Street
Trenton, New Jersey 08625

RE: **Dunn v. NJ Dept of Law & Public Safety, DYFS, et al.**
 Docket No.:   MRS-L-3559-08
 Our File No.: 2103.44

Dear Ms. Bakonyi:

Enclosed please a copy of the Court's January 28, 2013 Order Confirming the November 15, 2012 Arbitration Award and Entering Judgment, which has been executed by Judge Hansbury.

Kindly take the necessary steps to provide this office with the appropriate payment/s satisfying the Judgment, upon receipt of which we will, of course, file a Warrant to Satisfy Judgment with the Court.

Should you have any questions or concerns, please don't hesitate to contact me.

Very truly yours,

THE ROTOLO LAW FIRM

E. Carr "Woody" Cornog III, Esq.
ECC/emm
Enclosure
William P. Dunn IV i/c/o Leslie & Jennifer Dunn (w/enclosure)

THE ROTOLO LAW FIRM
A Professional Corporation
502 Route 22 West
Lebanon, New Jersey 08833
(908) 534-7900
File No.: 2103.44 ECC/eml

Attorney for Plaintiffs: WILLIAM P. DUNN IV, (Administrator Ad Prosequendum for LESLIE V. DUNN and JENNIFER L. DUNN, minor daughters and heirs-at-law of Sandra A. Dunn, deceased, and Guardian ad litem for LESLIE V. DUNN and JENNIFER L. DUNN, individually)

WILLIAM P. DUNN IV, (Administrator Ad Prosequendum for LESLIE V. DUNN and JENNIFER L. DUNN, minor daughters and heirs-at-law of Sandra A. Dunn, deceased, and Guardian Ad Litem for LESLIE V. DUNN and JENNIFER L. DUNN, individually)	: SUPERIOR COURT OF NEW JERSEY : LAW DIVISION –MORRIS COUNTY : : DOCKET NO.: MRS-L-3559-08 : : : Civil Action :
v.	:
STATE OF NEW JERSEY, DEPARTMENT OF LAW & PUBLIC SAFETY, DIVISION OF YOUTH AND FAMILY SERVICES, URMENE REMEY, (individually and as an agent/ employee of DYFS), NICK MANGOLD (individually and as an agent/employee of DYFS), BERYL LICHTER (individually and as an agent/employee of DYFS), DONNA HEWITT (individually and as an agent/employee of (DYFS), JOHN DOES 1-10 (fictitious name for an unknown and unquantified group of individuals) and XYZ CORP. 1-10 (fictitious name for an unknown and unquantified group of corporations, partnerships and/or other entities)	: ORDER CONFIRMING ARBITRATION : AWARD AND ENTERING JUDGMENT : : : : : : : : : : : : : : :

THIS MATTER having been opened to the Court by the Rotolo Law Firm, attorneys for

William P. Dunn IV (Administrator Ad Prosequendum for LESLIE V. DUNN and JENNIFER L.

DUNN, minor daughters and heirs-at-law of Sandra A. Dunn, deceased, and Guardian ad litem

for LESLIE V. DUNN and JENNIFER L. DUNN, individually) for an Order confirming the

Arbitration Award rendered on November 15, 2012 and entering Judgment thereon, pursuant to

R. 4:21a-6(b)(3), and the Court having reviewed the moving papers and the opposition submitted, if any, and for good cause having been shown;

IT IS on this 28th day of January 2013,

ORDERED that Plaintiffs' Motion to Confirm the Arbitration Award is hereby granted and Judgment is hereby entered as follows:

1) In favor of Plaintiff Leslie Dunn against Defendant State of New Jersey, Division of Youth & Family Services in the amount of ████████

2) In favor of Plaintiff Jennifer Dunn against Defendant State of New Jersey, Division of Youth & Family Services in the amount of ████████ and it is further

ORDERED that a copy of this Order shall be served upon all parties within 7 days of the date hereof.

_____ , J.S.C.
STEPHAN C. HANSBURY, JUDGE
SUPERIOR COURT OF NEW JERSEY

Opposed ___
Unopposed ✕

Acknowledgments

I would like to thank a few people who were helpful during our family's time of crisis. Scott & Sally Noyes and Craig & Sally Curtiss both of Harding Township. Both of these families were supportive and very helpful towards our family after Sandy's passing with their own free time and friendship.

Wayne Bolton whose sermons while attending The New Vernon Presbyterian church began the healing process for me in those dark early days.

Victor Rotolo of the Rotolo Law Group located in Lebanon Township New Jersey who believed an injustice had taken place within our household when no one else cared to listen. Victor thank you for all your help and support.

E. Carr "Woody" Cornog III, Esq. boy oh boy I thought my handle of William Pennington Dunn IV was a long one Woody but that's what decedents of Irish peasant families do. Woody you did it and brought about the closure and I am forever in your debt.

Gordon Ward the leader of the New Vernon youth ministry at the church we attended and published author. Gordon thank for all the advice while on this endeavor, it was Gordon who read this original manuscript in November of 2014 and told me I had written something important. That one is out of my hand and will be determined by a higher power.

Cheryl Whitmore my cousin residing now in North Carolina the first person to read the original manuscript and supported this whole heartedly. Cheryl all your phone calls were truly inspiring and helpful.

I finally wish to thank a lady by the name Gloria Weichand who somehow by divine intervention or as Gordon coined "Godincidence" appear when needed. Gloria said to me in December of 2014 the last time we spoke "Bill you know what you need to do now, follow your heart and let it take you where you are meant to be." Gloria I am not sure where this endeavor will lead me but have determined to follow my heart.

I am not sure as to where this written journey will take me and some may not agree with a few pages written in the appendices. I have always said the following when speaking to perspective investment clients "everyone has an asshole and an opinion and if selected as your advisor you better hope this asshole's opinion is right". Generally in regards to the financial markets my opinion is correct, with regards to this book the jury is still out. It will be up to the reader to decide.

Regards to All
Bill